THE ENGLISH
BREAKFAST

THE ENGLISH BREAKFAST

THE BIOGRAPHY OF A NATIONAL MEAL WITH RECIPES

AN ENGLISH BREAKFAST-TABLE.

KAORI O'CONNOR

B L O O M S B U R Y

LONDON · NEW DELHI · NEW YORK · SYDNEY

Bloomsbury Academic
An imprint of Bloomsbury Publishing Plc

50 Bedford Square
London
WC1B 3DP
UK

175 Fifth Avenue
New York
NY 10010
USA

www.bloomsbury.com

First published 2013

© Kaori O'Connor, 2006, 2013

Kaori O'Connor has asserted her right under the Copyright, Designs and Patents Act, 1988, to be identified as Author of this work.

British Library Cataloguing-in-Publication Data
A catalogue record for this book is available from the British Library.

ISBN: PB: 978-0-8578-5454-4
ePub: 978-0-8578-5491-9

Library of Congress Cataloging-in-Publication Data
A catalog record for this book is available from the Library of Congress.

Typeset by SAGE India
Printed and bound in Great Britain

This book is dedicated with love and thanks to

Kato Ono Yamashiro, my grandmother

Martha Yamashiro, my aunt

Madge Yamashiro O'Connor, my mother

Kira Eva Tokiko Kalihilihiokekaiokanaloa Ffion Lusela
Hopkins,
my daughter

CONTENTS

CHAPTER ONE

The Biography of a National Meal

The English Breakfast is the best-known national meal in the world, a unique cultural and culinary symbol of England and Englishness, in edible form. As Countess Morphy (1936) put it: 'Breakfast is the English meal par excellence. . .one of the great national institutions of England'. But how did it attain this distinction, what can a national meal tell us about the nation that eats it, and is there more to the English breakfast than bacon and eggs?

This is a biography of the English Breakfast, a culinary detective story and a cookbook, rolled into one. It presents the history of the English Breakfast, the myths that surround it, the social changes that shaped it, and the enduring sentiments and appetites it evokes, concluding with a collection of authentic Victorian and Edwardian recipes for many forgotten delights of the breakfast table and sideboard from the heyday of this greatest of all meals.

* * *

In 1933, the food writer Robin Douglas gave a lyrical account of returning to England following a holiday in France. After crossing the English Channel on the night ferry, he drove through the Sussex countryside on a perfect day in late spring, until the 'the most delicious smell in the world, a blend of wallflowers, warm earth, frying bacon and coffee' drew him into the typically English welcome of breakfast at a roadside inn. For Douglas, as for countless others, the English Breakfast was both the symbol and substance of home, its aroma the very essence of England.

The English Breakfast is served on the small mountain trains that climb the Swiss peaks to resorts like Klosters where the English pioneered winter sports. It is offered on cruise liners that ply sea lanes originally developed for trade and migration, and appears in all parts of the tropics that used to be part of the Empire, unsuited to the climate though it may be. Back at home—where, as the writer Somerset Maugham famously observed, 'To eat well in England you should have breakfast three times a day'—it is the one meal that is not confined to particular times, but is served all day in ordinary cafes up and down the land, as well as in chic London restaurants and hotels. Surveys of visitors to England regularly find that breakfast is the English meal that, above all others, tourists look forward to eating, while on holiday themselves, the English consistently order English or 'cooked' breakfasts as they are often called

now, even if they don't cook and eat them in their own homes. What is this apparent power over plate and palate exercised by the English Breakfast?

MAKING NATIONAL CUISINES

Far from being a footnote to history, anthropologists and historians have established that food is its very substance, the building blocks of nationhood and identity. Arjun Appadurai (1988) has shown how, in the early days of independence when Indian society was fragmented, the creation of a standard 'Indian' cuisine supported by a new genre of popular cookery books, was a major factor in achieving national unity. The development of a national cuisine played a similar role in the emergence of modern Italy (Helstosky 2003) and in the formation of local identity in the new Caribbean nation of Belize (Wilk 1999), while Ishige's (2001) study of Japanese food shows the stages through which a much older national cuisine comes into being.

Food links body and spirit, self and society. It is both symbol and substance. National cuisines or dishes inspire strong passions, embody national values and are believed to be linked to the nation's character, health and fortunes. As the philosopher and gastronome Jean Anthelme Brillat-Savarin put it—'The destiny of nations depends on the manner in which they eat'. The anthropologist Mary Douglas (1975) has shown that to decipher a society's meals and cuisine is to understand the society itself. As the English food writer P. Morton Shand (1929) observed, 'The cookery of a nation is just as much part of its customs and traditions as are its laws and language'. It is through food, rather than political rhetoric, that people experience the nation in everyday life (C. Palmer 1998). To consume national dishes is not just an act of eating —it is the creation of the nation within the self.

The recipe for making national cuisines might read like this—take history, environment, culture, geography, politics, myth, chance and economics, and stir well together—but the mixture would never turn out the same way twice. Douglas (1997) captured the essence of food in just four words—'food is not feed'. Cuisines are not just cookery techniques, recipes and ingredients—they are culture and history in edible form. All societies make different choices about food—how it is cooked, which foods are appropriate for which meals, when meals should be eaten, which foods are 'good' and 'bad', and much more. Different foods and ways of eating mark the boundaries between social classes, genders, ethnicities, religions and regions. Social, political, historical and economic changes are reflected in changes in foods and ways of eating—what Fischer (1989) called 'foodways'. That is why different societies—or the same society in different periods of history—can begin with similar ingredients, and end up with entirely dissimilar cuisines.

* * *

The English writer George Orwell knew about food. He experienced the realities of *haute cuisine* by working in restaurant kitchens in Paris, where only a double door separated filthy sculleries and slaving minions from elegant customers dining in splendour. He wrote lyrically about English cooking, praising crusty English cottage loaves and Oxford marmalade, and in *A Nice Cup of Tea* he explained his eleven rules for obtaining a perfect brew at great length. He understood the politics of food and the pain of hunger, and food used as an instrument of power is a recurring theme in *Animal Farm* and *1984*. Above all, Orwell was aware of the strength of tradition. As World War II raged and enemy bombers flew over London, he wrote in *The Lion and the Unicorn* (1940):

Yes, there is something distinctive and recognizable in English civilization. It is a culture as individual as that of Spain. It is somehow bound up with solid breakfasts and gloomy Sundays, smoky towns and winding roads, green fields and red pillar-boxes. It has a flavour of its own. Moreover it is continuous, it stretches into the future and the past, there is something in it that persists, as in a living creature. What can the England of 1940 have in common with the England of 1840? But then, what have you in common with the child of five whose photograph your mother keeps on the mantelpiece? Nothing, except that you happen to be the same person.

And above all, it is your civilization, it is you. However much you hate it or laugh at it, you will never be happy away from it for any length of time. The suet puddings and the red pillar-boxes have entered into your soul. Good or evil, it is yours, you belong to it, and this side the grave you will never get away from the marks that it has given you.

Few accounts are as illustrative of the power of tradition, and the subtle ways in which culture, cuisine and nation are linked. 1940, 1840, 1740, 1640, 1540, the centuries seem to merge and differences fall away in the face of an all-embracing English identity both ancient and resilient, reaffirmed at the start of every day through the eating of the national meal. But tradition is not always what it seems, because when Orwell was writing about solid English breakfasts with good bread and marmalade, the national meal of eternal England was actually less than a hundred years old.

This celebrated meal is also a culinary mystery. Early English cookbooks have recipes for lunch and for dinner, but no recipes at all for breakfast. Large breakfasts do not figure in English life or cookbooks until the nineteenth century, when they appear with dramatic suddenness. Why and how did breakfast come to be England's national meal, and what is the 'real' English breakfast?

The development of cuisines, as Sir Jack Goody (1982, 1998) and others have shown, is a long and complex process. Over time, basic ingredients and cookery techniques begin to acquire particular associations, cultural meanings, socioeconomic significance and identity—a process that anthropologists call 'the cultural biography of a thing' (Kopytoff 1986). This identity is maintained over time, even though some of the ingredients, recipes and methods may change (Wilk 1999). National cuisines can be latent, existing on an implicit, taken-for-granted level until they are 'rediscovered', called into prominence by social conflict or crisis. As such, national cuisines are sensitive barometers of both change and fundamental values. Every national cuisine has a history, and every national meal has a biography that begins with the ingredients and becomes a cultural narrative over time.

Some food historians, notably Flandrin and Montanari (1999) have questioned the very concept of 'national' cuisines, arguing that long-established regional cuisines do not stop at shifting political borders. This regional approach may be appropriate in Europe where borders have always been fluid but it is less successful in the case of island nations like Japan and Great Britain where identity has been consolidated by geographical isolation. In any case it is seemingly impossible to separate nations from what they think of as their national cuisines, whether or not the cuisines are truly representative and even if they are entirely invented, as can be the case with new nations. The challenge is how to come to grips with the subject.

Many aspects of the process by which a national cuisine is formed can be seen in Naomichi Ishige's *The History and Culture of Japanese Food* (2001). Ishige traces the development of Japanese cuisine from prehistory to the present, showing how various edible elements came to be present in Japan, how they took on cultural meaning, and how various dishes and ways of eating became inextricably linked with Japanese national identity. The same approach has been taken here to the biography of the English Breakfast.

* * *

The ingredients of the English Breakfast arrived in England long before the meal itself came into being. The variety and abundance of England's produce has long been renowned, but archaeology has revealed that many of the foods and techniques now thought of as typically English, were imported from the continent in the course of successive waves of migration over thousands of years. The most notable contribution came from the Romans, who arrived in 43AD and, after a campaign against the Celtic inhabitants—described by the writer Diodorus Siculus as a fierce and savage people 'looking like wood demons with hair like a horse's mane'—established the island south of what is now Hadrian's Wall as a province of the Roman empire, giving it the name Britannia.

Over the three and a half centuries that they were in Britannia, the Romans are credited with introducing walnuts, cherries, types of beans and peas, rabbits, onions, leeks, carrots, parsley, radishes, spelt, fennel, mint, thyme, turnips, parsnips, pheasants, partridges, fallow deer, guinea fowl, mulberries, medlars, cucumbers, sweet chestnuts, a superior kind of domesticated chicken, cultivated apples, plums, pears and grapes. Cattle, sheep, pigs, and goats were already present, but the Romans introduced better breeds and husbandry practices. They brought vegetable gardens, orchards, cheese-making with rennet, bread baking in ovens, boiling fruit down to make jams and jellies, sausage-making and different ways of preserving hams and bacon.

This largesse was not accidental. Roman imperialism was political, economic, cultural—and culinary. They saw theirs as a civilizing mission and, once the fighting was over, they aimed to 'Romanise' their subject peoples by spreading the Latin language along with Roman values, customs, dress, architecture and cuisine. Praising Agricola's fairness in dealing with the Celtic tribes, the Roman historian Tacitus observed 'the result was that those who had just lately rejected the Raman tongue now conceived a

desire for eloquence. Thus even our style of dress came into favour and the toga was everywhere to be seen. Gradually too they went astray into the allurements of evil ways, colonnades and warm baths and elegant banquets. The Britons, who had no experience of this, called it 'civilization' although it was part of their enslavement'. It has been said that after a conflict, the victors re-write history. They certainly re-write menus. Since antiquity, food has been used in this way as part of what the sociologist Norbert Elias (1994) later called 'the civilizing process'.

From the Roman point of view, the Celts of Britannia and the Continent were richly deserving of culinary conquest. Julius Caesar claimed that the Britons were so barbaric they did not know how to sow crops. Strabo thought the people of Gaul little better than animals—'To this day, they lie on the ground and take their meals seated on straw. They subsist principally on milk and all kinds of flesh, especially that of swine, which they eat both fresh and salted'—and was particularly appalled by the people of the Fenni tribe who, he reported, 'live in an astonishingly barbaric and disgusting manner using wild plants for their food', while Tacitus thought the German tribes primitive in the extreme—'Their diet is simple: wild fruit, fresh game, curdled milk. They banish hunger without great preparation or appetising sauces.' To the Romans, sauces were the very essence of civilised eating.

Roman descriptions of Celtic eating and provisioning practices were intentionally oversimplified, in order to show the benefits of Roman culinary influences in the best possible light. In fact, the pre-Roman Celts of Britannia and the Continent ate a late Iron Age diet that included wild and cultivated grains and seeds, the meat of sheep, cattle and pigs; game; wild fruits, roots and herbs, with fish and shellfish along the coasts and rivers. Small-scale agriculture was practiced. The staple dish was porridge or stew made from grains and seeds, to which meat, vegetables and herbs could be added according to season and circumstance. The most common method of cooking was boiling in a cauldron over an open fire. Spit-roasted meat was highly esteemed, but roasting consumed more fuel than boiling and also required young, tender cuts of meat. It was therefore an elite food and, along with beer or mead, was served at the feasts that were at the heart of Celtic culture. 'No race' wrote Tacitus, 'indulges so lavishly in feast and hospitality. To close the door against a human being is a crime. Everyone, according to his property, receives at a well-spread board'.

Feasts were occasions when Celtic leaders could demonstrate their wealth and power, and strengthen their position by offering lavish hospitality to followers who would then be bound to them through the material and symbolic act of having taken their food. The importance of the feast is demonstrated by the presence in elite Celtic graves of large knives and platters for carving and serving roasted meats, and valuable cauldrons, some still containing traces of mead (Arnold 2001). Fuelled by copious drinking, feasts could continue for days, Tacitus noting with disapproval 'To make day and night run into one in drinking is a reproach to no man: brawls are frequent, naturally, among heavy drinkers: they are seldom settled with abuse, more often with wounds and bloodshed. Nevertheless the mutual reconciliation of enemies, the forming of family alliances, the appointment of chiefs, the question even of war or peace, are usually debated at these banquets; as though at no other time were the mind more open to obvious, or better warmed to larger thoughts.' Tacitus could not have made it clearer that this was not the Roman way of doing things.

* * *

Exactly who ate what, when, and how during the Roman occupation of Britannia is difficult to determine. Elite Romans continued to eat in the Roman manner, or as near to it as circumstances allowed. They imported Roman staples such as olives, almonds and spices which could not be grown locally; and also quantities of fine wine, although they learned to drink and enjoy the local mead. The remains of Roman townhouses and villas in the countryside show that they also imported fashionable dining practices. In the Roman homeland, elite dwellings not only had special rooms dedicated to dining – they had different dining rooms for winter and summer (Cosh 2001). Ideally, summer dining rooms faced south east, were light and airy and had wide doors for viewing the garden or countryside. Winter dining rooms were supposed to face west toward the setting sun to maximise light, and had narrow doors to reduce draughts. Excavations of elite Roman and Romano-British sites have confirmed the use of the Roman dining arrangement of three couches, each capable of holding three persons, placed in a U-shape around a central table, and also the existence of seasonal dining rooms. In less grand establishments there might be a single dining room, with heating at one end only, so dining could take place at the heated end in winter and at the other in summer.

The extent to which Romanised Britons followed Roman culinary practices on a regular basis is not known, but excavations of elite Romano-British residences have revealed the presence of sizeable hall-type outhouses containing the remains of both cauldrons and cauldron chains, indicating that feasting and traditional Celtic cookery continued among the elite Britons alongside Roman practices. While the common people were unaffected by elite dining modes, archaeologists using methods that include comparing the contents of latrines from Roman army camps with those from latrines in Romano-British centres, have established that Roman foodstuffs and techniques were gradually spreading across the land (Bakels and Jacomet 2003).

Also beginning to take root were Roman ways of thinking about food and eating. There were really two conflicting Roman foodways: two separate cuisines and attitudes to eating. The early republic of Rome was an agricultural society in which people lived simply in the countryside, growing their own food and practicing the country virtues of frugality, discipline and diligence while devoting themselves equally to the land and to public service if they were men, or to family duties if they were women. Their cuisine was basic, involving foods that were nourishing, plain, hearty, simply prepared and locally produced, cereal porridge being a Roman staple. This unadorned food was believed to strengthen both the body and the character, serving as the foundation for the honesty, morality and dignity (*gravitas*) that were considered the qualities of civilized beings and especially of elite Roman gentlemen. The purity and virtue embodied in rustic food cooked at a modest country hearth had a strong symbolic value to the Romans of the republic. There were three meals in a Roman day, eaten companionably in unpretentious surroundings, but only lunch and dinner were meals of any substance. Breakfast was light, usually consisting of just fruit or cheese with bread. Often it was not eaten at all, or was so insignificant as not to be mentioned. Moderation in all things was expected, and excessive eating and drinking met with disapproval. Even in ancient times, Cicero's maxim—'You should eat to live, not live to eat'—was well known.

However, as Rome's empire grew and the republic became an imperial state, wealth and luxuries flooded into the Roman heartland, changing the traditional way of life. The patrician elite who idealized the simple virtues, plain food and country life of early Rome, disapproved of the foreign trade in luxuries. They particularly condemned exotic foods, believing them to be a corrupting influence responsible for weakening the empire, destroying the old Roman values, imperilling cultural stability, encouraging self-indulgence rather than public service and ruining the nation's health. Others, grown newly rich, embraced all that their wealth could buy—foreign wines, spices, fruits, rare delicacies and elaborate ways of preparing and serving them. The new luxuries led to new ways of eating, epitomised by the banquets that became legendary for excesses of all kinds, including dishes that contained live birds or other creatures, *entrées* that consisted of several kinds of fowl or animal stuffed one inside the other, foods that were disguised to look like something else, or dishes that looked more like pieces of sculpture than food, all heavily dressed with herbs, spices and sauces.

The heavy consumption of foreign goods was centred in the cities, while in the countryside people ate and lived in a more traditional manner. Country-dwellers included peasants and patricians, because in addition to their town houses, the old elite liked to have a place in the country—preferably a farm rather than an opulent villa—where they could escape what they saw as the increasing decadence of the cities, exotic food and excessive consumption, and return to the simple country life. The conflict between the foodways of the patrician elite and the *nouveaux riches*, the old ways of the republic and the new ways of the empire, between local produce and imported food, and between plain cooking and exotic complex cuisines only ended with the fall of Rome itself. When the Romans left Britannia at the beginning of the fifth century after nearly four hundred years, their culinary legacy included Roman ways of thinking about food that would one day lead to the English Breakfast. These included an idealisation of country life and the country gentleman; a belief in the virtues of food that was home produced and plainly cooked; and the acceptance of the idea that there were different cuisines for country and for town.

* * *

The end of Britannia was followed by a turbulent period when culinary concerns were initially displaced by more pressing considerations. Conflict broke out between the southern Romanised Britons, the Celts from the west, and the northern Picts and Scots from beyond Hadrian's Wall. Then, during the fifth and sixth centuries there was a migration of Germanic colonists from different Continental tribes who became known collectively as Anglo-Saxons. The Romanised Britons, one of whom may have been the inspiration for the figure of King Arthur, were subdued and assimilated by the newcomers. The Anglo-Saxons set up a number of independent kingdoms in the south and central areas of the former Britannia, fighting among themselves as they sought to expand their territories. There was another wave of inward migration that resulted in the establishment of Danish colonies along the east coast in the ninth century, and further warfare. The times called for warriors, and this was a society of heroes.

The landscape portrayed in the literary epics of the time was a perilous place of wolf-slopes and windswept headlands, menacing forests and trackless plains, where mortal enemies, wild animals or supernatural forces lay everywhere in wait, and where the din of battle alternated with the silence of death. Leaders were in constant competition to gain and hold their positions and lands. Bonds of obligation and loyalty between leaders and retainers were forged and maintained through the giving of gifts such as arms and gold rings, through the sharing of war spoils, and above all through the holding of feasts. As with the pre-Roman Celts, feasting was at the very heart of this warrior culture. Feasts were far more than social events, they were also religious occasions when the gods were asked for aid and thanked for victory, as well as a legal arena in which public vows of loyalty could be made and other agreements entered into. Instead of

Anglo-Saxon Glass Vessels

the stone townhouses and villas of the Romans, the Anglo-Saxons built large timber halls for feasting on a large scale. This is the heroic scene still fixed in the popular imagination—the 'high mead hall' of Beowulf —noisy with fellowship, furnished with benches drawn up to long tables, light from the warming fire glinting on treasure and rich hangings. Feasting was the ideal pastime, and 'hall-joys' were relished and remembered from one feast to the next, but in these unsettled times foods of the land that required no cultivation or husbandry, like game and semi-wild animals and plants, were relied upon. In the surviving literature of the early Anglo-Saxons, there are few references to food, but many to drink, which was quaffed in prodigious quantities from horns and drinking cups that did not have flat bottoms, so they could not be put down until the vessel was empty.

This was a life in which there were no certainties, when courage, loyalty and bravery were the greatest virtues. Death was best met in battle, fighting gloriously for one's lord. The greatest tragedy was to outlive lord and companions, and to become an outcast far from fellowship and feasting, a theme of the great Anglo-Saxon elegy *The Wanderer* (Crossley-Holland 1982):

> 'Where has the horse gone? Where the man?
> Where the giver of gold?
> Where is the feasting-place?
> Where the pleasures of the hall?
> I mourn the gleaming cup, the warrior in his corselet, the glory of the Prince.
> How that time has passed, darkened under the shadow of night
> As if it had never been.'

As conditions became more settled, a rural lifestyle developed, with hamlets and small farms appearing in the still heavily forested countryside where the plants and animals brought by the Romans had now become naturalised. Inevitably, food and eating practices changed. The Anglo-Saxons are credited with introducing rye, and the Danes with bringing in new ways of curing and preserving fish. Gradually, a distinctive cuisine began to develop that consisted of the basic food ingredients from Roman times, prepared in a simpler, plainer way than that practiced by the Romano-British elite, and which combined pre-Roman, Anglo-Saxon and Danish elements.

* * *

Pork was the staple meat, and pigs were herded in the forests where acorns and beech-mast that gave their flesh a fine flavour. Fresh pork was usually eaten only once a year, in late autumn when pigs were killed in order to avoid the expense of feeding them over the winter. Otherwise pork was salted, smoked or pickled, prepared in the form of hams, bacon, sausages, meat puddings and mixtures of cereal, offal, herbs, blood and fat stuffed into a casing for cooking, like a modern-day haggis. Wealth was reckoned in flitches of bacon, which were prepared in quantity for domestic use, for the payment of land-rents and the settling of debts, and as gifts. Boiling, which was particularly suitable for salted meats, continued to be the main method of cooking, which was reflected in the ubiquity of broths, soups and gruels containing cereals like barley, vegetables, beans and peas. Cheese and butter were made, and eggs were boiled or fried in pans greased with fat. The fields and forests provided a wide array of seasonal berries, game, wildfowl and roots, as well as herbs and flowers for flavouring. A unique feature of English cuisine was the widespread use of flowers like elderflower and cowslip in sweet and savoury cookery. A preference for baked loaves continued among the elite, a Roman legacy, but ovens were a luxury and the common people ate griddle-cakes cooked next to the fire. Sauces, and especially savoury fruit sauces, another Roman favourite, were popular. The arrival of Christian missionaries and the founding of monasteries re-introduced the old Roman idea of moderation with regard to food. Gluttony became a sin, and a complicated Christian calendar of meatless days and fasts was imposed, resulting in a dramatic rise in fish-eating. It proved impossible to do away with feasting, but feasts were now held in honour of Christian saints, and loyalty to the church was substituted for loyalty to a war leader.

Many of the elements of the English Breakfast were now present—except for breakfast itself. As with the Romans, breakfast was the least important meal of the Anglo-Saxon day, and many people seemed not have eaten one. In the monasteries, only two meals a day were commonly taken, one at noon and the other in the early evening. Some people only ate once a day, as a demonstration of their religious piety. Or perhaps they were only seen to eat once a day because a great deal of furtive eating went on, in order to avoid being accused of gluttony. There are accounts of people stealing away from feasts, where they were expected to consume in moderation, to carry on eating and drinking in the toilets, out of the public gaze. The rich ate more and better food than the poor, but social differences were not as wide as they had been under the Romans. Free men were either nobles or commoners, and everyone ate what was recognisably the same kind of food, or at least agreed on what good food was. If this was old England, its symbolic dish was not roast beef but boiled pork.

However, what had been Britannia was not yet a unified nation. The small Anglo-Saxon kingdoms were gradually absorbed into a few larger ones that faced fierce attacks by marauding Danes against whom Alfred, King of Wessex,

conducted a long campaign. An apocryphal story relating to the period is the tale of Alfred and the burnt cakes. Forced to seek refuge in a swineherd's hut, the king, travelling in disguise, was asked by a peasant woman to tend the griddle-cakes baking by the fire, Alfred became so preoccupied in thinking about the Danes that he let the cakes burn, for which the woman was said to have given him a sound thrashing, not knowing he was the king, and Alfred accepted his punishment without reproof. This tale was used through the following centuries in different ways to illustrate aspects of personal virtue and national identity, and the cakes themselves —the plain food of common folk—entered the iconography as emblematic of the worthiness of simplicity, an example of the way in which particular foods can assume special meanings. Ironically, it was only when Old English had become established as a common language, and political unity seemed within reach, that another wave of migration—the Norman Conquest of 1066 led by William of Normandy—swept the Anglo-Saxons from power.

* * *

The Normans' first hostile engagement in England was not a pitched battle, as is generally thought. The Bayeux Tapestry which depicts the Conquest clearly shows that it was an act of culinary outrage. This is a hugely significant moment and image for English society and cuisine. In Latin, the embroidered text of the tapestry explains what is happening in the panels which are arranged as a sequence leading up to the death of King Harold. 'Here the horses come out of the ships. And here the soldiers hurried to Hastings to seize food. Here the meat is cooked. And here the servants served it up. Here they made a feast. And here the Bishop blesses the food and drink'. The Normans are shown riding through the countryside, stopping at an Anglo-Saxon farmstead and compelling the occupants to provide an ox, sheep and pig. The next section shows the poultry and joints from the seized provisions being readied for spit roasting while bread is being prepared in an oven. Finally, Duke William and his guests, including his half brother Bishop Odo, are served the roasted meat by servants, before hastening to defeat the forces of Harold Godwinson. The main elements of the tapestry—seizure of Anglo-Saxon property, preferences for particular kinds of food, and a hierarchical form of dining—set a social and culinary pattern that would prevail for centuries to come.

The Norman elite spoke French and were part of a cosmopolitan aristocratic culture that linked the princely courts of Europe. The Anglo-Saxon nobles and commoners spoke English, led a largely rural existence, were insular in their outlook and had been in the country long enough to feel a unifying sense of dispossession and 'Englishness' as opposed to the 'Frenchness' of the newcomers. Initially, there were fundamental differences between Norman and Saxon in all regards, and just as there were now two main languages and cultures, there were two cuisines—plain Anglo-Saxon food, considered to be 'low' or peasant food by the Norman elite, and the French 'high' cuisine of the royal court and the nobility. At its most extreme, Norman courtly food can be seen as a version of the luxurious cuisine of the late Roman Empire, which had been favoured by the Roman *nouveaux riches*. Complicated to prepare, highly spiced, richly sauced and containing many rare and foreign ingredients, it was served in quantity and presented with great show at lavish banquets. In royal and princely courts across Europe, banqueting food became ever more elaborate and theatrical, a cuisine of artifice intended for display. Many of the banquet dishes were sculptures or tableaux prepared purely for show and amusement, such as castles moulded out of pea paste, platters of greenery dressed with the lifelike stuffed skins of birds and animals and, later, large models of exotic animals or galleons in full sail made of expensive sugar (Mintz 1985). The point of food of this kind was to show that the giver of the banquet could afford to spend vast sums on food that could not be eaten.

Banqueting foods were not consumed on a daily basis, but among the elite ordinary foods prepared in the French manner, which was seen as a sign of refinement and superiority, became the preferred way of eating. French continued to be the language of fashion and power in England for some three hundred years after the Conquest, but the tyranny of French cooking went on for much longer. There was, however, one omission. Despite its luxury in other regards, the elite French way of eating did not include breakfast as a substantial formal meal.

Even up to the time of Louis XV, many French kings ate no breakfast at all or just took a drink, preferring three or four hours to pass between arising and the eating of the first of two daily meals. If taken, breakfast was extremely light, usually consisting of just some bread. There are several possible reasons for the disregard of breakfast. First, a concern for religious observance—eating before morning prayers or before the first main meal of the day was disapproved of by the church, although some secret breakfasting did take place. Second, in the kitchens of the period,

From the Bayeux Tapestry

several hours would be necessary to produce a meal considered worthy of the elite, and eating early was therefore not practical. Third, it was recognised that labourers needed to eat more frequently and as heartily as possible to keep up their strength, so forgoing breakfast or breakfasting lightly was a sign of social superiority, an indication that one did not need to work. Generally, the higher one's social status, the later one took the first meal of the day, whatever it was called. In the countryside, peasants and farmers might well eat heartily before noon if food was available, but they did not do so immediately on arising. The animals and fields usually required immediate attention, so it was usual to tend to these duties before settling to a midmorning meal that was often cold, because there had been no time to cook, or because it was too costly in fuel terms to do so.

After 1066, some Anglo-Saxon nobles forfeited their lands and others became subaltern partners of the Normans, serving as their lieutenants although seen by the Normans as their social and cultural inferiors. The Norman incomers are estimated to have numbered no more than 15,000 in a total population of just over a million at the time of the Conquest. As most of the Normans were male, intermarriage with Saxon women was extensive. Within a century of the Conquest, some contemporary sources suggested that the Norman and Saxon populations were so intermingled through marriage that it was difficult to tell them apart. But other accounts of the period depict a society still riven by hatred and resentment, with the Saxons—the sufferers of 'exquisite tortures'—continuing to see the Normans as a separate and hated race of interlopers, against whom they carried on a long campaign of covert resistance. Under the feudal system fostered by the Normans, Anglo-Saxon free commoners lost many rights they had previously enjoyed and social divisions widened.

* * *

By the thirteenth century there was a social hierarchy with the king at the top, followed by the nobility or magnates and then the knights. Then came those of the middling sort, comprised of people such as wealthy merchants and the growing urban elite. Next came free commoners and, lowest of all, the peasants. The word 'knight' comes from a Saxon root, showing that many Saxons had attained knightly rank. Yet even though some Saxons had prospered and the Normans now spoke English, there

were still two cultures, the 'old' England of the
Saxons and the 'new' England of the Normans,
which came to include parts of present-day
Ireland and Scotland and, from 1283, Wales.
It was from among the knightly families that
a new social group emerged who would be
closely linked to the English Breakfast. These
were the squires. Initially fledgling knights
or the descendants of knightly families who

were unwilling or unable to take on the expense and responsibilities of knighthood,
squires—who came to include the younger sons of titled families who had no title
themselves—stood midway in status between nobles and commoners in a different
way than merchants did. Being of noble or distinguished blood even if at some
remove, they were considered socially superior to merchants, however rich the latter
might be. Squires and their families evolved into the peculiarly English institution
called the gentry who kept alive the traditional values, practices and cuisine of the
Anglo-Saxons and developed the unique English country lifestyle.

As time went on, the 'squirearchy' or gentry became lesser landowners, basing
themselves in the countryside away from the urban centres of power where they
had little influence. Enjoying a fair degree of autonomy within their estates, the
gentry could revive and maintain the traditional way of life that had been lost in
the immediate aftermath of the Conquest. This, more than increasing national
prosperity, changes in grain prices, foreign wars or advances in sheep husbandry
accounts for the strong identity that the country gentry had from the outset, which
they consolidated by taking a generally inward-looking 'little England' perspective,
intermarrying, involving themselves in local affairs, eating food prepared in the 'old
English' manner and indulging wholeheartedly in country ways and pursuits such as
hunting, creating a country lifestyle and community that they saw as entirely separate
from, and equal if not superior to, that of court and town. In this, they considered
themselves to be the cultural heirs of the Anglo-Saxons and also of the patrician
Romans, of whom Horace had written: 'Happy the man who, remote from business,
after the manner of the ancient race of mortals, cultivates his paternal lands with his

own oxen, disengaged from every kind of usury. . . shunning both the bar and the proud portals of men in power.'

Culinary time is very different to historical time. Sometimes it passes with alarming swiftness, sometimes very slowly indeed. For centuries, the eating patterns of everyday life continued much as they had on the eve of the Conquest. Two meals a day, with many meatless days in a week, continued to be the ideal in the eyes of the church, but by the end of the fifteenth century the number of meals that might be taken in a day increased, and scattered references to breakfast began to appear in the budgets and accounts of elite households. However, breakfasting very much depended on social status. The 1478 household ordinances of King Edward IV specified that only members of the royal household down to the rank of squire were allowed to eat breakfast. Not all elite households breakfasted, and for those that did, breakfasts were not lavish, consisting of bread, beer or wine, with boiled meat or fish and eggs on meatless days, taken after morning mass, with the first important meal of the day served some hours later, at or shortly before noon, a practice that continued through the Tudor period.

The existence of separate cuisines had also continued. The food of court and town remained elaborate, becoming more complex as new foreign elements were added. By contrast, to look at English domestic country cookbooks of the seventeenth century is to see Anglo-Saxon cookery, which included earlier Roman and Celtic elements, still recognisable in what had now matured into what became known as 'good plain English cooking'. This was not food for the poor or for peasants, but a cuisine in its own right relished by the country elite, a defining part of their social identity. Here are porridges, plain or with fruit; pease pottage and baked beans, vinegars made with elder and primrose; hams of mutton and veal as well as pork; many cures of bacon; herb and meat puddings boiled in cloth, slow-cooked stews, sweet and savoury pies, boiled and roasted joints. There are recipes for cowslip cream, mutton broth, braised game and wildfowl, pigeon pie and fish pie, breads and buns, herb sauces and fruit jellies. Familiar patterns recur in the preparation of dishes—onions, carrots and turnips were used to give flavour, along with bunches of sweet herbs, while spices were rarely and sparingly used.

Gentry women did not usually cook themselves, but they supervised the household and instructed the cooks, and they thought food sufficiently important to compile books of recipes to hand on down through the family. Most, if not all of the food, was locally produced on the landowner's estate or farm. The rhythm of daily life and the times of meals was determined by nature and agricultural considerations, with the first full meal, called dinner, still taken at noon. If a journey was in prospect or some strenuous early work had been done, something might be taken earlier, such as cold meats, cheese or boiled eggs, with ale or beer, but this did not have the status of a regular, formal meal. Dinner at mid-day was still the main meal of the day, a substantial repast that included pies, savoury puddings, roast and boiled meats, fish, stews and pickles. With traditional English food went the customary English hospitality of old. Travellers could reasonably expect to find a welcome at the gentry's country houses which, especially since the overthrow of the monasteries, had become centres of influence in local society. Dotted about the countryside on estates of several thousand acres, these comfortable establishments seemed the very embodiment of timeless stability, security and social prestige.

From this most English *milieu* emerged the unique figure of the English country gentleman. The idealised gentleman was the embodiment of gentry virtues and values, a man whose status came from true worth and good family, not from recently acquired rank. A born leader, his word was his bond. He carried out his civic responsibilities like the Roman patricians of old, and treated his tenantry—for whom he might hold a dinner or a dance once a year—with the fair yet firm affection of a father. He cared for the land as he cared for his family, and in the countryside he set the tone for everything from church affairs to agricultural policies. The love of country burned in his heart, and he identified the nation's welfare with his own.

The English gentleman was a man of principles and dignity who always showed grace under pressure. He took an interest in the less fortunate, and engaged in acts of charity. He disdained fashion, and enjoyed plain, honest English country food. He was vigorous in pursuit of sports, and many country gentlemen believed that the perfect way to die was on a hunting field in England. The gentleman was resourceful, brave and, above all, he was manly. Tobias Smollett wrote lyrically of the gentleman's country comforts that he contrasted with 'town grievances'—cider from his own orchards, a table furnished from his own grounds, and rising with the sun to take pleasure in seeing his tenants thrive under his auspices. The English country gentleman was admired abroad as well as at home, and the poet Gerard Manley Hopkins spoke for many when he wrote 'By the by, if the English race had done nothing else, yet if they left the world the notion of a gentleman they would have done a great service to mankind.'

* * *

The Civil War (1642–51) that divided the country was fought on English plates as well as on English battlefields. The lavish French cookery popular at the court of Charles I and his French queen, Henrietta Maria, was replaced by plain English cooking and abstemious attitudes to eating under the Puritan regime of Oliver Cromwell, only to have French food and self-indulgence return to court circles with the restoration of the monarchy under Charles II. Goody (1982) notes how simple cookery and a puritanical approach to food was characteristic of the low church, *petit bourgeoisie* and revolutionary groups, while *haute cuisine* was associated with the aristocracy, political and mercantile establishments and high church. Beneath these historical specificities, differences in cuisine can be seen as part of a moral dialogue, as they had been in ancient Rome. The differences between the preferred foods of Cavaliers and Roundheads also expressed the deep cultural divide that separated them, as had been the case with the Anglo-Saxons and Normans. To the Puritans, excess and indulgence with regard to food was seen as symptomatic of the social and political ills that had come upon the land during the Stuart administration, exposing the nation to material as well as moral danger. The cultural historian David Hackett Fischer (1989) has shown how, transported to the American colonies, English Puritan foodways became the foundation of the culinary culture of New England, surviving today in signature dishes such as baked beans, fruit pies and New England boiled dinners, and in the Yankee tradition of disciplined eating.

Back in England, culinary time again ran slowly. Shorn of the excesses of Puritan austerity, plain English cooking flourished once more. Country houses, country gentry, country cooking—all seemed immutable and timeless. Then, quite suddenly, things began to change, and although many factors were involved, it is convenient to focus on three that would have a particular impact on the English Breakfast—tea, towns and technology.

Tea transformed English life, at all levels of society. The national thirst for the drink was a principal impetus in the establishment of England's international trading empire, which brought many foreign goods and influences into the country in addition to tea, resulting in profits that created a sizeable new group of *nouveaux riches*. Domestically, tea changed centuries-old patterns of consumption, making breakfast into an established social meal for the first time. When tea was introduced to England in the 1650's, the upper classes—the only ones who could afford it—made tea drinking the height of fashion, and were soon holding breakfast parties where tea was offered to guests, along with bread, butter jam and two other foreign novelties, coffee and chocolate. This was the period when toast won a special place in the heart of the nation, a German visitor describing it in this way (in Girouard 1978): 'One slice after another is taken, and held to the fire with a fork till the butter soaks through the whole pile of slices'. In this case, necessity was the mother of invention.

 English houses were so cold that it was impossible to spread the equally cold butter on anything but freshly toasted bread. It became fashionable to have a separate room devoted exclusively to eating breakfast. New furniture and new serving ware had to be provided for this new meal of breakfast, and the first breakfast tables

appeared, smaller and lighter than dining tables and
often round, followed by imported tea ware and
then the first domestically-produced teapots and
teacups and finally by whole breakfast services of
matched cups, saucers, milk ewers, slop and sugar
basins and bread and butter plates. As time went
on, tea and coffee services grew more elaborate, and
breakfast tables got bigger, although the food at these
breakfasts still consisted of bread, toast or cake. As
tea grew cheaper, it became a popular mania in all
classes of society, helping to popularise the practice
of taking breakfast. However, even in Jane Austen's
time at the end of the Georgian period, among people
of leisure a good two hours elapsed between arising
and eating, and this time was spent shopping, letter-
writing or taking exercise.

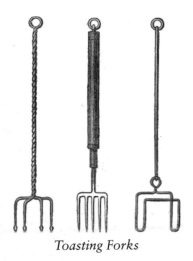

Toasting Forks

* * *

As agriculture gave way to industry, the bases of the nation's economy and of individual
prosperity shifted. Labourers deserted the countryside for the growing towns and the
new factories made possible by innovative technology. As England became the first
industrial nation, the whole rhythm of daily life changed. Machinery and not nature
dictated the hours of sleeping, working and especially eating. Increasingly, workers
were expected to eat before they came to work, in order to labour efficiently and to
save their employers the expense of giving them time off to eat after starting work.
The value of land was falling, and many of the gentry faced financial difficulties and
social uncertainties. Simultaneously, the lot of the workers began to improve and the
growing professional middle class along with those involved in foreign trade became
wealthier. All started to entertain social aspirations that were potentially destabilising
at a time of social unrest in Europe. A strong anti-industrial and anti-business feeling
grew up in many quarters. Echoing the concerns of the patrician Romans of old,
there was widespread fear that foreign influences and imported goods, especially
foreign edibles often glossed as 'French food', might weaken the fibre of the nation.
Much of this can be seen in the following patriotic ballad by Richard Leveridge,
written in 1735 but popular throughout the nineteenth century. The 'Boiled Pork of
Old England' would have been more accurate, but it would not have made as fine a
song.

The Roast Beef of Old England

'When Mighty Roast Beef was the Englishman's Food
It ennobl'd our veins and enriched our Blood:
Our Soldiers were Brave and our Courtiers were Good:
Oh! The Roast Beef of Old England,
And Old English Roast Beef.

But since we have learned from all vapouring France,
To eat their Ragouts, as well as to Dance.
We are fed up with nothing but vain Complaisance,
Oh! The Roast Beef Of Old England
And Old English Roast Beef

Our Fathers, of old, were Robust, Stout and Strong,
And kept open House, with good cheer all day long.
Which made their plump Tenants rejoyce in this Song,
Oh! The Roast Beef of Old England
And Old English Roast Beef

When good Queen Elizabeth sate on the throne
E'er Coffee and Tea and such slip-slops were known;
The World was in Terror if e'er she did frown,
Oh! The Roast Beef of Old England
And Old English Roast Beef

Oh! Then we had stomachs to eat, and to fight:
And when wrongs were a-cooking to do ourselves right,
But now we're a . . . I could, but good Night.
Oh! The Roast Beef of Old England
And Old English Roast Beef!'

The loss of England's American colonies and the events of the French Revolution increased these concerns, as did the accelerating rates of industrialisation, urbanisation and social change. Traditionalists who saw England as a land of proud countrymen were slung by Napoleon's remark that it had become a nation of shopkeepers. There was a widespread fear of national decline, exacerbated by what was seen as the decadence of the Georgian aristocracy, members of which were given to excesses of behaviour, dress, dandyism, dilettantism, drink and consumption which critics compared to those that had brought about the fall of the Roman Empire. In this volatile period there grew up a deep nostalgia for a more secure past, and a heart-felt need to affirm traditional English identity and values, unify the population and strengthen the national vision and sense of purpose.

In response, there came an upsurge of patriotism in many forms, including literature, art, architecture and popular culture. This new nationalism looked to an idealised, even mythologized past, with the medieval period and the reign of Elizabeth I, Gloriana, celebrated as golden ages, and historic pursuits such as archery revived as an elite sport, but the strongest and most important theme to emerge in the new nationalism was the reassertion of traditional Anglo-Saxon identity and virtues. There were many popular romances with Anglo-Saxon characters and settings, notably Sir Walter Scott's *Ivanhoe*, in which Saxons of noble character and antecedents are seen struggling under the 'Norman yoke', and Edward Bulwer-Lytton's heroic *Harold the Last of the Saxon Kings*. Both turn suffering and defeat into victories in which Saxon values ultimately triumph over those of the Normans, as the English language triumphed over Norman French. As Bulwer-Lytton put it, England was still a Saxon land. In *Ivanhoe*, food becomes a metaphor for cultural values, differences and identity, the simple cookery and home-produced ingredients of Cedric's great hall contrasted with the spiced, complex and imported foods served at Prince John's banquet (Vanden Bosche 1987). As Cedric the Saxon declares 'Far better was our homely diet, eaten in peace and liberty, than the luxurious dainties, the love of which hath delivered us as bondsmen to the foreign conqueror.'

Personages from the Anglo-Saxon past became cult figures, especially King Alfred, who became the object of what Simon Keynes (1999) called Alfredophilia and then Alfredomania, in the cause of constructing 'Englishness'. King Alfred was reinvented for popular consumption as a thoroughly English monarch who personified royal virtue, was the originator of the constitution and patron of the English language, becoming the very symbol and embodiment of English nationality. The Hanoverian royal family, as foreign as the Normans had been, took a particular interest in King Alfred, seeking Englishness by association. The story of

Alfred and the burnt cakes found its way into every schoolroom history of England, with Alfred presented as the first English gentleman, managing to retain his dignity and show graciousness in challenging circumstances. Alfred was the subject of history painting in the grand style and of many illustrated history books, both popular and scholarly. His portrait busts graced town halls, and statues of the king marked public buildings. Even as much of the countryside fell empty as the workers were drawn to the towns, country life and the English landscape were glorified—particularly as Krishnan Kumar (2003) has noted, Sussex, Wiltshire, Hampshire, Dorset and other southern counties that were at the heart of the old Anglo-Saxon kingdoms, and which came to represent the English countryside as a whole.

That not everything in these patriotic presentations and romanticised accounts was true or verifiable is unimportant. They were largely believed, and myths that are believed become social truths and self-fulfilling prophecies. The past was reinvented and reclaimed to serve the needs of the present. The Saxon heritage—the 'real' England, old and true—was presented as a unifying tradition in which all social groups could share. Finally, the stage was being readied for the public celebration of the English culinary tradition of good plain cookery, and the emergence of the national meal—the English Breakfast.

* * *

The accession of Queen Victoria in 1837 is a useful reference point. Under Queen Victoria, regard for the certainties of an idealised past and veneration of re-invented traditional values became a national passion that unified society in a time of great change. The early years of the Victorian era saw the rise of the new urban middle classes, and the decline of the traditional country gentry, many of whom could no longer afford to live off their land in the manner to which they had been so long accustomed. The former had wealth, the latter had social cachet and influence. Instead of one group seeking to overthrow the other as happened on the continent, the newly revived Anglo-Saxon heritage facilitated an accommodation in which the figure of the gentleman as social and moral ideal was key. Bertrand Russell suggested that the concept of the gentleman was invented by the aristocracy to keep the middle classes in order, but it might be more accurate to say that the gentleman was invented by the gentry to keep both the aristocrats and the middle classes in order.

Queen Victoria and the Prince Consort

Under Queen Victoria, aristocrats were strongly encouraged to conduct themselves with probity and sobriety in a gentlemanly manner new to many of them. Similarly, the *nouveaux riches*, the middle and the lower classes alike took the gentry as their model. As *Modern Etiquette in Public and Private*, one of the most popular etiquette books of the day put it—'High birth and good breeding are the privileges of the few, but the habits and manners of a gentleman may be acquired by all.' Men strove to become gentlemen, and women gentlewomen or ladies. Gentrification became their route to social acceptance and they re-cast themselves in the image of the gentry, as appropriate to their station in life, which of course many hoped to leave behind. Those bent on self-betterment wanted to learn everything they could about the gentry, and the object of the greatest interest was the English country house.

* * *

The possession of country estates had always been a defining feature of the aristocracy and the landed gentry. Initially, especially among the gentry, the land was much more important than the houses built on them, and the dwellings of even the wealthiest gentry could be surprising modest, given their worth reckoned in acres. In time, however, the house became an important statement of family position and tradition. As the writer Vita Sackville-West (1944), who grew up at Knole, the great Elizabethan country house in Kent noted, these houses were essentially part of the country, 'not only in the country, but part of it, a natural growth'. Moreover, they were part of a very particular country—an England 'green throughout; her seas, her woods, her fields all island-green. Green, quiet England. Old, quiet England'.

One elite ideal was to own all the land in all directions as far as the eye could see, another was to be entirely provisioned from one's own estates, so that all the food put upon the table had sprung from one's own soil, rivers, forests and moorlands. The upper class fondness for venison, game and salmon springs from the fact that these are all specific products of country estates, once largely available only to those who possessed them. Here, symbolism was as important as economic self-sufficiency. Brillat-Savarin might have had the English elite in mind when he said 'Tell me what you eat, and I will tell you who you are.' Eating the fruits of the land, simply and plainly prepared, was a kind of secular sacrament, binding one ever closer to the soil and nation.

Scattered across the countryside, each estate was a social world in miniature, whole communities made up of fieldworkers, artisans, dairymen, herdsmen, gardeners, cooks and servants, many of whose connections with the estate went back generations. At the top of the hierarchy was the gentry family itself. Each estate had its own internal rhythm based on the cycles of harvest and husbandry and the specificities of location —such as proximity to hunting country and good fishing rivers, or the possession of shooting moors. Elite families were a close and effectively closed and exclusive community linked by kinship and marriage over many generations, and this provided the network for the round of country house visits that were a major feature of country

life. Relatives and friends would travel across the countryside to attend house parties that might last for several days or several weeks, during which time hosts offered guests the chance to engage in local country pursuits. Two weeks shooting with cousins who had a grouse moor, a week elsewhere when the fishing was good, a long visit to in-laws when the deerstalking season was at its height, and days out with neighbouring hunts, along with activities of a less strenuous kind like sight-seeing and attendance at local dances and dinners were fixed points in country calendars.

A particular feature of these house parties was the food, good country fare that gave the host the chance to show off the excellence of the estate's produce, and the specialities for which the area was known—fine hams or excellent cheeses, smoked fish or rich cream—and which always in season included an abundance of game such as grouse, pheasant, and ptarmigan. This was the defining food of the English country gentleman, and the distinctive repast of country house parties was the meal that came to be called 'breakfast', but which was actually the first of the two main daily meals that had been eaten since early times.

This was a leisurely repast, usually taking place over two hours in the mid to late morning from nine to eleven, allowing guests to come to table when they liked. It was the only meal of the day not served by servants. Cold offerings and hot food in china and silver dishes were laid out on sideboards and tables, and guests helped themselves. Breakfast allowed the host to entertain more informally than was possible at dinner, and the absence of servants gave breakfasters a degree of privacy. Male guests were very often away from the house during much of the day engaged in sporting pursuits, so the opportunities for a full luncheon were limited, although picnics were popular. Breakfast was considered a masculine meal, in contrast to afternoon tea, which was considered a feminine repast. The decoration and furnishings of dining and breakfast rooms tended to enhance masculine associations, with dark furniture and ornate dark sideboards rather like secular altars, on which the food was displayed in the manner of offerings. Ancestral portraits—authentic or not—were a favoured embellishment, emphasising the links between past and present through food and communal eating, and demonstrating a respect for tradition. Breakfast food was hearty, manly viands in a manly age, and often the guests would have arisen earlier, and gone outdoors to work up an appetite. This was the interval Sir Arthur Conan Doyle's hero Sherlock Holmes referred to when he said—'There can be no question, my dear Watson, of the value of exercise before breakfast'. During country house parties, male guests were always expected to present themselves at breakfast, while women were often allowed to abstain. For a man to breakfast in his room was regarded as the height of effeminacy and this remark by Oscar Wilde—'I often take exercise. Only yesterday I had breakfast in bed'—would have outraged traditionalists.

Beyond great gates and behind high walls, their far towers and chimneys glimpsed momentarily above ancient woods like the flash of hunting pink in a distant field, country houses and their lifestyle exerted a compelling fascination on those outside the circle, coming to represent all that was best in England, and all they aspired to.

Two Lady's Kitchen Aprons from Beeton's Young Englishwoman *magazine, April 1871.*

3012.—SIDEBOARD AS LAID FOR BREAKFAST.

3018.—GUESTS' BREAKFAST AT COUNTRY HOUSE, SUITABLE FOR TWELVE PERSONS.

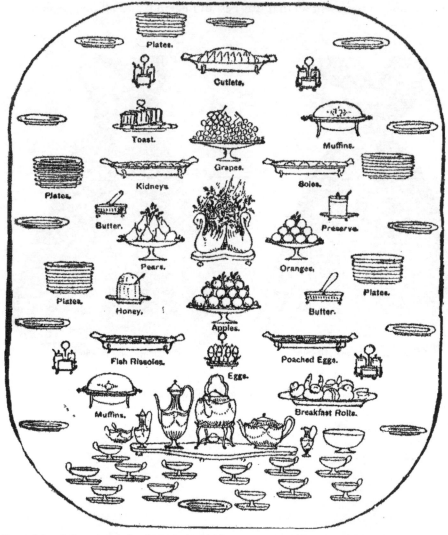

From Mrs. Beeton's Book of Household Management, *1901.*

CHAPTER TWO

The English Country House Breakfast

What is the 'real' English Breakfast? Bacon, eggs, good bread and marmalade, however well-prepared, leave behind a faint trace of dissatisfaction, like a smudge of jam on a plate. Is this all there is? Once there was much, much more. The original English Breakfast, the meal of distant memory and heart's desire, is the country house breakfast like those which Ethel, Lady Raglan, reminiscing about childhood in the great house of her grandfather, the Earl of St Germans, described in this way:

> I always remember what a great feature was made of the breakfasts at my grandfather's house parties at Port Eliot, and of the numerous courses that succeeded each other. There would be a choice of fish, fried eggs and crisp bacon, a variety of egg dishes, omelettes and sizzling sausages and bacon. During the shooting parties, hot game and grilled pheasants always appeared on the breakfast menu but were served of course without any vegetables. On a side table was always to be found a choice of cold viands; delicious home-smoked hams, pressed meats, one of the large raised pies for which Mrs Vaughan (the cook) was justly famous, consisting of cold game and galantine,

with aspic jelly. The guests drank either tea or coffee, and there were the invariable accompaniments of home-made rolls, piping hot, and stillroom preserves of apple and quince jelly, and always piled bowls of rich Cornish cream. The meal usually finished with a fruit course of grapes or hothouse peaches and nectarines.

Growing up at Wilton House in Wiltshire, a daughter of the Earl of Pembroke remembered breakfasts of hot sausages, bacon, egg, devilled kidneys and plaice, with a sideboard set with ham, tongue and game pie, and plenty of toast and marmalade (in Waterson 1985), while the writer J. B. Priestley (1970) recollected a country house visit where the breakfast offerings included porridge and cream, pots of coffee and of China and Indian tea, and a choice of cold drinks. There were two large sideboards. On one was set a row of silver dishes holding poached or scrambled eggs, bacon, ham, sausages, devilled kidneys, haddock and other fish, kept warm by spirit lamps. The second held cold meats including ham, tongue, beef, galantines and cold roast partridge, ptarmigan, pheasant and grouse in season. Looking back at Edwardian mornings, Lady Cynthia Asquith (in Streatfield 1956) recalled:

> Most households were cheerfully resigned to breakfast—then a fabulous meal—going on till half past ten or so, and the little blue flames under the array of lidded, silver chafing-dishes kept piping hot the crisp, curly bacon; eggs (poached, boiled and fried), mounds of damp kedgeree (made with salmon), haddocks swimming in melted butter, sputtering sausages and ruddily-exuding kidneys. First the young men of the party would line themselves with porridge immersed in thick yellow cream. Next they would pile some of the contents of nearly each hot dish on to their plates. This course consumed, they would ram down scones, thickly buttered and topped with home-made jam, marmalade or honey. Fruit from the walls, nets or hothouses of the kitchen garden wound up this minor meal.

In *Breakfasts, Luncheons and Ball Suppers* (1887:4), Major 'L' (Major James Landon) wrote:

> The Author thinks that in a country house, which contains, probably, a sprinkling of good and bad appetites and digestions, breakfasts should consist of a variety to suit all tastes. Fish, poultry, or game, if in season; sausages and one meat of some sort, such as mutton cutlets, or fillets of beef; omelettes, and eggs served in various ways; bread of both kinds, white and brown, and fancy bread of as many kinds as can be conveniently served; two or three kinds of jam, orange marmalade, and fruits when in season; and on the side table, cold meats such as ham, tongue, cold game or game pie, galantines, and in winter a round of spiced beef.

These lavish breakfasts, unique to England, never failed to astonish foreign visitors. When the American historian John Motley encountered one of these gargantuan meals for the first time, he noted—'When I reflected that all these people would lunch at 2 and dine at 8, I bowed my head in humiliation and the fork dropped nerveless from my grasp.' Even foreign cooks were taken by surprise. When Gabriel Tschumi, chef to King Edward VII, first entered the kitchens at Windsor Castle, he was astounded to see the ranges red hot at seven in the morning, preparing five-course royal breakfasts, and even more so to learn that the royal servants ate the same amount.

It was not only country houses and royal castles that were renowned for their breakfasts. In Oxford—home city of Oxford marmalade—the breakfast parties held in the colleges of the university were legendary, like this one which took place in 1884 (*Cassell's Family Magazine*, in Aylmer 1995:10):

> The feast commences with two enormous dishes of whiting and soles. After the edge of appetite has been blunted on these trifles, the serious business of the day begins. A couple of "spread eagles" i.e. Fowls squashed flat and embellished with mushrooms, face a mound of sausages enclosed in a rampart of mashed potatoes, and are supported on either hand by a regiment of boiled eggs and a solid square of beefsteak. These are backed up by a reserve of omelettes, sweet and savoury, anchovy toast, more graphically than elegantly known as "dirty Toast"—and "squish"—a synonym for marmalade.

A NEW WORLD IN COOKBOOKS

In Victorian England during the nineteenth century, the parallel rise of the print media and of the middle classes produced a literature that was a central part of the civilising process in which gentrification, ostensibly about social advancement and improvement, was actually a form of social control. From the viewpoint of the upper classes, it was desirable that the *nouveaux riches* and middle classes become gentrified to a degree, but not so gentrified that they would pose a threat.

Codes of correct behaviour sprung up that were far more elaborate than those the aristocracy or gentry had observed themselves on a daily basis, but which served to keep a social distance between them and the aspiring middle classes. Social life became a minefield, with the newly rich and those below them under tremendous pressure to avoid showing by thought, word or deed that they were not 'one of us'. Manners

Egg cutter for removing the tops of eggs.

became a national obsession. In the intense atmosphere of social competition, incorrect dress for an occasion, inability to use the correct tableware, ignorance of correct form when paying calls, along with a thousand other possible *faux pas* could, it was feared, lead to social death. For those new to society, formal dining was regarded as a particular ordeal. As *Modern Etiquette in Public and Private* cautioned its readers —'The rules to be observed at table are numerous and minute, and none of them can be violated without exposing the offender to instant detection'.

Not surprisingly, a whole new genre of popular literature appeared—etiquette books, books on the management of household and servants, books of deportment, books of home decoration and books of advice of all kinds, including how urban women could learn to enjoy a country life. All promised to help the aspiring middle classes negotiate this unknown social territory. There were handsome volumes for the well-off, plainer editions for the middling market and cheap paper-covered six-penny editions for readers of the poorer sort who saw no irony in being told what the correct form would be if presented to the Queen. The literature of gentrification and self-improvement was also a literature of fantasy. It depicted a highly idealised world, in which few people actually lived and behaved exactly as described on an everyday basis, a world to which in any case very few of the readers would actually ever gain full entrée. Even Isabella Beeton, who wrote authoritatively on the management of large numbers of servants, only employed two herself, although three was the minimum number normally in service in a middle class household (Hughes 2005). Nonetheless, these books acted as a conduit of dreams and aspirations, and in the climate of the times, to know how things should be done—even if the opportunity to put knowledge into practice never or rarely arose—was regarded as a worthy accomplishment in itself, a form of proto-gentrification. Out of all the new publications, cookbooks were among the most avidly read.

Anthropologists have long recognised that cookbooks are not just collections of recipes. In all cultures and periods of history, cookbooks have been unique records of a society's systems of production and distribution, ideas about gender and domesticity, social and cosmological schemes, systems of class and hierarchy, and visions of the ideal life (Appadurai 1998; Sahlins 1976; Goody 1982, 1998; Mintz and Du Bois 2002; Sutton 2005; Magee 2005). As Humble (2005) has pointed out, cookbooks reflect the fantasies and fears associated with food as much as they describe what people actually ate. But no cookbooks ever produced rival those of England in this period for detail, depth and scope because it was a society that was in the process of reinventing itself *en masse*.

Victorian and Edwardian cookbooks are as much about social class as about cuisine, and as much about morality as about meals. Gentry family cookbooks of the seventeenth century launch straight into the recipes. Explanations were unnecessary, everyone knew 'the way things are done', from the mistress down to the cooks and servants. Many gentrifying Victorian cookbooks, by contrast, were virtual encyclopaedias. They began from the premise that although their readers might know how to cook, they did not know how to cook and serve in the 'right way.' In addition to social realignments, improving prosperity and increasing imports meant that the middle and working classes now had access to quantities and qualities of foods previously enjoyed only by the wealthy, to which they needed to be introduced. Many cookbooks included daily menus, on the assumption that readers had to be taught the correct form in composing meals. Social values as well as victuals were on the culinary agenda. Few Victorian cookbooks begin without a moralising introduction on the importance of hygiene, regularity, nutrition, economy, efficiency and health, proceeding on to deal comprehensively with matters of practicality, provisioning and presentation from instructions for using kitchen equipment and shopping economically to ornamental napkin-folding, and this is before the recipes even began.

Different cookbooks were addressed to different audiences. Mistresses of the grandest households never saw a cook-book, culinary and domestic matters being left to her cook, housekeeper, and kitchen and garden staff. Cookbooks intended for mist-resses of less substantial homes emphasise the social aspects of dining and entertainment generally, followed by a section of recipes for the cook. Sometimes, cookbooks of this kind came in a two volume set, the volume for the mistress of the house containing social information, notes on etiquette and table setting, menus and names and descriptions of suitable dishes but not the recipes for them, while the second volume, for the cook, contained recipes and nothing else—a kind of cookbook apartheid.

Poultry and Game from Mrs. Beeton's Book of Household Management

Some cookbooks were intended for the growing number of professional cooks who were employed by the new middle classes, and these were often compendiums of hundreds of recipes representing a much wider range than many professional cooks have today— possibly a much wider rage than any one Victorian cook possessed. French dishes and English dishes with French names were given prominence in order to cater for the employer's social aspirations. Then there were inexpensive cookery books aimed at lower middle class households, many of which kept at least one live-in servant or a daily who may also have cooked, and finally there were cookbooks for the working classes, where the woman of the house was the sole cook and servant. Even in the humblest publications, gentry cookery—including recipes for roast pheasant and venison—was often described in detail, enabling readers to share in the gentry lifestyle vicariously. Apart from exercising the imagination, this was accomplished by following advice like this from *The Wife's Own Book of Cookery* (Bishop 1864:31)—'The receipts here given, which are on too large a scale for a small family, may have their proportions equally reduced and an excellent dish will be the result. In some instances, also, the more expensive ingredients may be left out without destroying the integrity of the receipt, discretion and judgment being alone required in these cases.'

By far the most significant element in Victorian cookbooks was the domestic ideal embodied in the figure of Coventry Patmore's *'The Angel in the House'*, the wife devoted to the interests of her husband, and who made their dwelling, however great or small, 'Home Sweet Home' at the sacrifice of her own independence. The nineteenth century was a time of gender polarisation—of masculine activity in the public arena and feminine activity in the private sphere especially within the home, where food was a matter of the greatest importance. As the writer of *Margaret Sim's Cookery Book* (Walford 1883:ix) cautioned:

> Friends and readers, whatever else you have, and whatever you have not, each, even to the poorest among you, possesses (oft doth he wish he did not!) a stomach. . . Trifle with your business, your property, your time, and your friends—trifle, I say, with all of these if you are fool enough; but, fool or not, lend an ear to him who would warn you from trifling with your stomach.

Throughout the Victorian and Edwardian period, cookbooks promoted the ideal of feminine domesticity, none more assiduously than the encyclopaedic *Book of Household Management*. Compiled by Isabella Beeton and first published in book form in 1861 by her husband Samuel Beeton, proprietor of the popular *Englishwoman's*

Domestic Magazine, it begins 'As with the Commander of an Army, or the leader of an enterprise, so it is with the mistress of a house'. It was to this book and couple that Sir Arthur Conan Doyle referred in *A Duet, with an Occasional Chorus* which took married life as its theme. In it, the heroine says 'Mrs. Beeton must have been the finest housekeeper in the world. Therefore, Mr Beeton must have been the happiest and most comfortable man,' to which the hero responds that Mrs. Beeton's book 'has more wisdom to the square inch than any work of man'.

The Book of Household Management is a remarkable social document that both reflected and perpetuated the aspirations to gentrification of the new middle class. Isabella Beeton died in 1865, but the book—compiled by different editors—continued to be published under her name, with new sections added to reflect changing practice. In the first (1861) edition of her book, this is all Isabella Beeton had to say on the subject of breakfast—'It will not be necessary to give here a long bill of fare of cold joints, &c, which may be placed on the side-board and do duty at the breakfast table. Suffice it to say that any cold meat the larder may furnish, should be nicely garnished and be placed on the buffet' followed by a few suggestions and no recipes. When a new edition of the work now called *Mrs Beeton's Book of Household Management* appeared in 1888, it had a new fulsome chapter on breakfast including menus and table-settings.

There was plenty of competition. Georgiana Hill's *The Breakfast Book* had appeared in 1865, and Mary Hooper's *Handbook for The Breakfast Table* in 1873. The anonymously-written *Breakfast and Luncheon at Home* came out in 1880. In 1884, Miss M. L. Allen's *Breakfast Dishes for Every Morning of Three Months* was published. 1885 saw the publication of *Breakfast and Savoury Dishes* by R.O.C. (Rose Owen Cole). In 1887, 'Major L'—Major James L. Landon—brought out a book on breakfasts, luncheons and ball suppers as enjoyed by the country house hunting set. He divided breakfasts into three types—those suitable for large parties, those for breakfasters of robust constitution, and those for ladies and for gentlemen of sedentary occupation and a certain age who, he suggested, should not eat meat more than once a day, in order to avoid gout. *Fifty Breakfasts* by Colonel Kenney Herbert appeared in 1894. The publication of *The Breakfast Book* by Rose Brown and *The Dictionary of Dainty Breakfasts* by Phyllis Browne (Sarah Sharp Hamer) both followed in 1898. *The Young Ladies' Journal* devoted a special extra supplement to the subject of *Breakfast and the*

AN ENGLISH BREAKFAST-TABLE.

Breakfast-Table. Breakfast cookbooks were entirely new, and they came into being quite suddenly because people had to be told how to prepare and present a meal that had never really existed in this way before. Culinary time had speeded up, and the English Breakfast had arrived.

* * *

These were among the factors that had elevated breakfast to its new prominence. By 1887, the year of Queen Victoria's Golden Jubilee, England was the most prosperous nation in the world, with an Empire that embraced a quarter of the world's population. The *nouveaux riches* and middle classes had taken to the country with enthusiasm. Some with great new wealth had purchased extensive lands and built grand houses, others had purchased smaller estates with houses already on them—even if they knew nothing about how estates should be run and tenants managed. Still others rented country houses from impoverished gentry, rented shooting rights, and even rented horses to hunt with. Instead of leading a country life in the traditional manner, they opted for style over substance and developed a more luxurious version of gentry ways. Their houses were too comfortable, their house parties too ostentatious, their repasts too lavish to be strictly authentic. A case in point was Waddesdon Manor, built in 1883 by Baron Ferdinand de Rothschild in the French chateau style and furnished with antique French furniture, draperies and *objêts* that were gilded, swagged and inlaid to such a degree that some members of the old guard found the opulence oppressive—which did not stop them from taking the hospitality offered.

In Baron Ferdinand's time, breakfasts at Waddesdon began before the guests got to the breakfast room. They were awakened by footmen in powdered wigs, followed by a servant with a trolley of early morning drinks who invited them to choose tea, coffee or a peach grown on a wall in the famous Waddesdon greenhouses. Those who chose tea were asked if they preferred China, Indian or Ceylon, with lemon, milk or cream and, if milk, whether they wanted Jersey, Hereford or Shorthorn. On the new country estates, much of the working agricultural land was disposed of or converted into decorative landscapes. Instead of using the natural produce

Roofed Peach-house

of the land as a medium of competition, owners now built extensive and expensive greenhouses where their gardeners grew foreign rarities such as nectarines, grapes and semi-tropical flowers under artificial conditions to embellish the table. Greenhouse peaches were regarded as the ultimate luxury fruit.

Some of the old gentry were able to carry on as before, but in the end it was the newly rich incomers who helped to continue the countryside tradition, albeit in modified form. The wealth and influence of the old gentry lay in land, and as the cities became the centres of wealth, the country gentry were increasingly forced to seek work off the land for the first time, joining the rising urban middle classes who had always worked. A substantial breakfast before leaving home became the new order of the day, and the meal upon which the old gentry modelled the new morning meal was the country house breakfast, which they transplanted to the city and served at an earlier hour. For

ORDER OF THE HOUSEHOLD

Morning Prayers, 8.45 A.M.
" Forsake not the assembling of yourselves together."

MEALS.

Breakfast (Kitchen & Nursery)	.	8 a.m.
„ (Dining-Room)	.	. 9 „
Kitchen Dinner „	. .	. 12.30 „
Luncheon . .	. . .	. 1.30 „
Kitchen and Nursery Tea .	.	5 „
Dinner .	. . .	. 6.30 „
Kitchen Supper	. . .	. 9 „

Post Arrives. 9 A.M.
" Kind words in which we feel the pressure of a hand."
Post Departs. 5 P.M.
"A timely written letter is a rivet in the chain of affection."
Pleasures and Duties in due order linked.

Evening Prayers, 10 P.M.

people faced with downward social mobility, 'keeping up standards'—keeping cultural capital intact in the face of economic change—is a means of maintaining identity, and for the newly-employed gentry, eating a 'proper' breakfast became something of an article of faith that was quickly taken up by the gentrifying middle classes. As time went on, country house parties and breakfasts themselves were affected by social changes. More and more of the guests worked, so house parties were often restricted to weekends—called 'Fridays to Mondays'—and breakfasts became less leisurely.

While the timing of meals had always been somewhat flexible among the country gentry, the times and composition of meals were now supposed to be as orderly and regular as possible, reflecting the changed realities of commercial and family life. Since time was now money, every minute had to be properly accounted for in the new moral and material economy. As *Mrs. Beeton's Book of Household Management* (1888) put it, 'order and punctuality are so important to the comfort and happiness of the household that every mistress should fix stated hours for meals &c which ought to be strictly observed by every member of the family' and even provided a Household Order for the day, beginning with pre-breakfast prayers. As Arnold Palmer (1985) pointed out, not every businessman could afford to leave so late for his office. In *Our Mutual Friend*, Charles Dickens's Mr Podsnap, a man 'in marine insurance', famously got up at eight, shaved close at a quarter past, breakfasted at nine and went to the city at ten, but humble clerks and shop or factory workers had to start the day much earlier.

* * *

Religious practice, the upholding of the great social tenets of respectability and responsibility, and the embracing of a Christian way of life were defining features of the new Victorian middle class. Religion offered them stability and moral certainty during a time of great change, and promoted the Protestant work ethic which further legitimised the status of the self-made man. These social aspects of religion had less appeal to the gentry and aristocracy in many of whose houses prayers were often perfunctory, reduced to a simple grace before meals, or dispensed with altogether, although they shared with the middle classes that Christian sense of certainty and superiority that justified the expansion of Empire. In many middle class households by contrast, the devotions that began the day—led by the head of the household, and including the family servants—along with the meal that followed were highly significant, being ritual enactments of spiritual, social and family values sealed by the taking of food. The Religious Tract Society, an influential Christian organisation, even published cookbooks like *The Girl's Own Cookery Book* (1882), which began with the words and music for a hymn suitable for grace before or after a meal. Over time, lengthy morning prayers were discontinued, but the breakfast meal retained a distinctive sacramental quality, put in secular terms by Leigh Hunt in this way— 'Breakfast is a forecast of the whole day. Spoil that and all is spoiled.'

The special status of breakfast was enhanced by further changes to other meals. During the working week, lunch as a sociable or family meal disappeared except among the leisured classes. Instead, lunch became a gendered meal increasingly taken outside the home, men lunching with men at their place of employment, club or eating establishment, while ladies lunched with other ladies, or did not lunch at all. Thus the evening meal became the prime occasion for formal entertaining. In town, and in the grander country houses, including those of the *nouveaux riches* which tended to employ French chefs, French cookery was still considered the *sine qua non* of fashionable dining, an old prejudice that was given fresh impetus by the celebrated chefs who came to England from France after the revolution, including Louis Ude, Antoinin Carême, Alexis Soyer and Auguste Escoffier.

French food was not universally popular in English society. The senior figures in John Galsworthy's *The Forsyte Saga,* which followed the fortunes of a family who had risen from agricultural work to city wealth in three generations and is considered the best literary portrayal of the Victorian new men, disliked 'Frenchified' food and the French custom of serving *hors d'oeuvres*. Instead, they liked nothing better than a plainly roasted saddle of mutton. Nonetheless, the long-established practice of two styles of eating, English and French, had continued despite the fact that most of the eighteenth century had been spent fighting the French. Now, however, Victorian patriotism demanded a thoroughly English emblematic repast, just as the new employment patterns required a hearty one. The French hold over lunch and dinner still obtained in fashionable and cosmopolitan circles, but there were no such things as a French breakfast or substantial French breakfast foods in any meaningful sense. So breakfast time became the bastion of Englishness, and breakfast emerged as the national meal.

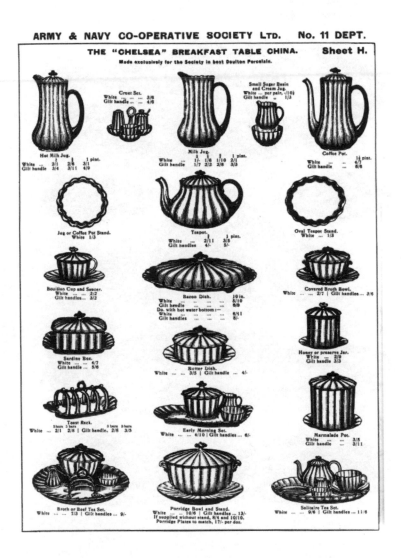

FISH.

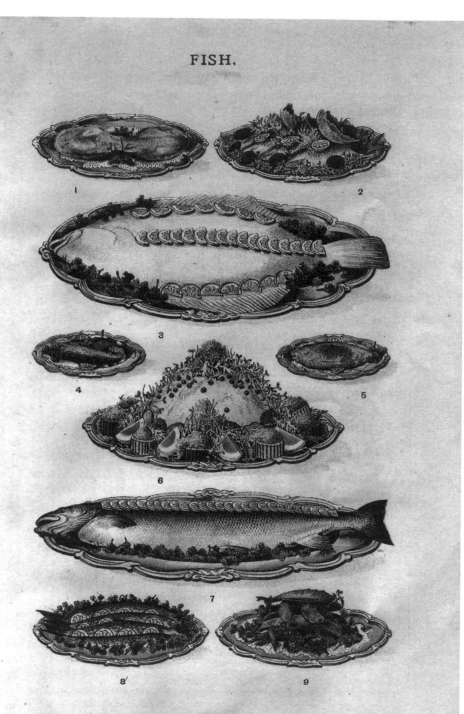

1.—Scallops au Gratin. 2.—Red Mullet. 3.—Turbot. 4.—Cod Steak. 5.—Fried Sole.
6.—Mayonnaise of Salmon. 7.—Salmon au Naturel. 8.—Brown Trout. 9.—Smelts.

CHAPTER THREE

English Breakfasts

As nearly as possible, English Breakfasts approximated to the old country ideal of locally produced or identifiably English food whether naturalised or not, cooked in a traditional manner and served bounteously. The country house breakfast was and remains the beau ideal, and *Mrs Beeton's Book of Household Management* included a diagram for the proper setting of breakfast table and sideboard in the country house manner.

Of course, there was not just one English Breakfast—there were many, depending on who was eating, when and where. During the reign of Edward VII, the English Breakfasts served at the Palace ran to several courses served promptly at nine in the morning. This was a breakfast served to the King in 1904 (Tschumi 1954): he liked his bacon cut precisely a quarter of an inch thick. Even for this most English of meals, the daily menus in the royal household were written in French as they were in grand households, a sign of the continuing contradictions and complexities signified by the differences between *haute* and national cuisine.

Breakfast—Windsor Castle
February 11, 1904

Petites soles frits
Haddock à l'Anglaise
Oeufs en cocotte
Oeufs pocher
Bacon à l'Anglais
Poulets frilées à la diable
Becassines sur canapés
Les viands froides à la gélee

The sumptuous breakfasts served in aristocratic households during country house parties have already been described. Daily breakfasts when guests were not present were less lavish, the menu depending on the preferences of the household and on the season, but the nobility and gentry certainly ate well even when only *en famille*.

The catalogues of establishments like The Army and Navy Stores in London show full breakfast services with items like special china boxes to hold the sardines that were a popular breakfast choice, covered muffin dishes, large porridge tureens with matching stands, broth bowls, bacon dishes with domed lids and a wonderful array of ingenious serving dishes with spirit lamps or hot water compartments for keeping food warm. The breakfasts of the new country set tended to include more hot food, and fancier dishes called by French names, although this did not mean that they were French in origin.

Another type of country breakfast favoured by the old-fashioned hunting, shooting and fishing squirearchy was the plain and hearty repasts like those of bygone days, in which cold roast and boiled meats played a central part, like this meal from *Jorrocks' Jaunts and Jollities* by R.S. Surtees (1838):

> About a yard and a half from the fire was placed the breakfast table; in the centre stood a magnificent uncut ham, with a great quartern loaf on one side and a huge Bologna sausage on the other; besides these there were nine eggs, two pyramids of muffins, a great deal of toast, a dozen ship-biscuits, and half a pork-pie, while a dozen kidneys were spluttering on a spit before the fire, and Betsy held a gridiron covered with mutton-chops on the top.

For the working classes, the basic cooked breakfast of bacon and eggs with tea and toast was a happy sufficiency, when they could get it. Often, in the poorer homes, cooked breakfasts could only be afforded once a week,

FOR YOUR MORNING TOAST

CHIVERS

Olde English

MARMALADE

The Aristocrat of the Breakfast Table!

on Sunday, and then only for the man of the house. Yet despite the differences, all felt they were eating the English Breakfast.

In its variations, the English Breakfast retained implicitly aristocratic associations derived from its country house roots as well as an aura of long-established tradition so convincing that the antiquity of the English Breakfast was taken for granted. The belief that a decent English Breakfast was the mark of a gentleman, even if he now had to go to work, was capitalised on by Chivers, the jam makers, in their advertisement for Olde English marmalade.

In the country and at weekends, breakfast could be a leisurely and elaborate meal, but in town during the working week, time was a priority and practical considerations came to the fore. Among the urban middle classes, the favourite workday breakfast settled quickly into variations on the theme of bacon, ham, eggs and fish. The lack of variety in breakfasts is a topic returned to time and time again by all breakfast cookbook writers. As Phillis Browne, author of *The Girl's Own Cookery Book* (1882) put it:

> I never feel uneasy about the health of a friend who can eat a thoroughly good breakfast. Unfortunately, however, there are comparatively few people nowadays who are able to do this. The majority of folks nibble a little bread-and-butter or toast, get through a small rasher of bacon, or break an egg, and discover that it is either stale, too hard, or too soft; swallow a cup of coffee, and then declare they have breakfasted. Indeed, I have known gentlemen who made their breakfasts chiefly off their newspapers.

Rose Brown explains that the object of her *Breakfast Book* (1898):

> . . .is to give real and practical help to the often perplexed housewife to whom the only answer to the ever-recurring question 'what shall we have for breakfast?' seems to be the monotonous dirge 'Eggs and bacon, bacon and eggs,' varied occasionally by snacks of fish or preserved meat of some kind.

Many breakfast cookbooks set out to whet the morning appetite by offering a choice of savoury dishes such as hashes, puddings and tasty things on toast that have disappeared from modern tables.

Even in poor households, an attempt was made to introduce variety. *Our Daily Fare* (1899) sets out several weekly breakfast menus, with full costings. Suggested breakfasts for a family of four children and two adults, to cost no more than one pound per week in total for food for all meals, or four shillings per head, were given as follows. Sunday: bread and butter, milk, toast, jam, tea or coffee. Monday: three rashers bacon, porridge, bread and butter, tea or coffee. Tuesday: Rizine (rice pudding), bread and butter, toast, jam, tea or coffee. Wednesday: potato pie, bread and butter, jam. Tea or coffee. Thursday: bread and butter, milk, beef rissoles, tea or coffee. Friday: boiled eggs, dripping toast, bread and butter, tea and toast, tea or coffee. Saturday: porridge, bread and butter, toast, tea or coffee. However, the cost in

shillings and pence was only part of the total, the cost in time was arguably more burdensome.

Breakfast and Savoury Dishes by R.O.C. (1883), intended for a less modest household, gives a money and time costing for each recipe. The cost of preparing two pounds of potted beef, sufficient for a number of people, was two shillings and nine and a half pence, but the cost in time was two hours and a half. Pigeon pie cost four shillings and eight and three quarters pence to make, and one and three quarter hours time to prepare. Varied cookery placed a heavy burden on the Angel of the House or her kitchen servants and cook.

Variety and the tempting of the masculine appetite were means to a greater end. According to Mary Hooper, author of *The Handbook for the Breakfast Table* (1873):

> If men could, before leaving for their business, have a suitable breakfast, how great a boon it would be to them! And how many lives, now sacrificed to the pressure of the times, might be prolonged if the physical powers were more duly sustained during the early part of the day by a good breakfast.

The anonymous author of *Our Daily Fare and How to Provide It* (1899) cautioned:

> We would advise all young housekeepers to try and make this meal a pleasant and varied one, it being, particularly for a man going to business, a most important one. . . Give a little time to the arrangement and preparation of breakfast, make the table look nice and have everything to hand for with business men there is seldom time for waiting with this meal—and do not let it be the hurried, slovenly one it so often is.

Indeed, breakfast was seen as the proving ground of a woman's domestic artistry. As Mary Jewry urged in *Warne's Domestic Cookery* (1879)—'A lady's taste and nicety are very perceptible at the breakfast-table. . . A nicely-laid, pretty, appetizing breakfast is a great promoter of good temper and harmony through the ensuing day'.

* * *

The 1800's are often described as the 'masculine century', a period of fundamental shifts in gender roles and expectations. A man's mission, whatever his place in society, was now seen to be the earning of a livelihood, or the custodianship of inheritance, that would support his domestic establishment and family, while the role of women became the sustaining of masculine enterprise, not least through the provision of the meal that prepared him for his daily work. Breakfast was and is the meal men take most seriously, and the 'Tabular Introduction' on the elements of the perfect breakfast included later in this volume fairly represents the masculine point of view

on the subject in a timeless and amusing way. The possession of a breakfast room became a mark of gentility in the new suburban homes. Even Mr. Pooter, the lower middle class city clerk in George and Weedon Grossmith's (1892) *Diary of a Nobody* had a breakfast room.

The very future of home, hearth and, ultimately, the nation and Empire, was thought by many to depend on the English Breakfast. A profound belief in the moral virtue of good, plain English cooking and the English Breakfast had been institutionalised in the English public schools, which taught the sons of the middle classes to be gentlemen. A unique feature of English public schools was fagging, the system in which younger boys became the informal servants of older boys, one of the fag's duties being to prepare breakfast-type snacks for them on demand. As P. Morton Shand observed in 1929:

> Only public school fags can make perfectly golden, perfectly crisp and yet perfectly spongy toast, for the simple reason that they are properly beaten should any one of the eight, pluperfect, decrusted triangles, which constitute a fag-masters traditional portion, evince the slightest sign of scraping, uneven cutting, excessive thickness or imperfect saturation with butter. . . The public school system seems to me amply vindicated in that it teaches boys to make toast and. . .to prepare such simple dishes as buttered eggs, or to fry bacon and kippers to perfection. . . That is a good deal in return for an education that probably teaches them little else of real utility, for these are just the very things that nine out of ten servants cannot be taught to do. . . It may be an abominable action to beat a boy for a bad translation of Livy. . .but it is certainly laudable to beat him for clumsily burning one's toast. King Alfred, the first English fag, when put to the task, learnt that one must suffer stinging rebukes before one can hope to begin to con over one's lessons in the school of life.

The public schools fed the military, the Church and the professional Civil Service, who carried the English breakfast to the far-flung outposts of the British Empire. The advertising imagery of the period reveals that the semi-mystical semi-commercial ideal of England in the form of iconic export commodities, breakfast foods prime among them, were a vitally important element in the joint progress of trade and civilisation (Opie 1985). Cargo ships on the empire routes carried consignments of

English breakfast ingredients from establishments like Fortnum and Mason and the Army and Navy Stores—tinned Wiltshire bacon and Dorset butter, tinned whole roast grouse and game pies, English clover honey, York and Bradenham hams, five kinds of marmalade and jams galore. All across the globe there were many establishments like the Britannia Restaurant, situated 'within two minutes' walk of the jetty' at Colombo, which provided 'carriages, guides, jinrickshaws—and breakfasts at any time'.

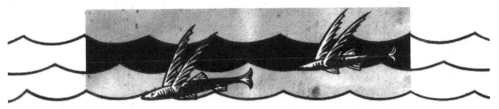

Cunard
White Star

R.M.S.
"HOMERIC."

September 21, 1935

Breakfast

Sweet Melon   Grape Fruit   Apples   Oranges
Cold Baked Apples
Preserved Figs in Syrup   Compôte of Prunes
Juices : Orange   Prune
H-O. Oats   Boiled Hominy
Grape Nuts   Post Toasties   Triscuits   Shredded Wheat
All Bran   Force   Krumbles   Corn Flakes
Tribrek   Bran Flakes   Puffed Wheat
Rice Flakes   Bisc-O'Rye

Onion Soup au Gratin

Fried Mullet   Lochfyne Herring, Ring Potatoes
Fried Whiting   Halibut Fish Cakes

Eggs : Fried, Turned, Poached, Boiled and Buttered
Omelettes : Plain, Fines Herbes, Lorraine, Parmentier, Parsley

Hashed Mutton and Walnuts
Scotch Collops   Turkey Liver Sauté, Bordelaise

Potatoes : Sauté and Creamed Mashed

TO ORDER FROM THE GRILL (10 to 15 Minutes)
Wiltshire Bacon   Cumberland Ham
Mutton Chop   Lamb's Kidney Brochette
Chipolata Sausage   Cambridge Sausage

COLD BUFFET :
Roast Beef   Boiled Ham   Roast Mutton
Galantine of Chicken   Breakfast Sausage
Radishes   Spring Onions   Lettuce

White and Graham Rolls   Hovis Bread   Crescents
Wholewheat Bread   Raisin Bread   Vienna Bread   Rye Bread
Pulled Bread   Cottage Loaves   Scotch Oatcake   Brioches
Parkerhouse Rolls   Energen Rolls   Toast Melba
Hovis Scones   Mixed Fruit Buns   Devonshire Scones   Waffles
Buckwheat and Griddle Cakes, Maple Syrup

Marmalade   Honey   Jam
Coffee   Instant Postum   Kaffee Hag
Indian, Ceylon and China Tea   Iced Tea and Coffee
Cadbury's Cup Chocolate
Horlick's Malted Milk, Plain or Chocolate Flavour

*Passengers on Special Diet are invited to make their
requirements known*

ORIENT LINE.

TOURIST

Breakfast

STEWED MIXED FRUIT WITH RICE

OATMEAL PORRIDGE
FORCE   GRAPE NUTS

KIPPERED HERRINGS

BROILED BREAKFAST BACON

EGGS : FRIED AND TURNED
TO ORDER : BOILED EGGS

TRIPE FRITTERS & CRISP FRIED ONIONS

PURÉE & PAILLE POTATOES

SALISBURY CAKES WITH SYRUP

COLD SIDEBOARD :
HAM D'LIGHT   ROAST LAMB

WHITE & GRAHAM ROLLS   TOAST
FRUIT BREAD
SCOTCH OATCAKES   PRESERVES
TEA   COFFEE   COCOA

S.S. "ORSOVA."
WEDNESDAY. 30TH MARCH. 1932

The makers of the Empire sailed out on ships that began every day with English breakfasts, offering different menus to different classes of passengers. The breakfasts in First Class, like the 1935 Cunard menu for the R.M.S. Homeric, were legendary, but even Tourist Class menus like the 1932 example from the Orient Line's S.S. Orsova which sailed between London and Australia is substantial and satisfyingly English.

Abroad, wondering how the inhabitants of such a small island could have built such a large empire, many foreigners concluded that it must be due to English food, particularly the English breakfast. This view was not discouraged, because as Tacitus had noted so long before, civilising through cuisine is a powerful force, and it was also of great benefit to the English export trade. Inevitably, as foreign imports and new foods like curry came in to England, there were periodic reassertions of the need to purify the national palate by eating only home produced food, as had once happened in Rome. But foreign influences crept in, as witnessed by the popularity of dishes like kedgeree and Bombay duck (dried fish) for breakfast.

There were other variations of the traditional breakfast—the Welsh breakfast included the seaweed laverbread, served with bacon, while the Irish breakfast boasted white and black puddings (blood sausages). Scottish breakfasts were known for the excellence of the baked goods and porridge, and for smoked fish, particularly finnan haddock and kippered herring, which often took the place of bacon. The absence of bacon from Scottish breakfasts was once attributed to a superstitious fear of the pig by the Scots, but in fact resulted from the unsuitability of Scottish terrain for pig-rearing in the traditional foraging manner. These meals have always been treated as regional variations of the English Breakfast, at least by the English, not as national dishes in their own right.

It has never been considered correct to call the meal the British Breakfast, even though the country became formally known as The Kingdom of Great Britain in 1707, and has been The Kingdom of Great Britain and Ireland since 1800. The English Breakfast is the national dish of a mythic and indivisible England, a repast that, despite differences in execution, binds its people together as one.

The English Breakfast came through the Great War of 1914–1918, only to begin a new battle on the home front. Throughout the 1920's, the growing taste for all things modern and American made the English Breakfast seem very old-fashioned, although to its partisans that was its very appeal. On the table, the greatest enemies were grapefruit and packaged cereals, both American imports. Grapefruit was widely believed to burn away fat, helping women to achieve the newly fashionable slender silhouette. Convenience was the real advantage of packaged cereals, but it was sold as a health food so wives serving it to husband and family need not feel guilty at giving them short shrift, and it often had a hidden moral agenda—the American brothers Will and John Kellogg, whose eponymous company went on to invent and produce the world's most famous breakfast cereals, were ardent supporters of vegetarianism. Economy was also a consideration. As one large American producer of convenience food put it—'It is all ready for your table. It saves your materials and saves your fuel'. These packaged repasts did not meet with universal approval in England. P. Morton Shand echoed the opinion of many when he wrote disdainfully—'No one who can get good porridge would ever want to eat those nauseating American proprietary cereals.'

Other factors were even more threatening to the future of the English Breakfast. Pre-war society was dependent on a large population in domestic service, and of all servants the cook was arguably the most important. In 1905, *The Lady's Realm* magazine had advised its readers 'The first meal of the day is difficult to vary sufficiently to tempt capricious appetites unless one possesses a first-class cook.' While many cooks learned their trade as apprentices to cooks working in households, there were also a number of schools that taught cookery to women who wanted to become professional cooks. In the early twentieth century and particularly after World War I, the appeal of domestic service declined sharply and servants became both scarce and more expensive to employ. Schools that had formerly catered to working or lower middle class women now had a new clientele, young

women of the middle and gentry classes who could no longer afford to employ a cook, and could not learn cooking from their mothers, who had never cooked for themselves.

Manufacturers of cooking stoves like the Valor-Perfection quickly capitalised on this development with advertisements that suggested their equipment could do much of the work of a human cook. But even with the best equipment, domesticity had diminishing appeal for a growing number of independent young women, many of whom were admirers of Virginia Woolf who declared in *Professions for Women* (1931) that 'killing the Angel in the House was part of the occupation of a woman writer.'

Inevitably, the problem of culinary monotony increased. The complaint with which *What Shall We Have For Breakfast?* by Agnes C. Maitland (1926) opens is representative of the period:

> In most English middle-class households breakfast is of all meals the most uninteresting. The monotony of fried bacon and boiled eggs is seldom varied, except by an occasional dish of fish, or bacon and eggs fried together. This, no doubt, is partly due to the early hour at which breakfast must be taken in most homes, and partly to the want of resource and knowledge of an ordinary English cook.

Between the wars, the defence of English cooking in general and the English breakfast in particular was conducted energetically in the pages of *The Times*, the newspaper of choice of the gentrified middle class. Mustard—an essential breakfast condiment—from the low fields around Norwich, marmalade and jam from Dundee, the herrings of Lowestoft and Yarmouth, succulent Wiltshire bacon and the unrivalled flavour and beauty of English plums were celebrated in prose by *Times* writers. The old conflict between French and English cookery continued. In 1914, C. Herman Senn O.B.E., French by birth but long resident in England where he became chef at the Reform Club wrote in *The Times*: 'It has too long been the fashion to decry the English as against the foreign cook.' This theme was revisited regularly by contributors to the letter pages and by the paper's own correspondents. Many readers of *The Times* followed the correspondence over breakfast served in the restaurant cars of railway trains carrying them in to work in the city. The breakfast menu of the Great Eastern Railway offered passengers porridge, haddock, cold fowl and ham, sausage, bacon and eggs, cutlets, steaks and chops, in addition to tea, coffee and fruit of the season.

In the early 1920's, a regular feature in *The Times* called 'The Woman's View, from A Correspondent' masked the identity of Lady (Agnes) Jekyll, who

wrote amusingly on matters of interest to women, frequently about food. Of all meals, the one she wrote about most often was breakfast, beginning one piece— 'Breakfast is the most difficult meal of the day, whether from its social or its culinary aspect. Many of us feel like that man who, meeting a bore, said, "If you have got anything to say to me, I wish you would kindly say it to somebody else".'

A feature on the country breakfast table written by Lady Jekyll for *The Times* on October 29, 1921, perfectly captures the status of the English Breakfast at a time when women of the gentry and middle classes were facing the prospect of cooking for themselves—one suspects not always successfully. This may have been the beginning of what the noted food writer Jane Grigson (1979) called the 'lack of professionalism' that she believed did substantial damage to traditional English cookery in the years after World War I.

A Country Breakfast Table

By Lady Jekyll

We show very little imagination in our breakfast fare. Is it because we have not had the French to help us in devising just the right dishes, or because we have slowly sunk into a series of grooves and make no effort to rise above them? Or again, is it that on this point our men are unexacting, and prefer the well-known round of herrings, haddock, kidneys, sausages, and eggs and bacon, while so many women, owing, perhaps, to the dictum that it is good for the figure to forgo breakfast, have given up eating it? In the country, however, the courage even of the slimmest woman has been known to fail and, faced with a houseful of healthy visitors, the hostess must set her wits to work.

Of course, no breakfast table is complete without eggs and bacon, and the British male is apt to say 'hands off' here; but there is variety even in the method of serving eggs and bacon, and it is worth while experimenting, even if the experiment is a failure. There was once an American who converted whole housefuls of English folk to eating their marmalade with their bacon instead of after it, so perhaps, in these more adventurous days, there may be an enthusiastic reception for another somewhat similar recipe:

The ham and eggs are fried in the ordinary way, with the addition of golden syrup or molasses, and cooked just enough for the syrup to begin to set but not to stiffen. Potatoes, mashed in milk, are piled in the centre, and the ham and eggs served round with the contents of the frying pan poured over all. Is it worth risking? You may well find it so. But if the conventional Englishman turns down his thumbs and will not be lured to eat sweets with his bacon, do not be disheartened, but next morning omit the mashed potatoes and molasses and add slices of potatoes fried, with the bacon, to the regular dish, and he will not fail to praise this innovation.

The defence of English cookery in general and the English Breakfast in particular was carried out in a wider arena than the pages of *The Times*. In reaction to what some saw as the Americanisation of the nation, there had been an upsurge of interest in folk

and regional cuising, leading to the foundation of
the English Folk Cookery Association by Florence
White who began her 1931 book *Good Things
in England* with the ringing words 'This book
is an attempt to capture the charm of England's
cookery before it is completely crushed out of
existence.'

   Travelling the English countryside, Florence
White gathered recipes for traditional food, still
eaten regularly, that had been largely unchanged
by the passage of time—mutton hams, frumenty
and mead, demonstrating what anthropologists
have long known about the innate conservatism
of food, and the special way in which it carries history. There were many recipes
involving bacon and ham, reflecting what has been called the persistence of the
English predilection for fried bacon, apparently little changed since the days that
William Shakespeare in *King Henry IV Part I* had Falstaff shout 'On bacons, on',
using the derogatory term for the common people, who were called after their
customary food.

   Along with good, plain English cookery went the moral undertones with which
it had so long been entwined. The best explicit statement was made by a naturalized
Englishman, Joseph Conrad, in the preface he wrote for a cookbook by his wife
Jessie, first published in 1925:

> Good cooking is a moral agent. By good cooking I mean the conscientious preparation
> of the simple food of every-day life, not the more or less skilful concoction of idle feasts
> and rare dishes. Conscientious cooking is an enemy to gluttony. . . The decency of our
> life is for a great part a matter of good taste, of the correct appreciation of what is fine
> in simplicity.

Traditional English cooking flourished until 1939, when war was declared. World
War II struck the English Breakfast a blow from which it has never fully recovered.
For one thing, at least in the cities, fresh eggs and bacon were hard to come by.
Foodstuffs were strictly rationed and people ate what they could get. In 1940, the
food writer Ambrose Heath began his cookbook *Good Breakfasts* in this way:

> The lack of bacon has disturbed our native breakfast-dish and brought doubt and
> distress into many an early morning kitchen. The purpose of this little book is to help
> to dispel these two concomitants of war-time and still to promote what Izaak Walton
> called "a good, honest, wholesome, hungry breakfast".

However, his recipes for dishes like rabbit roll and cods tongues failed to meet
with general approval, and by the time the cookbook appeared many of the more
conventional ingredients Heath specified, like fresh eggs, had become virtually

unobtainable, and remained so until the end of the war. Fuel was also scarce, so as little cooking as possible became the rule. The English Breakfast was remembered wistfully by many, including George Orwell when writing *The Lion and the Unicorn*, but by then it was much more than a meal. It was the symbol of home, family, the land, custom, all that was worth fighting for, and all that had always been worth fighting for in a past beyond memory, but not beyond feeling.

Rationing continued for years after the war ended in 1945. When breakfast foods finally came off rationing, many people had got out of the traditional breakfast habit, and other things had changed. Men had less time for a leisurely breakfast at home, and women were going out to work in their numbers. In homes where they were still cooked at all, traditional breakfasts tended to appear only at the weekend, despite the continuing efforts to re-establish cooked breakfasts on a daily basis by the makers of cookers like Regulo, and by the suppliers of electricity and gas.

The English Breakfast persisted in outposts of Empire—the underwater explorer Hans Hass (1954) came upon a typical colonial scene in Port Sudan in the early 1950's, when he encountered the Commissioner breakfasting in lonely splendour in a large dining room at the Residence, seated at a long, polished table laid with toast, butter, coffee, grilled bacon and what Hass described as 'a fish swimming in oil'. The English Breakfast also continued to sail the seas, and at least on shipboard there seemed little doubt about its future. The Peninsular and Oriental (P&O) Line was still offering a special children's version of the English Breakfast on the S.S. Corfu in 1959.

Back at home, the English Breakfast has not disappeared entirely, but as the anthropologist David Pocock (1985) noted, since World War II breakfast has been the vulnerable point for all changes that make for speed and simplicity, as demonstrated by the present popularity of cereals, yoghurts and pre-baked goods such as muffins and croissants that do not even need to be toasted. There have been other broad changes in breakfasting practices. Even a brief look at Victorian breakfast cookbooks reveals striking differences between the present and the past—the Victorian preference for savoury flavours over sweet ones, their smaller consumption of sugar, and the virtual disappearance of offal such as kidneys of which the Victorians were so fond. The great variety of fish that once graced the breakfast table have been reduced to

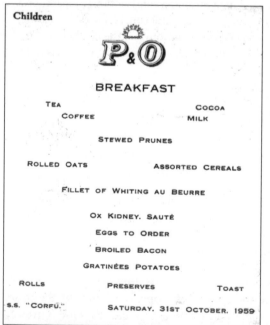

Children

P&O

BREAKFAST

TEA   COCOA
     COFFEE   MILK

          STEWED PRUNES

ROLLED OATS   ASSORTED CEREALS

     FILLET OF WHITING AU BEURRE

          OX KIDNEY. SAUTÉ

          EGGS TO ORDER

          BROILED BACON

     GRATINÉES POTATOES

ROLLS   PRESERVES   TOAST

S.S. "CORFU."   SATURDAY. 31ST OCTOBER. 1959

BETTER
BREAKFASTS
in the Regulo-controlled
NEW WORLD OVEN

just three—kippers, smoked haddock and smoked salmon—and even these are served infrequently. Fruit juices, mainstay of today's breakfasts, hardly appear. Coffee has eclipsed tea and cocoa as the favoured morning drink. Family breakfasts are rare, and increasingly breakfast is a meal for one. In the home today, the middle class cooked English Breakfast—usually a combination of eggs, bacon, sausage, tomato, mushrooms and possibly black pudding—still tends to appear, if at all, only at the weekend, usually on Sunday and especially if the main Sunday meal is in the evening, not at lunchtime.

The bounteous and leisurely English Breakfast survives in brunch, a meal that slips in and out of fashion. Effectively a country house breakfast without the game and with desserts and champagne, Bucks Fizz or Bloody Mary cocktails added, it is usually served on a Sunday morning from eleven o'clock onwards. But the English Breakfast is now usually seen only in its simplest incarnation—the bacon, eggs, baked beans and grilled tomato combination beloved of the English working man, ideally eaten in a simple workers' cafe. The democratisation of society in the post-war years made working class food fashionable—but it should now be clear that this is not all there is to the English Breakfast.

The country house breakfast was a meal eaten by the members of a particular class —and predominantly its male members—at a particular point in historical time when economic and social circumstances, including a substantial part of the population in domestic service, favoured it. As such, its heyday lasted roughly a century, from the accession of Queen Victoria to World War II. However, it was the outcome of a very much longer culinary tradition and socio-cultural heritage that included beliefs about the morality of food which had its roots in antiquity and in the historical specificities of contesting English and French foodways, and it was much more than just a meal. The English Breakfast was an ideal that people aspired to, and achieved when they could, if only occasionally. It became a symbol of the nation, reinventing it in the process; an emblem of gentility and a link to a past made real through belief. At home and abroad, it signified a certain social order and defined 'Englishness'. Once established as the national meal it was eaten in some form by members of all classes in a unifying cultural practice. And so it remains, even though its symbolism, mythology and history have been largely forgotten.

* * *

Having seen how English plain cookery developed and how and when breakfast came to be the national meal, it remains to show how the English Breakfast was once cooked, presented and served. There follow three very different Victorian and Edwardian cookbooks by leading culinary figures of the period that between them embrace the theory and practice of the English Breakfast, along with the text of *The Young Ladies' Journal Extra Supplement on Breakfast and the Breakfast-Table* and the masculine memorandum on the perfect breakfast mentioned previously. Taken together, they offer a feast of lost dishes that richly deserve rediscovery.

No attempt has been made to standardise the cookbooks, convert or introduce measures or adapt the recipes in any way. They are presented in full with their original page numbers and stand as works of their time. The books have been published in their entirety and the comparison between them is instructive. *The Breakfast Book* (1865) epitomises the conspicuous consumption that characterised the Victorian elite, among whom breakfast was often a meal for entertaining guests. *Breakfast Dishes for Every Morning of Three Months* (1884) reflects practices in humbler homes where considerable ingenuity was applied to avoiding waste and achieving variety, while *Fifty Breakfasts* (1894) emphasises the importance of forward planning in the preparation of breakfasts intended to serve as the sure foundation for the important business of the day ahead. Experienced cooks will be able to follow the recipes and instructions with little difficulty. Inexperienced cooks can begin with the simpler recipes, of which there are many. Those interested primarily in culinary

Breakfast for one.

and social history may read the cookbooks as texts, but it is hoped that they will try the recipes. When reading or writing about food, one should also be able to taste it.

Like all great cultural traditions, the English Breakfast has taken on a life of its own, larger and longer than any of the many peoples and things that have contributed to it over time. But a culinary tradition only goes on living if it is cooked from and eaten. The future of the English Breakfast—the next chapter in its biography and its next moments in culinary time—is in your hands.

GAME.

1—Barded Partridges.   2—Roast Partridges.   3—Roast Surrey Fowls.
4—Larded Guinea Fowl.   5—Roast Plovers.   6—Stuffed Capon à la Mayonnaise.
7—Roast Gosling.   8—Roast Pigeons.

U

CHAPTER FOUR

Breakfast and the Breakfast-Table

The Young Ladies' Journal

Women's magazines were a highly influential form of popular culture in the nineteenth century. Appearing weekly or monthly, these publications carried a lively mix of fashion features, serialised fiction, accounts of travel, gardening notes, poetry, letters from readers, household hints, recipes and free needlework patterns. The 1860's saw the appearance of the first magazines aimed at younger middle class readers up to the age of about twenty-five. It was often to magazines of this kind that young women initially looked for domestic and culinary guidance.

The two leading English magazines for young women were Beeton's *Young Englishwoman*, published by Samuel Beeton, and *The Young Ladies' Journal*, published by his rival, Edward Harrison. *The Young Ladies' Journal*, which appeared between 1864 and 1920, was noted for its special supplements on subjects such as the Dinner-Table, the Work-Table and Serviettes. The fourth supplement, the text of which follows, gives an excellent description of the way the English Breakfast was served, and the breakfast table arranged, in the mid-1880's.

BREAKFAST AND THE BREAKFAST-TABLE

Our Dinner-Table Supplement has met with such a hearty welcome from our numerous readers, so manifold have been their kind and complimentary comments thereon, that at the request of many of them we intend to describe the arrangements of the table, &c., for other meals. We continue with the Breakfast-Table, and preface our directions by remarking that for the health of all the members of a family, breakfast should be regarded as one of the most, if not the most, important meal of the day. It comes after a long fast, and is a prelude to the day's work. The gentleman who has business or professional duties should take a good breakfast at leisure, as in many instances it is uncertain at what time he may be enabled to have lunch; and to the young folks of a family who no longer have meals in the nursery, a good breakfast taken quietly is most desirable, as it helps them to sustain the strain of study, which healthy, well-nourished young people are much more likely to excel in than those whose appetites and digestion are at fault.

A fixed hour for breakfast is desirable, and it should be as closely adhered to as circumstances will permit. Breakfast is not a ceremonious meal, therefore those who are down at the appointed time are not expected to wait for others who are late. If visitors are staying in the house, it is the rule, when bidding them good night, to mention the hour for breakfast, and to ask at what time they would like to be called, if they would like hot water, or whether milk, tea, or coffee should be sent to them in their rooms. Those who make a habit of these little indulgences are sometimes unhinged for the day if deprived of them. Ladies, if at all delicate, should be offered breakfast in their rooms; it is often a relief both to hostess and guest when visitors accept this offer, as it saves any hurry to the guest, and gives the hostess time to make her preparations, necessary for the day.

There should be no confusion, no hurry over breakfast, and the food prepared for it should be carefully selected and cooked, so that it may be thoroughly appreciated and enjoyed, and the breakfast-table should be made to look as pretty and dainty as possible, to tempt those with delicate appetites to partake of the food prepared. A considerate housekeeper will therefore study to have on the table the viands that are best liked, varying the dishes as much as the season and her means will admit.

In houses where there is a breakfast-room, the meal is of course served in it; in others, the dining-room is used for breakfast. And one of the first things which the servant who attends to the room should be directed to do is open the windows and door, so as to thoroughly freshen and ventilate it, and free the room from any odour of smoke or food remaining from the previous evening.

If the arrangement of the house admits of a breakfast-room it is most desirable for several reasons; one is that it may be swept and dusted in some spare moments of the previous day, leaving only the fire-lighting (in the winter) and the laying of the cloth; another reason is that if any visitors or members of a family are late down, it does not interfere with the luncheon-hour, nor the preparation that may have to be

THE YOUNG LADIES' JOURNAL
EXTRA SUPPLEMENT (No. 4).

BREAKFAST, & THE BREAKFAST-TABLE,

Presented Gratis with the February Part of "The Young Ladies' Journal."

made for it. In large establishments, where a butler and footman are kept, they lay the breakfast-cloth and place cold meats, game, or poultry on the sideboard, after first covering it with a damask cloth, and furnishing it with a plentiful supply of cold plates, knives, forks, and spoons; the hot meats and other hot dishes are placed on a side-table. The cups and saucers are set to the right hand of each person, and the butler, footman, or parlour-maid, as the case may be, takes round the tea and coffee pots, pouring out which ever may be desired; sugar and milk are placed at convenient intervals, and to this one helps one's self.

In other houses where only one footman or parlour-maid is kept, the breakfast-table is laid as shown in our illustration, and after the mistress of the house has poured out tea and coffee they are handed to those at table by the servant, who waits until all present are served, then leaves the room to attend to other duties.

A parlour maid wears a print dress, white cap and apron, when serving breakfast, and she would clear away after the breakfast, taking the china and plate to the pantry, the dishes of meat, bread &c to the kitchen, and the meat plates to be washed up in the scullery.

It is not, however, with those who have a retinue of well-trained servants who should know their duties, that we consider it needful to give instruction, but to young wives and others who have to train servants that may not, and very frequently do not know, the proper method of arranging tables in accordance with what is considered the correct mode. These, we feel sure, will be at no loss if they look carefully at our illustration (on page 59 of this book) and read through the following directions, which we have endeavoured to make as clear and simple as possible.

First, then, the breakfast-table should, like the dining table, be a long one, and on it a baize cloth should be laid under the damask cloth. In the matter of cloths, attempts are made now and then to introduce damask cloths and serviettes for the breakfast-table with colours in the borders; others again with frills are seen, but we think that nothing looks so well as the cloth of pure white double damask, with serviettes to match, and that the only ornamentation really desirable is a handsomely embroidered monogram or initial letters worked on them. It is not the rule to put a tray on the breakfast-table, but a breakfast-stand is desirable, on which the tea-pot, coffee-pot or chocolate-pot should be set, with cream and milk jugs and a hot-water jug if a kettle is not on the table. The breakfast-stand may be a plated one, or it may be of china, or a wood mount filled in with porcelain tiles is both useful and pretty. Worked or beaded stands are no longer fashionable; although those who have them need not discard them, as it is always pleasant to see familiar things liked and valued. The stand is placed immediately behind the breakfast cups, which are arranged in a double or single row, according to their number, at the end of the table at which the lady of the house sits. Behind the breakfast-stand, the kettle, with lamp to keep it boiling, should be stood, and behind it a slop-basin.

To each person should be placed a small breakfast serviette, a breakfast-plate, fish-knife and fork, two small knives, and one fork. If a large number of persons are at table two or three additional cream and milk jugs and sugar basins should be placed at intervals on the table; this saves much trouble to the lady who presides. Hot milk should be served if coffee or chocolate are taken. Where there is a small breakfast-party, four breakfast cruets placed at each corner are sufficient; if a larger number, salt-cellars and small pepper-castors are set to each person. It is always nice to have a few fresh-cut flowers in a centre vase on the table; when they are scarce a flowering plant or plants may be substituted. The arrangement of the flowers, however, should be simple. In country houses, where flowers are abundant, a bowl filled with daffodils or wall-flowers looks pretty in the centre, and in the summer a bowl of roses has a charming effect. In early spring a couple of small low vases with violets make a room fragrant. It is not, however, considered to be in good taste to have any formal or elaborate arrangement of flowers on the breakfast-table.

On many breakfast tables honey, marmalade or jams, sardines, potted meats, &c are distributed over the table in appropriate receptacles, many of which are sold in very pretty forms and devices. One or two sorts of fancy bread, a bread-tray with a loaf and bread-knife, and one or two toast-racks with dry toast and hot buttered toast are served at some tables. The latter should be in a covered toast-dish. Pats of butter or little balls and shells, which may easily be made with butter-spattles, are served in glass, plated or coleport china dishes, and look well, garnished with small springs of parsley, or butter passed through a potato-press, nicely arranged, has a very pretty effect. An egg-stand of silver, electro-plate or china is used by some persons; others prefer to put hot boiled eggs into a hot, folded serviette; the water lily is a suitable one, directions for folding which were given recently in our Serviette Supplement. A second serviette should be folded into a square, made hot, and put over the eggs. Where they are liked very hot, the serviette containing the eggs may be put on a hot-water plate; if this mode is adopted an egg-cup and egg-spoon are put on each breakfast plate.

It is not the rule for a servant to wait at breakfast in small households. After laying the table, and making all needful preparations, she sounds the gong or rings a breakfast-bell, as the case may be, and goes away to attend to her morning work.

Those who really appreciate a good cup of tea should have the tea-caddy in the breakfast room, the teapot should be made hot with hot water, carefully drained, and the tea put in it, and as much boiling water poured on it as is required. Three minutes is the proper time for it to stand; tea that has stood for some time is unwholesome. Where it is liked and agrees with persons, chocolate and preparations of cocoa will be found to be more nourishing and sustaining for breakfast than either tea or coffee. Coffee suits some persons better than either tea or cocoa; where it is used, it should be freshly ground, and to ensure its being perfectly clear the Vienna coffee machine is excellent to prepare it in. Hot milk should be served with coffee.

The master of the house serves hot or cold meats, or hot fish; his place is usually at one end of the table; hot and cold plates are placed before him, and hot meats are frequently served on hot water dishes. Sometimes only the hot dishes are placed at the

end of the table, cold ones are put at the side, and some other member of the family
will serve them.

We will mention a number of dishes that are considered appropriate for the
breakfast-table. In some places it is easy to procure fresh fish, and, first among all
fish for breakfast, trout is the greatest luxury to most persons, next a sole, whiting,
and even dabs, are served at breakfast, when one can be certain that they are fresh
caught. They are very good, but, if not of the freshest, their introduction at breakfast
is the greatest mistake as the odour is just enough to debar one from partaking of
anything else. This objection extends to dried fish, such as bloaters and kippers;
these, so much relished by some, will entirely destroy the appetite of others. Dried
salmon, and good dried haddocks, are much esteemed in some households, and are
not open to the same objection. The remains of boiled cod or salmon, made up into
little cakes, are always liked at breakfast. Of course, the season must, in a measure,
guide the housekeeper in her selection of dishes. Cold game, raised game pies, cold
fowl, pigeon pies, raised pork pies, ham, tongue, pressed beef, galantine of veal,
brawn, collared head, &c., are among the savoury dishes preferred at this meal. In
hot dishes, devilled legs of fowls or turkeys, hot roast partridges or pigeons, kidneys,
sausages, and eggs dressed in various ways, ham or bacon, boiled and toasted, cutlets,
savoury omelettes, croquettes of fowl, meat or game, may all, or any of them, appear
in turns on the breakfast-table. When watercress is in season, it is wholesome and
nice for breakfast; mushrooms, too, are regarded as a real delicacy, and tomatoes,
cooked and uncooked, are esteemed by many persons. On other tables, baked apples,
stewed pears, gooseberry-fool, dishes of fresh strawberries, raspberries and currants,
are appreciated as breakfast dishes in some houses; rolls, scones and other fancy
bread are liked by some persons.

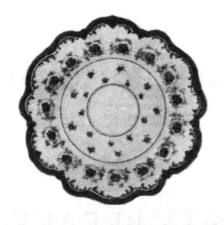

CHAPTER FIVE

The Perfect Breakfast

'A Mere Man'
(Sir Frederick William Andrewes)

Preceding the three breakfast cookbooks is this 'Tabular Introduction' to *The Dictionary of Dainty Breakfasts* by Phyllis Browne (Sarah Sharp Hamer). The pseudonym 'A Mere Man' masked the identity of the writer, Sir Frederick William Andrewes, Professor of Pathology in the University of London and a pioneer in bacteriology.

The Dictionary

OF

DAINTY BREAKFASTS

BY

PHYLLIS BROWNE

WITH A TABULAR INTRODUCTION

BY

A MERE MAN

v

INTRODUCTORY.

A breakfast should consist:—

- A. Of a fundamental dish.
- B. Of one or more trifling accessories for the benefit of (1) those who are so hungry that the fundamental dish does not suffice, and (2) those who feel so sick that they cannot touch it.
- C. Of fresh fruit, stewed or tinned fruit, jam or marmalade.
- D. Of drinks.
- E. Of bread, toast or scones.

A. FUNDAMENTAL DISHES.

These may be considered under the heads of:—

1. Ham or bacon, alone, or in combination with other articles.
2. Eggs cooked in various ways.
3. Fish and allied products.
4. Certain internal portions of the animal economy.
5. Meats of different kinds, hot or cold.

1. Ham or bacon.
   - (a) A cold ham or gammon of bacon may serve as the fundamental dish or as an accessory dish.
   - (b) Fried or broiled ham, or bacon, alone. This cannot be recommended as a primary dish, except for those who are feeling chippy as the result of the evening previous.
   - (c) Combinations of fried ham or bacon with other substances. These are much to be commended: the more important substances with which bacon may be combined are as follows:—
     - (α) Poached or fried eggs.
     - (β) Sheep's kidneys, stewed, with a thick, nourishing gravy.
     - (γ) Liver: the pieces should be small and very well cooked.
     - (δ) Mushrooms.
     - (ε) Tomatoes, or even bananas (not much to be commended).
     - (ζ) Oysters or scallops.

2. Eggs cooked in various ways.
   - (a) Simply boiled: these are more properly to be regarded as accessory trifles.
   - (b) Poached, on toast.

(c) Fried: these are impossible, apart from bacon.

(d) Scrambled or buttered. They should never taste of vaseline.

(e) Tomatoed eggs: much to be commended.

(f) Omelettes. A perfectly plain omelette is not sufficiently nourishing as a *pièce de résistance*. It is better to add fragments of bacon, chicken, kidney, or tongue. Or it may appear as:—

Savoury omelette.

Omelette aux fines herbes.

Sweet omelette ⎫   (not very suitable at
Cheese omelette ⎭   breakfast).

Tomato omelette.

(g) Eggs may also be cooked in recondite and fancy ways, such as *"œufs à l'Aurore,"* "sunshiny eggs," "hashed eggs with gravy," and last, but not least, "curried eggs".

3. Fish and allied products.

(a) *Real fish*. The following kinds are suitable:—

Salmon cutlets (when salmon is down to IS.).

Trout (when you can get it).

Fried soles (if expense is no object).

Lemon soles, filleted.

Fried plaice or brill.

Cod cutlets.

Fresh herrings (in season).

Bloaters: these should be gently smoked and not salted. It is best not to split them, or remove the backbone, as by these processes the natural anatomy of the fish is disarranged, and you get your mouth full of bones. It takes ten minutes longer to eat a bloater the backbone of which has been removed; and there is an added risk to life.

Kippers: the same remarks apply to these; there is risk in eating them, and they are usually too dry and too salt.

Whiting: these should be quite fresh.

Mackerel: split and fried, or better stuffed and baked.

Smelts: these should be quite fresh.

Sardines: ⎫
Anchovies: ⎭ these are accessory trifles.

Dried haddock: not too often.

Skate: an unpleasant dish, rather to be deprecated.

Sprats : excellent, if you don't mind the smell all over the house.

(b) *Crustacea.*

Lobster, if you can afford it in London.

Dressed crab.

Curried prawns: perhaps the best breakfast known to man.

(c) *Molluscs.*

Oysters, even tinned ones, stewed in cream: many will avoid fresh oysters on account of the dangers of typhoid. Good scalloped.

Scallops.

(d) *Products of fish, etc.*

Cod's roe: excellent.

Herring's roe, on toast: an admirable accessory.

Kedgeree, from the remains of yesterday's fish (not very good).

4. Certain internal portions of the animal economy.
   (a) Sweetbreads: too dear in London as a rule. The proper sweetbread is the thymus gland; the pancreas is frequently foisted upon the unwary, but it is tough; it may be known by its elongated shape.
   (b) Kidneys (sheep's or even pigs'): these may be fried, but are better stewed with gravy. They may be eaten with bacon.
   Kidneys stewed with mushrooms are a dream.
   (c) Liver: with bacon, *vide supra.*
   (d) Brains: lamb's brains fried in bread crumbs are not bad, but rather cloying.
   (e) The heart is scarcely suitable for breakfast.
   No other viscera are suitable.

5. Meats of different kinds.
   The very robust are willing to eat chops and steaks at breakfast. Men in training commonly do so. A joint of cold meat may often be seen on the sideboard in country houses; your hunting man eats this. The ordinary person eschews butchers' meat at breakfast.
   The following meats are suitable:—
   (a) Cold tongue—tinned or otherwise. Ox or sheep.
   (b) Cold pheasant or grouse, when a present of game has arrived.
   (c) Grilled or devilled fowl: principally the bird's legs.
   (d) Cold fowl or duck, left over from the night before.
   (e) Fricasseed fowl with bacon round the edge.
   (f) Any sort of fowl or game (or rabbit) may be served as a curry.
   (g) Sausages (pork or beef).
       (1) Fried or grilled.
       (2) Sliced and curried.
       (3) As sausage rolls.
   (h) Meat pies, of sorts.

(1) Pork pie—cold. Those imported from Yorkshire and Northampton-shire are the best. They should be large: the smaller varieties contain an undue proportion of crust.
(2) Cold pigeon pie—containing also steak and egg.
(3) Cold veal and ham pie—containing egg.
(4) Cold beefsteak and kidney pie—containing egg.
(5) Game pie.
(6) Lamb pie.
(*i*) Hot cutlets: veal or mutton—with or without tomatoes.

Fried or chip potatoes may be served with any hot meaty breakfast dish, and, indeed, also with certain varieties of hot fish.

B. ACCESSORY DISHES.
1. Boiled eggs.
2. Cold ham or gammon.
3. Sardines, in the tin or on toast.
4. Anchovies: the best are filleted ones in oil.
5. Potted meats of all kinds, tinned, or homemade when the tongue gets too low to be cut any longer. The works of a tongue, such as the lymphatic glands embedded in the fat at its root, pass unnoticed in the potted article.
6. Shrimp, bloater, or anchovy paste.
7. Mushrooms on toast.
8. Herring's roe on toast.
9. Porridge and its allies, Quaker Oats and other farinaceous foods. These may be eaten at the beginning of breakfast, as a foundation, or at the end, to fill up the cracks.
10. Cold sausages of sorts.

C. FRUITS AND VEGETABLE PRODUCTS.
Fresh fruit—especially oranges—apples, pears and other fruit in season. These are best eaten at the beginning of breakfast, in large quantities. They are better at breakfast than at any other meal of the day.
Tomatoes.
Stewed rhubarb.
Tinned pears, peaches, apricots, etc.
Jam and marmalade.
Honey or honeycomb.
Cream is good with them all, especially Devonshire cream. The best way of eating Devonshire cream is, however, unquestionably with cheap, black, highly-flavoured treacle.

D. DRINKS.

Tea or coffee.   Cocoa.

When fresh fruit is taken at the beginning of breakfast, a glass of hock is a suitable accompaniment.

A glass of good light beer is excellent after breakfast, as they know very well at Westminster school.

E. BREAD, ETC.

Stacks of hot buttered toast at each corner of the table.

Racks of dry toast.

Tea cakes and scones—hot and buttered.

Cut bread and butter.

White and brown bread.

Vienna and other fancy breads.

Hot rolls (for the reckless).

Hot cross buns on Good Friday.

PEACH.

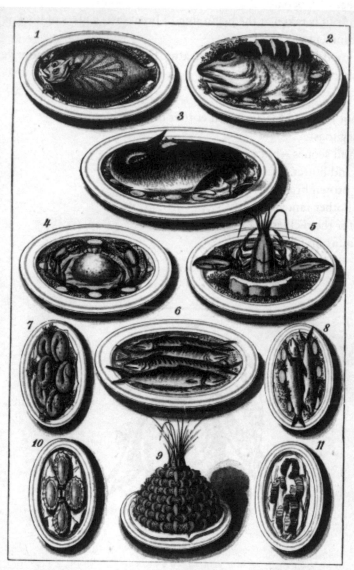

1. *Turbot.*   4. *Crab.*   7. *Whiting.*   10. *Scalloped Oysters.*

2. *Cod's Head.*   5. *Lobster.*   8. *Haddock.*   11. *Crimped Skate.*

3. *Salmon.*   6. *Mackerel.*   9. *Prawns.*

CHAPTER SIX

The Breakfast Book

A Cookery Book for the Morning Meal or Breakfast Table

Georgiana Hill

Brimming with social aspiration, this earliest of the three cookbooks perfectly captures the spirit of gentrification behind the rise of the English Breakfast. French terms are much in evidence, and there is a definite preference for the elaborate over than the simple. Written when breakfast was still in transition from a mid-day to a morning meal, it distinguishes between four kinds of repasts—family breakfasts, the *déjeuner à la forchette*, the cold collation and the *ambigu*. Many *ambigu* dishes were later dropped from the breakfast repertoire, but they would be highly suitable for a modern brunch. The text is leavened with such observations by the author as '*pastry-cooks, like poets, are born and not made*'.

Georgiana Hill was the author of *Everybody's Pudding Book*, or *Puddings, Tarts etc In Their Proper Seasons* (1862), *The Lady's Dessert Book* (1863), *Onions Dressed and Served in a Hundred Different Ways* (1870) and *Women in English Life from Medieval to Modern Times* (1896).

THE BREAKFAST BOOK:

A Cookery-Book for the Morning Meal,

OR

BREAKFAST TABLE;

COMPRISING

BILLS OF FARE, PASTIES, AND DISHES ADAPTED
FOR ALL OCCASIONS.

PREFACE.

What *shall* we have for dinner, is a question easily answered; but what *can* we have for breakfast is quite another thing. The object of this work is to solve the domestic difficulty. In the first chapter will be found assembled together the principal viands which are more or less in daily request for our ordinary breakfasts. Most of the articles enumerated are of a homely description. The second chapter is devoted to such quickly-dressed dishes as may be readily prepared at a short notice. They are alike suitable for ceremonial or domestic repasts. The succeeding chapters, with the exception of the one upon the subject of fish, treat principally of comestibles that housekeepers may prepare at leisure, and keep in readiness until wanted.

At the end are bills of fare for the several seasons of the year. These may be consulted, and selections made from them, in accordance with the means, tastes, and requirements of different housekeepers. Generally speaking, breakfasts may be classed under four heads: the family breakfast, the *déjeuner à la fourchette*, the cold collation, and the *ambigu*. The first is with us entirely made up of *hors d'œuvres*, or by-dishes, either hot or cold, which are served without sauce. In a *déjeuner à la fourchette* things are introduced in courses, similar to a dinner. Cold collations need scarcely be defined: almost all *recherché* things are proper for them, provided they are prepared for the purpose, so as to produce an ornamental effect. The *ambigu* is an entertainment of a very heterogeneous character, having a resemblance to a dinner, only that everything is placed upon the table at once; and *relevés*, soup, vegetables, and hot *entremets*, are held to be ineligible. Our everyday breakfasts are in a small way served *en ambigu*, inasmuch as broiled fish, cold pasties, devilled bones, boiled eggs, cold ham, etc., all appear together.

As a rule, dishes of grilled or tossed meat are to be preferred before those dressed after other methods; but bear in mind, that in the Italian tongue, the name of the morning meal is represented by the word *collezione*, or collection; and though it may be beyond our scope to banquet our guests with buffalo humps, reindeer tongues, lordly peacocks, stately swans, or Strasbourg pies, less pretending materials are seldom wanting to give the attractive variety which should constitute a *collezione*.

Browning Hill, Nov., 1865.

COLD COLLATION DISHES.

1—Pigeon Pie.   2—Raised Game Pie.   3—Cutlets and Peas.   4—Prawns en Bouquet.   5—Crême
    Chicken.   5—Plovers' Eggs.   7—Lamb Cutlets.   8—Larks Farcie.   9—Piped Ham.
    10—Boned Capon.

CONTENTS.

CHAPTER VII. PAGES 52–63.

FISH.

CHAPTER VIII. PAGES 64–69.

FISH PIES.

CHAPTER IX. PAGES 70–77.

BILLS OF FARE FOR BREAKFASTS THROUGHOUT THE YEAR.

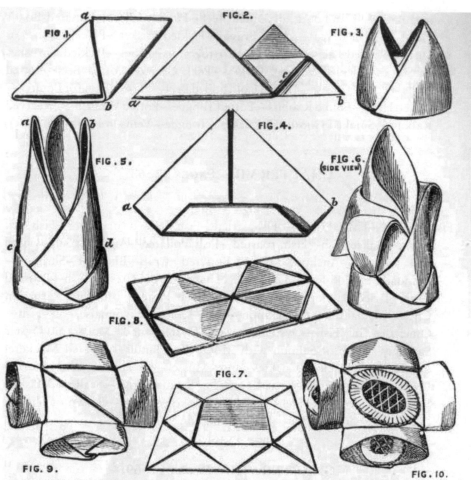

To Fold the Mitre.—The napkin must be folded in three, thus :—Fold one third over, turn it *backwards*, and thus make the three folds. Fold both ends to meet in the middle. Take the left-hand corner, *a*, and fold it across in a right angle. Take the opposite corner, *b*, on the left hand at the top, and fold it in the same manner ; you will thus form figure 1. Turn over and fold in halves lengthwise ; open the points, and you will have figure 2. Bend the point, *a*, towards the right, and tuck it in the groove, *c* ; turn the point, *b*, backwards towards the right hand, and tuck it in as at *a* ; you will then have figure 3—The Mitre.

The Water Lily.—Have a square napkin and fold it like a half handkerchief. Then take the two opposite points and make them meet on the centre one, which forms a square. Take the bottom corner, opposite the points, and roll it up as at figure 4. Turn the napkin over, and roll point *a* to about the centre. Take point *b*, and tuck it in the groove ; raise it, and you have figure 5—the Water Lily. Turn the corners over, and tuck them in at *c* and *d*. Turn back the second fold at the top—fig. 6.

Napkin Folded for small Tarts at the side and a Cake in the middle.—Have a perfectly square napkin ; turn the corners over so that they meet at the centre. Turn the four corners back to the edge, and you will have figure 7 ; carefully turn the napkin without unfolding it ; turn it over from two opposite sides into the centre at figure 8 ; turn it over again and make the other two ends meet in the middle you have then figure 9.

The Breakfast Book.

CHAPTER I.

THINGS MOST COMMONLY SERVED FOR FAMILY BREAKFASTS.

ANCHOVIES.

Some housekeepers send these to table either simply in the jars in which they were imported, or merely laid out in a dish, without the slightest attempt at decoration or good arrangement. Properly, they should be treated as follows:—Take six or eight pickled anchovies, wash them in vinegar and water, bone them, and cut the flesh in neat slices; dispose them prettily in a dish, with a garnish of the chopped hard-boiled yolks and whites of eggs, kept separately, a little parsley or chervil, and a few capers. Sprinkle with olive oil, and serve. *See* also Anchovy Toast, Canapés, Anchovy Sandwiches, etc.

BEEFSTEAKS.

Beef or rather rump steaks, for broiling, should not be much more than half-an-inch thick, or they will be hard on the outside before they are done through. Pepper them well, but do not salt them until previous to serving them, or the gravy will be drawn. Do them over an ardent fire, and only turn them once. When tossed, or as it is commonly called, *fried*, the pan should be made hot, then rubbed over with fat, and the steak put in. A quick fire is requisite. When done, pepper and salt it, and lay upon the top some pieces of either fresh or anchovy butter. Garnish with cresses, or little heaps of finely shred shalot, gherkins, or scraped horse-radish. Some prefer a beefsteak rolled, or served upon a sauce made by pouring a wineglassful of madeira, sweet ale, chili vinegar, or ketchup, into the pan, after the meat is taken up; or having an oyster or tomato sauce apart. Remember, whether tossed or broiled, beefsteaks should be done quickly; never suffer them to *go to sleep* over the fire.

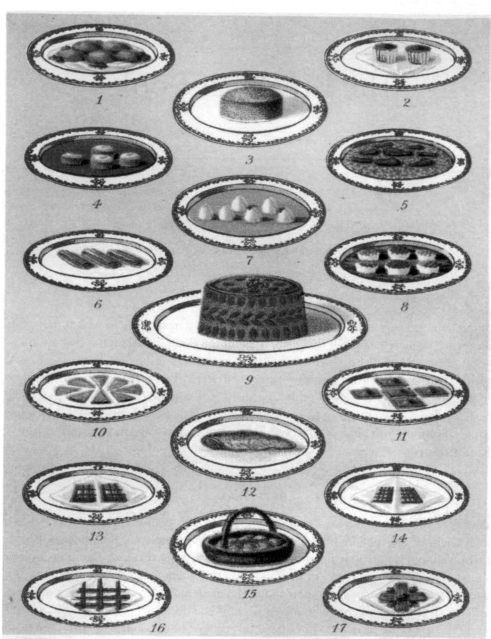

J. M. Kronheim & Co.   London

1. Fish Cakes. 2. Eggs in cases. 3. Savoury Calf's Foot. 4. Birds Nests. 5. Game on Aspic Jelly. 6. Curried Eggs. 7. Huitres au lit. 8. Eggs à la bonne femme. 9. Brawn. 10. Egg Toast. 11. Grated Ham & Toast. 12. Omelette aux fines Herbes. 13. Eggs à la Powerscourt. 14. Anchovy Toast. 15. Plovers Eggs. 16. Broiled Sheep Tails. 17. Kippered Salmon.

BLOATERS.

These may be scraped, peppered, rubbed over with oil, and either broiled, tossed in butter, or toasted before the fire. They are also very good if soaked in oil, and baked in a brisk oven. Drain, and serve them with crisp parsley. For an entrée they may be done thus:—Bone and skin the flesh, and place it in buttered paper cases, upon a layer of chopped mushroom, parsley, and chives, cover with some of the sauce, dust bread-crumbs on the top, and broil upon a gridiron, over a gentle fire. Bloaters are likewise excellent potted, to form fish-paste, which *see*. They are rightly in season from the commencement of October to the end of December.

BRAIN-CAKES, ETC.

The brains of the ox, hog, or calf, if properly treated, are very delicate eating, and admit of various ways of preparation. In almost all cases they require to be first blanched, by soaking in cold water, and afterwards thrown into boiling water seasoned with vinegar and salt. When cold, they may be sliced, and fried in butter, or made into coquilles (scallops). These need the addition of Parmesan cheese. Or they are exceedingly good as a mayonnaise. Intersperse pieces of cold brains with hard-boiled eggs and ornamental-shaped slices of cold tongue, pickles, etc.; sauce with a mayonnaise or ravigote sauce, and decorate with lumps of jelly, olives, sliced lemon, etc. Or directly the brains have been plain boiled, toss them in butter, and serve them *à la maitre d'hôtel,* or with either a shrimp or anchovy butter. For brain-cakes, beat the blanched brains to a smooth paste, add shred sage, seasoning, and egg, sufficient to give them the requisite consistency; fry them of a fine brown.

BRAWN.

This can generally be procured either at the pastrycooks or provision merchants; but as it is expensive to purchase, those who are partial to it should prepare it at home. When served in slices, it should be cut rather thin, and garnished with fresh parsley; but if sent to table in bulk, a white napkin should be arranged under it in the dish. The difference between brawn and pork-cheese consists in the skin of the meat being chopped-up and mixed with the other ingredients in the latter article, instead of being used to envelope it in, as is done in brawn.

CAVIARE.

Caviare, or preserved sturgeon-roe, is sold, pressed and unpressed, in canisters. In the latter, or whole state, it is employed in meat pies, ragouts, etc. Pressed, or in the form of a paste, it may be eaten spread upon bread and butter; with dry toast, or cut in thin slices, it may be tossed in olive oil, and served with lemon juice.

COD.

After salt cod has been properly soaked in water and vinegar, it may be cut into neat collops, wiped dry, peppered, well rubbed over with olive oil, and grilled until thoroughly browned; squeeze lemon over them, and serve. Or slices may be dipped into butter and fried. If ready-dressed, *see* Brandade of Codfish, Fish Croquettes, Fish with Parmesan Cheese, Curries, and Coquilles of Fish. Mustard, scraped horse-radish, and vinegar, are generally sent to table with salt fish.

COLD BOILED BEEF.

This, when intended to be introduced upon the breakfast-table, should, previously to boiling, be carefully boned, and skewered together in as nice a form as possible, and when cold, arranged in a white cloth. If served in slices, it should not be cut quite so thin as ham would be. *Vide* Vinaigrette, Remolade, Persillade, Cold Beef, Potted, etc. Some people make bubble-and-squeak with slices of cold boiled beef, fried with cold cabbage, but it is an inelegant and not over-wholesome dish.

COLD GAME OR POULTRY.

When either poultry or game is dressed expressly to appear at table cold, particular care should be taken to make it look as well as possible. For this purpose it is almost invariably first roasted, either plain or larded. When anything more *recherché* is aimed at, it may be boned and made into a galantine and braised. If served already cut up (unless when tied together again with white ribbon), the superior parts only should be made use of, and these should be tastefully garnished. For a collation, or a *déjeuner à la fourchette,* it is preferable arranged in a salad or a mayonnaise, or *en aspic* (in jelly). Ready-dressed game or poultry forms admirable curries, rissoles, croquettes, devils, scallops, salmis, etc.

COLD HAM.

A cold boiled ham is a welcome object at even the most distinguished tables. Epicures frequently prefer York hams to those of Bayonne or Westphalia. In curing the latter sugar is used, and the flavour of the Bayonne hams is owing to wine lees being employed in the pickle, while the superiority of York hams is due to the goodness of the salt made use of. Hams should always be neatly trimmed before being boiled; and unless they are exceedingly high dried, they are better without being soaked in water previously to boiling. Small-sized hams should be chosen for breakfast eating; for where the party in the house is not large, one gets tired of the sight of a frequently-presented joint of meat. Lately very miniature breakfast hams (some under six pounds in weight), are offered in the shops; but these are too suspiciously small to be tempting. Ham cannot reasonably be cut too thin. The remains of a ham are capable of being made use of as ham toast; in forcemeat; as ham cake; as an omelette; and as ham pie (*see* these things). Hams are sometimes roasted. To do them in this way, they are soaked in wine, the rind removed, and then slowly roasted. They should be well glazed, and served cold upon a white napkin. Hams are likewise to be coated over with melted suet or a coarse paste, and slowly baked.

COLD MEAT.

By this is commonly understood a joint of meat which has done duty at dinner the day before; and from carelessness housekeepers are often prone to introduce the most insipid joints, rather than take the trouble to prepare from them anything more relishing. The most admissible articles are cold roast beef, cold roast spare-rib, cold boiled pickled pork or gammon, etc. As for cold mutton and veal, in a general way, they should be avoided in favour of something more tasty and appetizing. When meat is dressed purposely to appear cold, it should, if possible, be rolled.

COLD TONGUE.

Ox or neats' tongues are held in higher estimation in England than they are elsewhere. They have the one great recommendation of making a show and of not being costly. When cured at home they are not half the price charged for them at the provision shops. When served, they should be agreeably decorated with ornamentally-cut paper. The remains of a cold tongue are very useful as a savoury addition to other meats. It is also very good *au gratin* (with breadcrumbs), potted, sliced, and devilled, grilled in paper cases, warmed up with Parmesan cheese, and forms a variety of made dishes. For extraordinary occasions, a tongue should be larded and glazed, or collared.

COLLARED MEAT OR FISH.

Scarcely anything is more convenient in housekeeping than collared meats. When once made they will, if properly attended to, keep well for some months. When presented at table in the piece, it should be surrounded with a white napkin, and a slice should be first removed from the top, so as to show a fresh cut. If served in slices, they should be garnished with fresh herbs or pickles. By way of variety, slices can be dipped into beaten egg and tossed in butter over a quick fire, or it may be used in sandwiches, or eaten with toast.

CURRIES.

Either poultry, fish, flesh, or game, whether previously dressed or not, may be quickly converted into a dish of curry. With the exception of mutton, which makes the most admirable of curries, white meats are considered the most suitable for this kind of dish. Beef, for some unfounded reason, is rarely curried. For ordinary repasts, a bordering of boiled rice round the dish may be omitted, sliced lemon serving the same purpose. Cold meat makes as good a curry as that dressed expressly. Cold boiled cod-fish browned, with a few onions, and curried, is excellent.

DEVILLED BONES, ETC.

The members of cold roasted poultry, game, rabbits, etc., should be slightly scored across in the thick places, then dipped into oil or liquid butter, and seasoned very highly with red and black pepper, salt, and, if approved of, a little curry-powder, then broil them over a pretty quick fire. Serve with a squeeze of lemon upon a chutney or piquante sauce. Cold chickens, pigeons, young ducks, and such things, when they are devilled whole, should be first split open at the back. When meat bones are devilled, some cooks merely first dip them into strong mixed mustard before they are grilled.

DRIED SPRATS.

These are seldom in the market until after 5th November. They should be separately wiped, as they are seldom over clean after undergoing the process of curing; then either toast them before the fire, or skewer them in rows and broil them quickly over a clear fire. Serve them as hot as you possibly can.

EGGS.

Although there are upwards of a hundred recognized methods of dressing eggs, almost the only established way in which they appear by themselves at family breakfasts, is *à la coque,* or boiled in their shells. The French manner of performing this is to make some water boiling hot, then take it off the fire, place the eggs in it, and let them remain exactly five minutes. Serve them enveloped in a white napkin, or in egg cups. Plover's eggs require full ten minutes boiling, and may be sent to table hot or cold.

FRIED POTATOES AND BACON.

Though a very homely dish, this is a very difficult one to dress satisfactorily, unless care and attention be bestowed upon it. In the first place, the bacon should be neither too thick nor too thin; it should be done quickly and thoroughly without being burnt. The cold boiled potatoes should be well chopped and peppered before they are put into the frying-pan, and turned about without intermission until the steam arises freely from them, for nothing is more objectionable than when they are barely warmed. The fire should be pretty brisk, but not fierce. Put the potatoes into a dish, and arrange upon them the slices of bacon *en couronne* (in a circle), round the margin.

FRIED EGGS AND BACON.

The slices of bacon or ham should be as nearly as possible of a size, and not too thick. Toss them in a frying pan until they are nicely browned, then break your eggs into the pan, and when they are sufficiently set firm, trim them neatly and place them upon the meat. The eggs may be poached, if preferred; they are then less rich, but not nearly so savoury.

FRESH FISH.

Fish being such an important adjunct to the breakfast table, I have devoted a chapter specially to it, which *see*.

FRIZZLED BACON.

Rashers, whether of bacon or ham, are quite an English institution; you will never even meet with the mention of them in Continental cookery-books. The meat should on no account be cut thick, and pains should be taken that it should be done to such a degree as to eat somewhat crisp, the fat being delicately browned. The most preferable way to dress it, is to toast it before the fire, either in a Dutch oven or in a bacon-toaster; but it is often broiled or tossed in a frying-pan. The latter method answers well enough for bacon, but it is apt to make ham soft. The rind should be taken off before cooking, and the ham may be peppered; bacon is better without seasoning.

HOUGH OF HAM.

A hough or knuckle of ham is a neat little dish for a small breakfast, being just enough to be disposed of at once. It is always served cold, and is sometimes accompanied with sliced hard-boiled eggs, interspersed with tufts of parsley, cresses, or other herbs.

HUNTER'S BEEF.

Hunter's beef, hung beef, Dutch beef, and pressed beef, are most useful household provisions, and if cured at home are less expensive in the end than even less pretentious articles. After they have been served a certain time in bulk, they can with great advantage be potted, or introduced in slices devilled, or *en persillade,* vinaigrette, omelettes, etc.

KIPPERED FISH.

If the fish be large cut it into long-shaped pieces, and dip them into oil, and broil them slightly. Should the fish be done entire, it may be scored in the thick fleshy parts, so as to let the heat reach it equally and quickly, as it ought not to be much dressed. Mackerel is exceedingly good simply toasted, and served with a little pounded loaf sugar sprinkled over it.

MEAT AND FISH PIES.

The value of savoury pies cannot be too highly insisted upon; they redeem the character of any meal, whether breakfast, luncheon, pic-nic, or supper. Even in summer they will, if well compounded, keep for several days; but care should be observed to put them by in a dry place, otherwise the crust becomes limp. Raised pies should invariably be served upon a damask napkin folded under them in the dish. *Vol a vents* being served hot, and requiring a good deal of pains to prepare them, we have omitted giving, although very generally served at *déjeuners à la fourchette;* the less aristocratic raised pies which we have contented ourselves with introducing are more in request for family repasts, and are most useful on account of their suitability for cold collations. *See* chapter upon Savoury Pies.

MUTTON CHOPS.

With the exception of sheep's kidneys, mutton chops are, beyond any other description of fresh meat, the most generally consumed for breakfast. Properly cut and well cooked they are as admirable a viand as we can command; but, unfortunately, the above conditions are not frequently observed. On the Continent mutton chops are mostly had from the best end of the neck, which is faultlessly divided into cutlets of an uniform thickness; these are divested of all the bone, with the exception of a portion of the rib; the skin is removed from the fat, the meat is made into a regular shape, it is smartly flattened with a side-stroke from the chopper, and when dressed is dipped into dissolved butter, and either tossed or grilled over a gay fire, and served with a clear gravy in the dish, and garnished with pickled gherkins or capers. Or they are broiled in paper cases *à la Maintenon.* A steak of mutton cut from a tender leg, and sprinkled with bread-crumbs and Parmesan cheese, then broiled, is a favourite dish in the South of Europe. Serve with tomato sauce.

OMELETTES.

Take four or six eggs, according to the size of the omelette required, break them into a basin, remove the treadles, add to the eggs, salt, pepper, and a tablespoonful of either milk or water: heat some lard or butter in a frying-pan, pour in the eggs, and fry them upon a brisk fire until the under side of the omelette is nicely browned. Observe, it should not be turned in the pan. Roll it or fold in the ends as you put it into the dish. Besides the foregoing ordinary omelette, the following things may be employed:— bacon, ham, tongue, dried sausage, kidney, Gruyére cheese, asparagus tops, truffles, oysters, cold meat, poultry, game or fish, green peas, tomatoes, mushrooms, savoury herbs, etc. When meat of any kind is used it may be either pounded to a paste and mixed with the eggs, or merely minced and put into the frying-pan, the eggs being afterwards poured upon it.

For a cheese omelette the Gruyére should be chopped up and strewn upon the eggs after they are in the pan. Parmesan cheese should be first grated and beaten up with the eggs before frying the omelette. Truffles, mushrooms, and peas, require to be stewed and placed upon the eggs, as soon as they are set on the under side in the frying pan. Veal kidney should be similarly prepared.

OYSTERS.

For *déjeuners à la fourchette* oysters are preferable *au naturel* (undressed), but for family breakfasts they are considered more savoury if broiled or fried. When they are scalloped, they are better if baked in a side-oven rather than before the fire, as in the latter method it often happens that the oysters are not sufficiently cooked. They are delicious if left in the deep shell, and a little lemon-juice, bread-crumbs, and pepper sprinkled over them; add a bit of butter, then place them upon a gridiron over a brisk fire, and let them remain till they begin to get plump. To fry oysters the larger sort should be chosen, beard and season them, dip them into a batter or beaten egg, and fry them quickly; serve with crisp parsley. Or they may be warmed up in a little cream, and dished with small sippets of toast. Abroad they are frequently formed into a ragout with Spanish chesnuts. They may likewise be made into patties, omelettes, etc. *See* also Curry, Oysterloaves, Oysters and Macaroni, etc.

PICKLED FISH.

No housekeeper should neglect, when any kind of fish is plentiful, to provide a supply for pickling. If made into a fresh pickle—that is, when some of the liquor is used in which the fish is boiled—it will only keep for a week or two, but when regularly preserved in strong vinegar and spices it will continue good for many months. At the provision shops hermetically-sealed canisters of fresh fish are sold: this is exceedingly well-flavoured in its way, but is expensive on account of the small quantity contained in each canister.

PORK CUTLETS.

In Spain, a pork cutlet and poached egg, with a squeeze of orange juice, constitute the breakfast of most of those who can afford to procure the luxury. The pork, which in its living state has been fattened upon sweet chestnuts, is cooked by being immersed in boiling olive oil, and rightly it merits its popularity. In England, pork chops or cutlets are usually not so esteemed: rubbed over with powdered sage, they are most commonly broiled, but as they need some time to cook, they are often found to be either smoky, burnt, underdone, or hard. They are better if boned, peppered, skewered round like little fillets, and tossed in butter. Serve garnished with barberries, and sauced with horseradish, tomato or piquante sauce. Pickles and mustard apart.

POTTED MEAT, GAME, OR FISH.

A very small quantity of any kind of cold meat can be converted into a paste and potted, and in this way make a much more refined-looking dish than it otherwise would. Slightly warm the outsides of the moulds, and turn it out to serve. Garnish with branches of bay or savoury herbs. Or, tolerably thin slices may be cut out and laid in a dish, with a decoration of green parsley; it may likewise be spread between thin bread-and-butter, or eaten with dry toast.

PRESERVED SARDINES AND TUNNY-FISH.

English people unfortunately entertain so strong a prejudice against anything prepared with oil, that in many houses the practice exists of dipping preserved sardines or tunny-fish into boiling water before they are deemed acceptable as an eatable; better forego the fish entirely than subject it to such treatment. They may be sent to table in the same manner as anchovies—which *see*. If preferred hot, dip them into beaten egg, and fry them, or serve them in croquettes, coquilles, *petits pâtés,* omelettes, etc.

RED OR WHITE HERRINGS.

As these can be procured throughout the year they deserve to be specially noticed. They are most generally tossed, toasted, or broiled, being first split open down the back. With a good fire, they are done in a few moments. Besides these methods, they may be dressed thus: take the flesh from the sides, free from bone and skin; throw it into boiling milk, ale, or water; let it remain two or three minutes, take it up, and either rub it over with fresh butter, and serve hot with buttered eggs, or let it become cold, arrange it upon a dish, mask it with herbs, and sprinkle it plentifully with olive oil. To do them with bread-crumbs, trim off the fins, tail, and head, open them at the back, dip them into dissolved butter, and then into a mixture of bread-crumbs, chopped herbs, and spices; repeat this operation, and broil them. In the South of Europe salt herrings are divested of their heads and tails, then put into boiling water for ten minutes, and afterwards served with very thin slices of lemon or sour apples and onion; olive oil and mustard apart.

SAUSAGES.

It is the usual practice to simply toss sausages in lard or butter, for if broiled they are apt to become smoky before they are properly done. As they take some time to cook, first prick them with a needle to prevent the skins from breaking. Garnish with pickled red cabbage, or apples sliced and tossed till nicely browned. Observe that underdone sausages are execrable.

SLICES OF HAM.

There is, after all, hardly anything more acceptable to the epicure than a savoury rasher of ham. It should be broiled upon or toasted before a brisk fire, then rubbed over with fresh butter, and sprinkled with pepper. Eggs fried or poached may be served with the ham if approved of. If you have reason to believe that the ham is too salt, dip the rashers for a moment or two into boiling water before cooking:—*See* also Ham Cake, Ham Toast, Omelettes, Ham Pie, etc.

SHEEP'S TONGUES.

Though certainly not a *recherché* comestible, sheep's tongues have their admirers. The tongues may be procured ready dressed at the provision warehouses, and eaten cold, or they may be prepared at home. Blanch them, that is to say, plain boil them until they will skin easily, and then simmer them in stock until they are tender. When cold you can slit them down the middle, rub them with butter, and brown them before the fire; or dip them into bread-crumbs and butter, and broil them; or do them with chopped herbs, etc., in paper cases; or sprinkle them with Parmesan cheese, and place them in an oven till they are browned. They may likewise be served cold with a ravigote sauce, or curried or devilled. Pickles, tomato, Lopresti, or chutney sauce should be sent to table with them.

SHEEP'S KIDNEYS.

Custom seems to have established but one method of dressing sheep's kidneys for breakfast, namely, *à la brochette,* or broiled. Split them open, but do not entirely divide them. Put a fine skewer through them to prevent their warping or closing together again: place them, inside downwards, upon a gridiron: as soon as they feel pretty firm turn them, and directly the gravy is well risen take them up; pepper, salt, and add to each a good piece of butter rubbed in some boiled parsley, squeeze a lemon over them, and put them into a hot dish. It is also admissible to toss them in butter, or cut them into thin slices, season them, dip them into batter, and fry them. They are also capital devilled, or chopped small after they are dressed, and made into croquettes or an omelette—for this purpose one kidney is sufficient for a moderate-sized omelette.

SHRIMPS, PRAWN, OR CRAYFISH.

When perfectly fresh, these and shellfish generally are peculiarly appropriate for breakfasts, or any other light repast, as they make such an ornamental effect at table. Dish them up carefully by arranging a white napkin in the form of a pyramid, and putting the fish round it: intersperse with fresh parsley:—*See* also Shrimp Pudding, ditto Butter, Patties, Croquettes, etc.

SMOKED HADDOCK.

This should be moistened with olive oil, placed upon a gridiron, and merely warmed through: indeed in some parts of Scotland it is sliced and eaten without being dressed at all. Many cooks subject it to the same treatment as salt cod, kippered fish or red herrings, to which you can refer.

SCALLOPED MEAT, GAME, OR FISH.

When comestibles of any kind are scalloped they are done in scallop or pilgrim shells, or tin pattypans made to resemble them. A very small quantity of cold meat goes a great way when scalloped, bread-crumbs, chopped egg, mashed potatoes, or forcemeat being added to fill up, Bake, broil, or do them in a Dutch oven before the fire, and serve in the shells.

SMOKED SALMON.

Dried salmon needs very little cooking. It may be sliced and broiled in oiled paper cases, or tossed in butter or olive oil, and served with lemon juice; or throw it into boiling water, and at the end of a few minutes take it up, and when cold arrange it as a salad, or with a remolade or ravigote sauce.

STRASBOURG, OR YORKSHIRE PIES.

The former of these are generally imported from the country in which they are made, but the latter may be very successfully prepared at home. The crust of Yorkshire pies is not intended to be eaten, but is kept to preserve the contents of the pasty; to avoid the inconvenience attending this arrangement, thick earthenware dishes, with covers to them, are now to be procured at the leading provision shops: these dishes are called *terrines*, and in them we can preserve our pies, or portions of pies, in safety. Meat pasties may also be made in these terrines, using them in place of crust, and merely lining them with thin slices of bacon fat or a layer of forcemeat or both: put some of the same upon the top, place on the cover, and bake as you would an ordinary pie. If preferred, the pies when cold can be turned out of the terrines by first laying the dishes for a few moments in boiling water.

SWEETBREADS.

These require to be blanched or parboiled, to whiten them. This being done, rub them with butter, and roast them, or cut them lengthwise, dip them into egg and bread-crumbs, and either fry them or broil them in paper cases; or, without cutting them, put into an oven and bake them; or slice them crosswise, and toss them in butter. Serve them with tomato sauce, and decorate them with slices of lemon or barberries, or very delicately-cut slices of toasted ham, bacon, or tongue. They are also capable of being converted into rissoles, scallops, or croquettes, and are exceedingly delicious curried. Cold sweetbreads are excellent as a mayonnaise, or with a remolade or ravigote sauce.

VEAL CUTLETS.

Chops or cutlets of veal require a good deal of careful cooking. They may be broiled with a coating of herbs, etc., in paper cases, but are really preferable for the breakfast-table simply tossed. When cut thin enough, they need not be beaten before they are dressed, for if the veal is quite fresh there is no fear of its not being tender. Garnish with sliced lemon and small pieces of toasted bacon.

WITH MARMALADE OR PRESERVED FRUITS OF DIFFERENT
DESCRIPTIONS, AND NARBONNE HONEY, ETC.

The foregoing constitute the chief comestibles current with most classes for the breakfast-table.

In the following chapter are given some made dishes which are expeditiously dressed, indeed the majority of them may be prepared under half an hour.

Ragouts, stews, fricandeaux, and fricassees, are purposely omitted, their name being legion, and a more considerable time being involved in their cooking than could be afforded by the generality of housekeepers.

CHAPTER II.

Made Dishes, etc., which may be quickly prepared.

BLANQUETTES OF COLD MEAT.

Take the white meat of cold roast turkey, rabbit, fowl, veal, or lamb, divest it of skin, cut it up and lay it in a stewpan. Clean and slice a few button mushrooms, throw them into lemon-juice and water; drain them, and toss them in butter and white stock, season to taste, and pour it hot on the meat; let it come to almost a boil, thicken with cream, and decorate the dish with small sippets of toast.

BROILED GAME, ETC.

The principal joints of birds, such as the wings and thighs, may be dipped into butter, and then into bread-crumbs, and grilled. Partridges, pigeons, and chickens may be done by first splitting them open at the back. The haunches of rabbits should have the shank-bones removed. As a rule, broiled poultry is preferable devilled, that is, rubbed over with hot spices before being dressed. Serve dry, or with a sauce made with the juice of a lemon, a glass each of Chili vinegar, wine, and ketchup, a dessert-spoonful of Bengal chutney, and a cup of gravy; add Cayenne pepper, if not sufficiently spiced. Steaks, or cutlets of pork, veal, lamb, or beef do better if cut as collops, that is to say, in pieces of a uniform size and thickness, without bone. It is a vexed question whether these should be turned frequently, or only once during the operation of broiling; but if the fire is precisely as it should be, and the meat of the requisite thickness, or rather thinness, once turning will be enough. Place them upon a hot gridiron rubbed with suet; watch the cutlets, and immediately there are indications of the gravy rising, turn them, and when the gravy comes to the surface of the top-side, the meat is done. With a good fire, mutton and beef are done in a quarter of an hour, but veal and pork require at least twenty minutes.

CALF'S LIVER AND BACON.

This is commonly tossed in butter; the liver sliced moderately thin, is first dressed, and the rashers of bacon afterwards; serve garnished with the latter. Calf's liver may also be fried: dip the slices into seasoned beaten egg and olive oil, and fry quickly. In France, similarly shaped pieces of liver and bacon are skewered together, then dipped into oil, and subsequently sprinkled with bread-crumbs, and broiled; season and serve. When tossed without the bacon, a glass of wine may be poured into the pan, and served in the dish, with the liver arranged *en couronne* round.

CAPILOTADE OF POULTRY.

This is a speedy way of warming up cold roasted fowl, turkey, rabbit, or pigeon. Chop up some shalot, and, if you have them, three or four mushrooms, sprinkle them over with flour, fry them in butter, and add two tablespoonfuls of gravy with some pepper and salt, and a glass of white wine. Cut up the meat, and simmer it for a quarter of an hour in this preparation. Serve with a garnish of pickled gherkins.

CIVETS OF GAME.

A civet is merely an expeditious method of dressing the flesh of hare, rabbit, or venison. Cut it into moderately small pieces. Toss a few slices of bacon in butter until both are well browned, put in the venison, hare, or rabbit, do it over a brisk fire for five minutes, add some capers and ready-dressed small onions, also herbs and mushrooms; let it simmer for nearly twenty minutes, and serve with sippets of toast round the dish. Remember the sauce should not be thickened in any way, except that the blood from the hare may be added.

CROQUETTES OF MEAT, ETC.

Mince any kind of cold meat, game, fish, or poultry, season it well; mix it with some gravy, thickened almost to a paste with yolk of eggs. Make it either into balls or rolls, dip them twice successively into eggs and bread-crumbs, and fry them brown. The lean should predominate one-third over the fat, or the croquettes will not be sufficiently firm. This is a relishing way of employing cold meat.

COLD MEAT, EN PERSILLADE.

Slice the meat, arrange it in a dish, pepper it, place some bits of butter on it, strain on it some shred parsley and shalot, moisten it with gravy, thickly sprinkle it with rasped toast, and put it into an oven for a quarter of an hour. A little Parmesan cheese may be added if the flavour is approved of.

COQUILLES, OR SCALLOPED MEAT, ETC.

In the English way of scalloping, the cold meat is chopped up, seasoned, and mixed with bread-crumbs: rightly the bread-crumbs should only be placed upon the top. Take any kind of cold roast meat, cut it into exceedingly thin slices of about an inch across, season it well, pour over it enough wine, gravy, and melted butter to moisten, place it in buttered scallop shells, sprinkle bread-crumbs pretty thickly on the top, and place them in a hot oven till well browned. Some sliced mushrooms are a great improvement. Cold rabbit, hare, sweetbreads, poultry, ox palates, calves' brains, *foie gras,* veal, and different kinds of fish, are specially adapted for coquilles. Serve in the shells.

CURRIES.

With Oriental people it is mutton, with the French it is veal, and with the English it is chicken, which most frequently form dishes of curry. Rabbit, too, is particularly good curried; but it is an unpardonable error to make use of flour in the composition of this dish. When cold meat is warmed up as a curry, it is only requisite to cut it up, and toss it in butter, then pour in some curry, mixed in either wine, gravy, milk, or lemon-juice and water. It may subsequently be thickened with tomato sauce, yolks of eggs, or cream. Fried onions, apples or cucumbers are often added. Serve surrounded with capsicums or other strongly-spiced pickles. For a curry made with meat not previously dressed: first, toss in butter some neat rashers of bacon; when done, take them up and put in the meat, which should be cut into moderately-sized pieces; if a rabbit or a fowl, the thick parts of the joints should have the flesh scored across; toss it till done, then pour in the curry, mixed as above directed; replace the bacon, stir it about till the meat is well coloured, and dish it up with the sauce poured over it. There are no fixed rules for the quantity of curry to be used; tastes differing and the strength of the powder varying; but it should always be *piquante* in flavour. A few chopped pickles, such as gherkins, shalots, etc., are an advisable addition.

DOLPETTES OF COLD MEAT.

Prepare the meat as for a hash—or some hashed meat that has become cold will answer the purpose—add to it some bread-crumbs, enough to stiffen the consistency, mix it together with the yolk of eggs, shape it into small balls, dip them into egg, roll them in bread-crumbs and grated Parmesan cheese, and fry them brown. Glaze them or serve them with tomato sauce.

FILLETS OF GAME, ETC., EN PAPILLOTES.

When things are said to be *en papillotes* they are entirely enveloped in folds of greased paper, *en caisse* they are merely laid in paper cases; in both instances thin slices of bacon fat are to be placed next to the paper, and forcemeat added at discretion. For papillotes, cut up and partially dress the meat by tossing it in butter, let it grow cold, well oil or smear over with butter some sheets of paper, lay in the bacon fat, spread forcemeat over the meat, place more bacon fat upon the top, fold it carefully up, and do it on a gridiron over a gentle fire until brown on both sides. The haunches of hares and rabbits should be larded. Cold tongue sliced, or sweetbreads, or sheep's tongues, halved, are very delicate done in this way. To do anything *en caisse*: turn up the edges of some pieces of oiled paper, put in some bacon fat, then the meat, which may previously have been roasted, spread more bacon fat on the top, sprinkle it with bread-crumbs, and put them into a brisk oven until nicely browned. To judge whether the oven be of the right heat, first try in it some bits of paper, and if they do not scorch put in the cases of meat.

FRIED POULTRY, GAME, ETC.

Cut it up, put it into a bowl with slices of onion, parsley leaves, crushed pepper, salt, and the juice of a lemon, or its equivalent, in white-wine vinegar. At the end of half an hour drain the meat, and wipe it dry; flour it, and fry it brown in butter, heap it upon a dish, and surround it with fried eggs.

GAME, ETC., À LA MINUTE.

In this manner may be dressed venison cutlets, young rabbits, leverets, larks, pigeons, chickens, mutton and lamb steaks, small birds, slices of calf's or lamb's liver, etc. Cut up the meat, season it and toss it in plenty of butter for from five minutes to a quarter of an hour, according to thickness. Small birds may be left whole, but poultry, hares etc., should be cut up. Pigeons, partridges, grouse, and such things, are to be simply quartered. When the meat is done, either thicken the butter with a little flour, add some white wine, and send to table decorated with sippets, or glaze the meat by first putting in a tablespoonful of jelly, and stirring all well about, and afterwards pour some gravy into the pan; when hot, add this to the dish of meat and serve. Game has a finer flavour if tossed in oil. The foregoing method differs from the ordinary way of tossing, inasmuch as the sauce is thickened. Rather thin fillets of plumed game, etc., may be dressed in the above manner, and arranged in a circle round the dish, placing a glazed sippet of toast between each fillet. After cutting off the fillets, the remainder of the bird does very well split open, grilled, and served with a remolade or chutney sauce.

HAM TOAST.

Scrape or pound some cold ham, mix it with beaten egg, season with pepper, lay it upon buttered toast, and place it in a hot oven for three or four minutes. Dried salmon, smoked tongue, potted meats, or any other relishing viands answer equally well upon toast.

HASHED GAME, ETC.

Detach the skin and sinews from cold meat of any kind, chop it fine, and put it into a stewpan with sufficient strong stock; season with pepper, nutmeg, and salt; thicken it with cream, and let it nearly boil. Serve with a garnish of poached eggs placed alternately—with small sippets of bread tossed in oil. With white meats fried oysters may take the place of the poached eggs. Hashed calf's head should have the brains made into small cakes fried for a garnish. With game, some chopped savoury herbs may be employed. Hashed meat is sometimes served *en croustade, i. e.* upon pieces of toast. Cut some slices of bread, either heart-shaped or circular, remove some of the crumb from the middle, fry them in butter, lay some hash upon them, place a poached egg upon each, and serve as hot as possible.

MARINADE OF COLD POULTRY, ETC.

Cut up cold roasted chickens, wood-pigeons, turkey, rabbit, or game; divest it of skin, and let it soak for nearly an hour in oil, wine, lemon-juice, or vinegar; season with sliced shalot, bruised bay leaves, pepper, salt, and shred herbs. Drain it, dip it into beaten eggs, and fry it either in oil or butter till it is well browned. Serve garnished with fried parsley. Some epicures prefer an onion or two cut up and fried with the meat.

MAYONNAISE OF COLD GAME, ETC.

Remove the skin from the flesh of cold roasted chicken, turkey, rabbit, partridge, or pheasant, cut up the meat, free from bone, put it into a bowl with salt, pepper, oil, chopped herbs, etc. Stir all together, and place it in a dish; put a circle of jelly round the edge; pour in a mayonnaise sauce (*vide*), and decorate it with hard-boiled eggs, slices of anchovy, pickled gherkins, capers, branches of tarragon, chervil, etc.

MEAT ROLLS.

Cut some very nice little thin fillets from any kind of meat not previously dressed, lay a small portion of forcemeat upon them, roll them round, tie them once across with a bit of thread, moisten them outside with yolk of egg, dust them over with bread-crumbs, season with pepper, put them upon a spit, and baste them with butter; ten minutes will do them. Send them to table with gravy in the dish, garnished with sliced lemon, crisped parsley, or scraped horse-radish.

MINCED POULTRY, MEAT, ETC.

After divesting the cold meat of every particle of sinew and gristle, mince it fine, and either simply season it, and put it into some boiling gravy, and thicken it with butter, rolled in a small quantity of flour, or add chopped mushrooms, sliced truffles, cucumbers, or onions, first tossed in butter; a little anchovy butter, white wine, or lemon-juice may be added. Decorate the dish with glazed sippets. Remark: the meat should not be allowed to boil after it is added to the gravy.

MIROTON OF COLD MEAT.

Beef, veal, and poultry, are considered the best suited for mirotons. Chop up two onions, fry them in butter until well browned, add a table-spoonful of gravy; with this mix some cold meat, minced fine, a few bread-crumbs, pepper, salt, and a beaten egg. Put it into a buttered mould, bake it till browned on the top, turn it out into a dish, and serve hot or cold. With veal add ham or tongue, and, if you like, some hard-boiled eggs, chopped small.

POULTRY ETC., À LA CHIPOLATA.

Cut up and season a rabbit, chicken, or pigeon, fry it quickly in butter, then add half a dozen small sausages; when these and the meat are done, take both up and put into the pan a dessert-spoonful of flour, some mushrooms, and a glass each of white wine and gravy; when this comes to a boil, return the meat and sausages, and add a dozen blanched Spanish chestnuts; give it a boil up, and serve as hot as possible. Ortolans, larks, and small birds generally, and fillets of capon or turkey, are excellent done thus.

RISSOLES.

Correctly speaking, rissoles are nothing more than fried patties. Thin slices of cold fish, flesh, fowl, game, cheese, or forcemeat, are to be laid between a very thin paste, the edges of which are to be then well fastened together. Fry them in hot lard or friture. Serve garnished with crisped parsley.

SALMIS OF GAME.

This method of serving is exclusively adapted to plumed game, such as cold roasted partridges; pheasants, plovers, quails, snipes, moor-fowl, wild ducks, ortolans, thrushes, etc. The smaller birds should be left whole; those of medium size, such as quails and small partridges should be merely halved; but when unusually large, they, as well as pheasants, require to be cut up. Remove the skin from the cold roasted game, divest it of the head, feet, pinions, and neck, put it into a stewpan with the juice of a lemon, two table-spoonfuls of gravy, a couple of glasses of wine, salt, spices, shalot, and shred lemon rind. Do it quickly for eight or ten minutes. Serve it arranged round the dish between sippets of toast; pour the sauce into the middle.

COLD SALMIS.

After warming up the game in gravy, as directed above, let it cool; dip the pieces into slightly-melted jelly, place them in a dish, and garnish plentifully with lumps of jelly.

SPORTSMAN'S SALMIS.

Cut up cold roasted birds, season them highly, and warm them up in three dessert-spoonfuls of salad oil, a glass of red wine, the juice of a lemon, and a little of the grated rind. When quite hot, serve with the sauce poured into the dish.

SALADS OF GAME, ETC.

The kind of meat most esteemed for a salad, is either pheasant, turkey, fowl, or rabbit. After it has been roasted and grown cold, cut up the meat, trim it, remove the skin from the best or white parts, put them into a bowl and season them, then arrange them in a dish; place round them the quartered hearts of white lettuces, and hard-boiled eggs also cut into four. Decorate with capers, gherkins, capsicums, fillets of anchovy, stoned olives, chopped herbs, shred shalot, etc. Pour over it a salad mixture of oil, vinegar, etc., and serve. You may intersperse it with small thin slips of ham, tongue, or anything else you may fancy.

TRUFFLES.

When things are said to be *à la Périgueux,* it is to be understood that they are flavoured with truffles—the most admired truffles being obtained from the neighbourhood of Périgueux. Truffles should be chosen of as round a shape as possible. Clean them with a brush and cold water, and serve them after any of the following fashions. Wrap them in thin slices of bacon fat, then roll them up in thick oiled paper, and do them in wood-ashes, or bake them in an oven. Or slice them and toss them in butter; serve with a thickened sauce of white wine and gravy. Or do them in a stewpan, lined with thin slices of bacon fat; add a bruised bay leaf, salt, and pepper, and enough champagne to cover them. Serve them in a napkin; this manner is called *en serviette*. Or mince them and toss them in olive-oil; add a little chopped parsley, pepper, a glass of white wine, and the same quantity of gravy. They may likewise be put into *petits pâtés;* or, with the addition of ham and bacon fat, they may be formed into a tourte.

VINAIGRETTE OF COLD MEAT.

Cut some cold boiled beef into small thin slices, arrange them in a dish, and season them with pepper, salt, chopped pickles, chervil, tarragon, vinegar, and oil. Decorate it with fillets of anchovy, gherkins, capsicums, and capers. Remember not to stir it up before serving. Cold tongue or sausage may be substituted for the cold beef.

CHAPTER III.

Sauces, suitable for Breakfasts generally and Cold Collations

---

ANCHOVY BUTTER.

Take six Gorgona anchovies, pick the flesh from the bone, fins, etc., pound it as fine as possible, and mix with it an equal weight of fresh butter. This is very relishing, either served upon dry toast, or as a sauce to other preparations.

CHUTNEY SAUCE.

Take eight ounces each of tamarinds, minced apples, tomatoes, pulped medlars, sultana raisins, grocers' currants, garlic bruised, ginger powdered, and brown sugar; the grated rinds and juice of four lemons, four ounces each of salprunella and red chillies bruised, a good handful of green mint chopped, and six pints of strong vinegar. Let this be all well mixed together. Keep it in a warm place for a month, and it will be fit for use; but age improves it.

COLD CURRY SAUCE.

Pound the hard-boiled yolks of six eggs, and add gradually four large dessert-spoonfuls of olive oil, one dessert-spoonful of strong curry-powder, and a good bit of Cayenne pepper. Mix with it sufficient lemon-juice to make it of the proper consistency to pass through a tammy. A sauce *enragée* is like the foregoing, with the exception of the curry-powder and lemon-juice, a little saffron taking the place of the former, and more oil being used to give it the required moisture. These sauces are invaluable with devilled dishes.

LOBSTER BUTTER.

Pound the eggs which are found under the tail of a hen lobster, and when they form a fine paste, mix with them an equal weight of very fresh butter, and pass it through a tammy.

LOPRESTI SAUCE.

Take six ounces each of the best mustard in powder and curry-powder, half an ounce of Cayenne pepper, four ounces of mustard-seed, three ounces of bruised garlic, eight ounces each of sliced shalots and salt; put it into a jar with three pints of very strong vinegar. Tie it down close, and keep it in a warm place by the fire for a week.

MAYONNAISE SAUCE.

Beat together the yolks of two raw eggs, a little vinegar, salt, and pepper; gradually add a sufficiency of fresh olive oil, and continue beating the whole until a smooth cream is formed. This sauce may be made to look green by adding a small quantity of spinach-juice.

MONTPELLIER BUTTER.

Take two pickled anchovies, a dessert-spoonful of capers, two or three gherkins, some peppercorns, the hard-boiled yolks of four eggs, a dessert-spoonful of tarragon vinegar, and a shalot; add the raw yolk of one egg. Pound all together in a mortar, until a sort of stiff cream is the result. Pour in enough olive oil to allow of its being passed through a sieve. Afterwards let it remain to become firm. Use as required for a cold sauce, with fish or meat.

RAVIGOTE SAUCE.

Take the hard-boiled yolks of six eggs, a pinch each of the leaves of well-cleaned tarragon, chervil, salad-burnet, mustard and cress, chives, and a tea-spoonful of capers, half a dozen gherkins, two ounces of preserved tunny-fish, and half a dozen anchovies. Pound all to a paste, then add a pound of the best fresh butter, two ounces of olive oil, and the juice of a lemon. Season with Cayenne pepper, mix well together, and keep it in a cool place.

REMOLADE SAUCE.

With equal quantities of oil and vinegar, mix a table-spoonful of the best mustard; add the raw yolks of two eggs, and a tea-spoonful each of finely-shred shalots and savoury herbs. Season with pepper and salt, and use as wanted, either for a salad mixture, or as a sauce for cold meat. A Tartar sauce is similar to the above, but omitting the eggs.

SHRIMP OR PRAWN BUTTER.

After picking them from their shells, pound the fish in a mortar, add a corresponding weight of fresh butter and some Cayenne pepper. Place the mixture in a *bain-marie*, and when the butter is melted, pass it through a strong sieve. Serve it cold as a *hors d'œuvre*. Remark: if intended to be kept for any length of time, the butter employed should have been previously clarified.

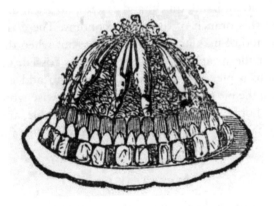

CHAPTER IV.

Savoury Pies for eating Cold.

As this is not an elementary work upon cookery, I shall not give detailed instructions for compounding pie-crusts, presuming that in every household there is some one who can make pastry good enough for the purpose. At the same time, I am fully convinced that pastry-cooks, like poets, are born, not made; for unless they are inherently light and cool of hand, quick, and careful, no given directions can qualify them successfully in this branch of domestic economy. There is, of course, a great similarity in the method of making all meat pasties; but when they are to be served cold, it is a rule that the meat should be first slightly tossed, or partially roasted, before it is made into a pie. This process is believed to add a greater amount of flavour, and to insure the pie keeping better than it otherwise would. To have a good effect, pasties should not be made large for the breakfast table, and when a raised pie can be conveniently had, it is more desirable than one made in a dish.

BEEF-STEAK PIE.

Have a very tender rump-steak; do not beat it if you can avoid it, as beating only draws out the gravy. Cut it into moderately small pieces, trim off the outer skin, and if too thick, remove some of the fat. Put the meat into a flying-pan which has been rubbed with butter and made quite hot. Just brown both sides of the meat, take it up, pepper it well, lay it in your dish, which should be edged with a good crust, pour in a good breakfast-cupful of strong gravy, seasoned with a little essence of anchovy or shrimp; but observe when either of these is used, salt should be omitted, as nothing is more objectionable than a predominance of the flavour of salt in a pie. Cover with a lid of crust, and bake for an hour in a tolerably quick oven. Custom has quite established a taste for the addition of fish with beef; thus oysters are often introduced in steak-pies, and lobster-sauce sometimes chosen with them. The oysters may be first bearded, peppered, dipped into yolk of egg, and slightly browned in a pan, or chopped up raw, and with other things made into forcemeat balls; these should be partially fried or poached before they are employed. Some epicures like a small quantity of Parmesan cheese, or some shred shalot sprinkled over the meat; but such peculiar flavours had better be avoided, though, if you can manage it, a gravy made from game of any kind, especially hare, is a material improvement.

CALF'S-FEET PIE.

There are sweet as well as savoury calf's-feet pies; the former are composed of currants, candied peel, wine, etc. For the latter, boil a pair of feet in plenty of water, until you can remove the bones easily, then line a terrine with thin slices of fat bacon, over this spread some rich forcemeat, put in the meat of the feet, add some mushroom-powder or truffles sliced, and some thin slices of cold tongue or smoked sausage, season well with pepper. Pour in a little strong gravy and a glass of brandy, cover with more forcemeat and bacon fat, put on the top of the terrine, and bake for an hour and a half in a rather slow oven. The flavour may be varied by substituting oysters, caviare, or other things, for the tongue, truffles, etc. Remark: the liquor in which the feet were boiled can be converted into jelly, but should not be put into the pie. Calves' sweetbreads, or kidney sliced, seasoned, tossed in butter, and mingled with the calf's feet, will be found to improve the pie greatly.

CALF'S-HEAD PIE.

Boil a small calf's head or half a large one, take all the meat from the bones, blanch and keep the brains separately, skin the palate, tongue, etc., and cut the latter into thin slices. Season with spices according to taste. Shake the meat for a few moments in a hot pan over a brisk fire. Put a rim of crust round your dish, lay in the meat, filling up with the yolks of eggs hard-boiled, pieces of the brains, forcemeat balls, and a little minced anchovy. Finish with a cupful of good gravy, and cover with a crust. A few flat sausages may take the place of the forcemeat balls, but they must be very highly seasoned, or the pie will be insipid. Oysters are likewise admissible.

CHICKEN OR FOWL PIE.

Carefully pluck, draw, and clean your birds. If chickens, simply split them open at the back; but if a fowl, cut it up. Rub the meat well with pepper, dip it into liquid butter, and broil it slightly over a clear fire. Make some rich forcemeat balls, being particular to use scraped marrow or bacon fat instead of suet; dispose the balls and the hard-boiled yolks of eggs amongst the meat when cold, and make it as a raised pie, or in an ordinary dish with a rim and top of crust. If it should be a raised pie, no gravy should be added; but otherwise pour in a cupful of relishing gravy. Should you prefer the chickens to remain whole, lay them with their breasts upwards. Some very thin slices of bacon may be added, if approved of, or you may lard the birds instead.

DUCK PIE.

Prepare a couple of young ducks, by scalding and drawing them; cut off their heads, necks, feet, and pinions; boil these down with the gizzards, an anchovy, and some seasoning, to make half a pint of strong gravy. Remove the fat from the insides of the birds, put in a good deal of pepper, rub them outside with butter, and roast them for twenty minutes before a quick fire; let them grow cold, cut them up, lay them with the livers in a dish edged with crust, add the strained gravy, the juice of a Seville orange, and a table-spoonful of stoned olives. Put on a lid of paste and bake for an hour. For a raised pie, bone the ducks and pour in some jelly after the pie is dressed.

GIBLET PIE.

Take two sets of goose giblets; reserve the livers, and boil the rest until perfectly tender; bone them, cut the gizzards and livers in halves, skim and reduce the liquor, season according to taste. When cold, lay the meat in the dish along with some collops of very tender rump-steak; add shred lemon peel and the gravy, which should be strong enough to jelly when cold; cover with a crust, and bake for an hour and a-half. In some parts of England a pudding of rich forcemeat is placed in the middle of the pie, and the meat arranged round.

GOOSE PIE.

For a green-goose pie, bone a couple of young geese, by first opening them down the backs; pepper them, and lay them one within the other; put them into a dish with a crust, and pour in a rich seasoned gravy, made from the bones and giblets; or make it into an oval-shaped raised pie, adding the gravy after the pie is baked. The livers of the geese may be made into a forcemeat with a few truffles, etc. A finer goose pie is made by boning a full-grown goose and a large capon; season both with spices; lay the capon inside the goose, and place upon the capon a small ox-tongue which has been boiled, skinned, and divested of the root end. Put the above in a thick raised crust, or in a terrine, garnished with some forcemeat, etc. Bake it for two hours, and fill up with jelly before serving. A pigeon may be substituted for the tongue, and the capon may be larded, if convenient.

HAM PIE.

Take some small slices of cold boiled ham, pepper them well. Cut up a fine fowl; toss it in butter till it begins to brown. Line a dish with a good paste; lay in first some ham, then some fowl; fill up the spaces with the yolks of hard-boiled eggs; add some mushroom powder, strew in some spices; cover with a layer of ham, pour in some gravy, put on a top crust, and bake it for an hour and a half. Remember, the ham should only be in the proportion of one-third the weight of the fowl, or the pie will taste too salt. Calves' sweetbreads are very good, employed instead of the fowl.

HARE PIE.

Cut up a full-grown hare, make a forcemeat with the liver, season it pretty highly with grated lemon-peel and spices; but do not use herbs if you intend the pie to keep. Add half a pound of butter, and jug the hare in a close stopped vessel for an hour. When cold, place all together in a crust, add a glass of port wine, and bake in a gentle oven for two hours. The meat of a leveret should be merely tossed in butter before being made into a pie, some strong beef gravy being added.

KIDNEY PIE.

Have a very fresh calf's kidney, with a good deal of the fat about it. Cut it into slices, and toss it quickly over a clear fire, but do not let the gravy be drawn. Beat some of the fat in a mortar, together with an equal weight of cold tongue, ham, or Bologna sausage, season well with spices, and make into forcemeat balls, with eggs, etc. Lay the meat in the dish or crust; add the forcemeat, a few hard-boiled yolks of eggs, and half a dozen sweet macaroons soaked in Madeira wine; sprinkle in some spices; pour in sufficient gravy. Bake for an hour. The kidney from a cold roasted loin of veal may be used, if not over-done; and oyster or sausage meat (first fried) substituted for the forcemeat.

LAMB'S-HEAD PIE.

Take two lambs' heads; open them, and clean them carefully, especially about the roots of the tongues; cut away the objectionable parts, but do not remove the brains. Pepper the heads, and lay them open in a dish, the cheek sides upwards; put some butter on them, and bake for an hour in a gentle oven. Take the flesh from the bones, cut the tongues and brains into slices, and when cold place all together in a dish with a rim of crust. Pour in the gravy which came from them in baking, add a little essence of anchovy, Cayenne pepper, and the grated rind of half a lemon. Cover with a lid of paste, and bake for half an hour, or until the crust is done. If preferred, it may be made into a raised pie.

LAMB PIE.

Take a shoulder of lamb; bone it, highly season it with spices, etc., sprinkle over it a little white sugar, roll it tight, and roast it for twenty minutes, basting it with butter. Let it grow cold, cut it into slices, squeeze a lemon over it, pack it in a raised crust and bake it for an hour. When done, pour in melted jelly of any particular flavour approved of. A few sultana raisins or grocers' currants, soaked in brandy, are often employed in this pie.

MUTTON PIE.

Commonly this is made with chops, either first tossed or stewed, or neither; it is far superior, if you take a fine loin of mutton, and cut the meat from it lengthwise, or saddle fashion; trim off all skin, suet, sinew, and superfluous flat, season the meat with plenty of pepper, and just toss it in a hot pan of butter for five minutes. When cold, place it in a dish edged with crust; add a little salt, a glass of port wine, and pour over it a gravy made by boiling down the bones of a well-hung woodcock, grouse, or other feathered game: by this means the pie will be equal to a venison pasty. Cover with a lid of crust, and bake for an hour. Some epicures prefer the addition of a small quantity of Parmesan cheese; or, four or five days before making into a pie, they rub the loin of mutton with sugar, and let it soak in a mixture of equal parts of vinegar and red wine. When a raised pie is preferred, the gravy should not be poured in until after the pie is baked.

OX-CHEEK PIE.

Carefully clean the cheek, season it well with spices, rub it over with fresh butter, and bake it gently till quite tender; skin the palate, and cut the meat into suitable-sized pieces; place it in a raised crust or pie-dish, add a little salt, a few forcemeat balls made with oysters, pour in a glass of Madeira, and the gravy rendered by the meat while baking; put on a top crust, and bake for an hour in a slow oven. An ounce of truffles may be introduced with advantage.

PARTRIDGE PIE.

Draw and singe the birds, cut off their feet and pinions, and either truss and lard them, or split them open at the back, and after broiling them a little, line them with a forcemeat of game, or thin slices of bacon fat; or, instead of this, they may be stewed for a time in very good game gravy until the birds are quite tender. Well-season them, and put all together in a raised crust, or in a pie-dish with a rim of paste; cover with a lid of the same, and bake for an hour. Some cooks are in the habit of laying a veal cutlet under the birds, and also add hard-boiled eggs, forcemeat, etc. When truffles are employed, this pie is called a *pâté à la Périgueux*, and the celebrated *Terrines de Nérac* are simply partridge pies made without paste, in covered dishes, lined with forcemeat, etc.

PÂTÉ DE PITHIVIERS.

This is a pasty composed of either larks, thrushes, snipes, plovers, or such like birds; each should be filled with a very delicate forcemeat, and wrapped in a very thin slice of bacon fat. Season them highly, and put them into a raised pie with the usual addition of forcemeat and bacon fat. Bake for two hours in a moderately-heated oven, and serve cold.

PERIGORD PIE.

This is made of different kinds of feathered game, mixed together. The birds should be larded, and interspersed with a high-flavoured forcemeat. This pie requires much baking, and should be enveloped in buttered paper, unless the heat of the oven can be conveniently regulated.

PHEASANT PIE.

Prepare your bird by singeing, drawing, etc. Extract the gall from the liver; pound the latter in a mortar, together with the meat from the breast of a partridge, two good teaspoonfuls of Bengal chutney, and a quarter of a pound of fresh butter. Put this inside the pheasant, baste it with butter, and roast it for a quarter of an hour before a quick fire. Let it grow cold, sprinkle it with salt, cut it up, add some pepper, place it in a dish edged with paste, and pour over it a little gravy made by boiling down the remainder of the partridge. Cover with a crust, and bake for an hour. Note: when gravy is recommended, it should not be compounded at random; a very strong decoction of meat, simply seasoned with pepper and salt, is all that is wanted; any vegetables boiled with it would only cause the pie soon to turn sour, and besides give it a brothy taste. The pheasant may be boned and larded, if preferred, and made into a raised pie.

PIC-NIC PIE.

Make some rich light pie-crust, roll it out as for a roley-poley pudding. Take some very tender rump-steak, carefully cut of an uniform thickness, remove every particle of sinew, skin, and fat; pepper it well, dip it into either olive oil or liquid butter, and broil it for five minutes over a clear fire, turning it once; lay it upon the paste, which should be somewhat larger than the steak; add a little salt, and strew over it either some chopped mushrooms or sliced truffles. Make it into a roll, securely fastening the edges with white of egg; glaze it with some of the same, and bake it for an hour. It does not signify whether the steak is in one piece or not, so long as it quite covers the middle of the paste. Slices cut as steaks from a tender leg of mutton may be treated in the same way.

PIGEON PIE.

After being plucked, cleaned, and drawn, the feet, necks, and pinions should be removed; the pigeons may either be stewed till tender and put whole into a pie, together with the liquor they were boiled down in, or they may be rubbed over with butter, then slightly broiled, and each cut into quarters; or the birds may be seasoned, and laid in a dish with their breasts downwards upon a fine rump-steak. Some cooks put a forcemeat ball into each, or a piece of anchovy butter, or pepper them inside, and place a thin slice of bacon fat in each, and strew hard-boiled yolks of eggs between them. A timbale of pigeons is made by lining a well-tinned stewpan with a raised paste, then putting in the birds, adding a lid of crust, and baking it slowly for two hours; let it grow cold in the timbale; when wanted, warm it slightly, and turn it out. French cooks mostly mince the meat which is added to a pigeon pie. Sweetbreads are an excellent addition.

PORK PIES.

A loin of young pork, sliced, deprived of its rind, and some of the fat removed, makes a very good pie, if properly seasoned. It may be baked in a dish with a top and sides of crust; but pork pies generally are made in a raised form; for this the meat should be boned, and the fat and lean equally distributed, and packed close, no gravy being added: these pies require to be well baked. By way of variety, half the pork may be made into sausage-meat, adding a little dried sage, and enveloping morsels of it in thin fillets of the remainder of the pork. For family use, delicious pies are made by frying a porker's liver in butter, and when cold pounding it in a mortar, together with a corresponding weight of bacon fat, and some spices; blanch the brains of the porker, and slice them, as well as the two kidneys and some of the lean meat.

Season all well. Lay the forcemeat of liver inside a raised crust, put in the meat and one or two bruised bay leaves; add a lid of crust, and bake it for two or three hours, according to size.

RABBIT PIE.

This is considered such an English dish that on the Continent it goes by the name *Pâté anglais*. Take the best joints of a couple of rabbits, cut them into pieces; season them highly, and toss them in butter till they are half done. Make a forcemeat with the livers and a like weight of bacon fat, a little anchovy butter, or a few oysters; season with sliced lemon rind, etc. Make it up as a timbale—that is, in a stewpan lined with crust, or in an ordinary dish; if in the latter way, pour in some strong gravy. Bake for an hour and a half. A large Ostend rabbit may be boned and larded with ham; or, when rabbits are plentiful, slices may be cut from the whole length of their backs, and wrapped round rolls of sausage meat, and packed in a raised crust.

SAUSAGE PIE.

Skin some Lyons or Bologna sausage; cut it into tolerably thin slices; divide these into quarters. Cover a pie-dish or stewpan with paste; lay in the sausage, interspersing it with peppered collops of veal or sweetbreads, and lumps of fresh sausage-meat, spiced, but not salted. If this sausage-meat can conveniently be made with the flesh of game or poultry, it is a great improvement. Pork cutlets may be employed in place of veal. Put on a lid of paste, and bake in a slow oven for two hours, if a large pie.

SMALL PATTIES.

The principal thing to be observed in making small patties is that the paste be exceedingly good; very little meat should be put in them, or they will be heavy. The game, meat, or poultry employed must be first pounded to a paste, or simply minced fine. Chopped mushrooms and truffles may be added. Cocks-combs, *foies gras*, ham, tongue, sausage, veal kidney, forcemeats of various kinds, caviare, sweetbreads, etc., are suitable for small patties. Immediately before baking your *Petits pâtés*, brush over the tops with egg. Twenty minutes will bake them.

STRASBOURG PIE.

Make a rich forcemeat with fat and lean pork, truffles, spices, etc. Get ready a raised crust, line it with thin slices of bacon fat, upon which spread a layer of forcemeat. In the middle place two very fat goose-livers, seasoned; add more truffles and forcemeat, finish with sliced bacon fat, a bruised laurel leaf, and a lid of crust. Fasten it very well where the paste joins. Bake it for two hours in a moderately hot oven.

SWEETBREAD PIE.

Blanch two calves' sweetbreads, pepper them, and toss them in butter for five minutes; add half their weight of bearded oysters, the grated rind of half a lemon, and the yolks of some hard-boiled eggs dipped into essence of anchovy, and peppered. Place all together in a dish with an edge of crust, pour in a little gravy and Madeira wine. Cover with a top of crust, and bake for an hour.

TERRINE OF HARE.

Bone a fine hare, save the prime parts, and make a mince of the remainder, adding the blood, the liver, a clove of garlic, and a pound of lean pork; season with salt, cloves, and pepper. Line a covered pie-dish with thinly-sliced bacon fat, put in part of the mince, a few sliced truffles, the meat of the hare, and the rest of the mince; pour in a glass of brandy, place two or three bay-leaves on the top, and some more slices of bacon fat. Hermetically fasten on the cover of the terrine by luting it with a little paste, and bake slowly for three hours. Serve cold.

TURKEY PIE.

Pick, singe, and draw the bird; open it down the back; bone, and lard it with tongue or ham. Rub it over with butter, and bake it a little in a brisk oven. Make a forcemeat of the liver with veal, or the white meat of poultry, oysters, spices, marrow, mushroom powder, etc. When cold, cut up the turkey, and either make it into a raised pie, surrounded with forcemeat and thin slices of bacon fat, or with these two ingredients put into a terrine without the addition of paste. A few blanched Spanish chestnuts may be employed in this pie. If made into an ordinary pie, boil down the bones and giblets until there is just enough gravy to pour into the dish. The turkey may be kept whole if preferred, and the meat from the breasts of pullets, or the backs of rabbits, used to fill up with. The yolks of hard-boiled eggs may be employed at discretion. A raised pie requires to be baked two hours, an ordinary pie one hour.

VEAL PIE.

Some cooks advocate stewing the meat before it is made into a pie, but if veal is fresh killed, and the meat cut from across the loin longitudinally, it cannot fail to be tender.

First toss it quickly in butter, and either cut it into small collops, and roll them round portions of forcemeat, composed of pounded ham, veal fat, etc., and make it into a raised pie, or make it into an ordinary pie, with gravy and seasoning, and half an ounce of unpressed caviare to each pound of veal. Without the latter, or forcemeat, it is sometimes served as a sweet pie, by employing raisins, grocers' currants, candied fruit, etc., in its composition. A savoury veal pie is improved by a few stoned olives and the yolks of some hard-boiled eggs. It should be highly seasoned with red and white pepper, nutmeg, etc. Bake according to size.

VENISON PIE.

Cut your meat into moderately small pieces; boil down the bones to make gravy. Season the meat, and properly distribute the fat and the lean in a dish edged with crust. Pack the venison pretty close, cover with a lid of crust, and bake slowly for four hours. If preferred, the venison may be first jugged for two or three hours, to make it tender, and afterwards put into a raised pie.

WOODCOCK PIE.

Pick clean and singe your birds; take out the trail, make it into a forcemeat with the livers, some bacon fat, etc. Split open the woodcocks at the backs, rub butter upon them, dust them plentifully with pepper, and broil them a little over a clear fire. When cold, lard them and make them into a raised pie in the usual way. Snipes similarly treated are excellent.

YORKSHIRE PIE.

Bone a large goose, a turkey, and a couple of ducks, first splitting them open at the backs. Boil down an old hare with plenty of spices, until the bones fall freely from out of the flesh. Make it with other things into a rich forcemeat; add it to the birds, and place them inside a thick, raised crust; fill up at the sides with two or three braces of partridges or woodcocks, cover it perfectly close, and bake it four hours. When done, pour in the hare gravy and some fresh butter, just melted, fasten up the hole, and keep it for at least a week before cutting it. Of course this pie can be modified by using a duck, a fowl, and a partridge, instead of the first-mentioned birds, and filling up with hard eggs, flat sausages, ham balls, or small birds, etc. In all cases the breasts of the birds should be placed upwards.

CHAPTER V.

SAVOURY PUDDINGS, SAUSAGES, AND DISHES REQUIRING TIME TO PREPARE THEM.

SAVOURY PUDDINGS.

By these we do not mean puddings made with a crust, such as are served as *entremets* at a dinner, but small spiced puddings, which come under the denomination of *hors d'œuvres,* or by-dishes suitable for breakfasts, and other light repasts. In place of paste they are enclosed in skins, and are broiled or tossed, as fancy dictates. The skin from the necks of geese and turkeys, when left in lengths sufficient for the purpose, are very convenient when the regular skins cannot be procured from the butchers.

DEVONSHIRE WHITE PUDDINGS.

Take a pound of shred pork fat, a quarter of a pound of cleaned currants, half a pound of grated bread, half a pint of clotted cream, a quarter of a pound of loaf sugar, and the yolks of six and the whites of two raw eggs. Mix these ingredients well together, fill the skins, and boil them for half an hour. Roast, fry, toss, or broil them, as wanted. Plainer puddings are composed of herbs, swelled groats, boiled onions, or leeks, suet, or chopped fat. Very rich puddings may be made with beef marrow, blanched almonds, cream, eggs, spices, sugar, and sweet wine.

FRENCH WHITE PUDDINGS.

Take equal parts of the white meat of cold fowl, bread-crumbs, boiled onions, and cream. Pound the meat to a paste, season it well, add the other ingredients, mix all together with the yolks of two raw eggs; put it into skins, and boil them for a quarter of an hour. Grill them in paper cases, or toss them in butter, before serving. When cream cannot be procured use milk.

GAME PUDDINGS.

Season and beat to a paste the flesh and liver of a cold roasted pheasant or hare. Make a little strong gravy by boiling down the bones, etc. Mix sufficient bread-crumbs in this, add the meat, with a third its weight of scraped veal fat. Make it of the requisite consistency with fresh raw eggs, and either put it into skins, or roll portions of it in flour, and poach them in boiling water. When cold, dip them successively in butter and bread-crumbs, and broil or fry them brown.

PUDDINGS À LA RICHELIEU.

These are made similarly to the preceding, with the exception that the flesh of either poultry or game may be used, and mashed potatoes and butter are substituted for the bread-crumbs and gravy. Black puddings are not bad in their way, but they are not among the things we would make to set before our friends.

STRASBOURG PUDDINGS.

Chop up the livers of two fat geese, add an equal weight of pork fat, minced very fine, and four onions boiled in gravy; sprinkle in a little dried sage, add pepper and salt, mix together with bread-crumbs and cream; put it into skins, and treat in the usual way. Hog's or calf's liver, first boiled, and a third of bacon fat added, may be employed as above, and rice boiled in milk may take the place of bread crumbs.

DRIED SAUSAGES.

BOLOGNA SAUSAGES.

Take of beef suet, bacon, beef, pork, and veal, of each half a pound; chop all fine; add some shred sage, marjoram, and penny-royal; season highly with pepper and salt. Fill it into large skins. Prick them with a needle, boil for an hour, and hang to dry.

CERVELAS, OR SMOKED SAUSAGE.

Chop together the lean of pork and bacon fat, letting the latter predominate one-fourth. Season it with pepper, salt, coriander, allspice, and nutmeg. Put it into skins, make them into lengths, smoke them for three days, then boil them in a liquor seasoned with herbs, vinegar, etc., and either serve cold upon a napkin, or slice and toss them in butter.

LYONS SAUSAGE.

One pound of beef, two pounds each of fat bacon and fresh pork; chop the beef and pork very fine, and merely cut up the bacon in square pieces. Season with coarse pepper and saltpetre. Put it into skins, tie them in lengths, and put them into a pan; sprinkle them with saltpetre, and let them remain a week; then smoke them for three or four days, and afterwards steep them for forty-eight hours in red wine, with the addition of sage, thyme, and bay leaves. Smoke them again, and keep them wrapped in paper till wanted.

ITALIAN SAUSAGE.

Take the leg and shoulder of a young porker, remove the fat and rind, and with a knife scrape the lean into a paste. Add half its weight of bacon fat, roughly cut up; season with pepper, cloves, mace, and nutmeg. Stuff the mixture into skins, and smother them in pounded saltpetre for eight days. Smoke them till sufficiently dry, and afterwards rub them with olive oil and the ashes from burnt vine branches.

SPANISH SAUSAGE.

Roughly cut up equal parts of the fat and lean of a full-grown hog. Beat together some salprunella, pimienta, or Spanish red pepper, cayenne, a clove or two of garlic, and a small quantity of powdered turmeric. Soak the whole in half Malaga wine and strong vinegar for a week; put the mixture into large ox skins, and keep them in a dry place. Toss slices in olive oil, and serve, garnished with pickled green capsicums.

Fresh Sausages, Etc.

MUTTON SAUSAGES.

Beat together in a mortar a pound of the lean of tender raw mutton, half a pound of veal fat, three anchovies, four ounces of bread, two dozen fresh oysters, bearded, two boiled onions, two raw eggs, and plenty of seasoning. Moisten with the oyster liquor and a little lemon-juice. Put it into small skins, and prick them with a needle before frying them.

PORK OR BEEF SAUSAGES.

For ordinary sausages:—Three pounds of fat and two pounds of lean pork, well seasoned and finely chopped; add half a pound of bread crumbs, soaked in milk. If intended to be made into flat sausages, mix with the beaten yolks of eggs. For Oxford sausages, add finely-shred herbs, according to taste. The above sausage-meat will keep well for a week or ten days, if properly seasoned. Excellent beef sausages are made by mincing equal parts of fat and lean of tender beef, with or without the addition of bacon fat. Season well with pepper, salt, and a small quantity of shred shalot and parsley. A good bit of bread, soaked in Rhine wine, makes the sausage lighter.

TRUFFLE SAUSAGES.

To one pound of lean pork add half a pound of bacon fat and three ounces of fresh truffles; season with salt and spices; chop it fine; mix with it a glass of champagne or some lemon-juice, and proceed as with other sausages.

VEAL SAUSAGES.

Take one pound each of lean veal and bacon fat, four anchovies, the hard-boiled yolks of four eggs, a little powdered sage, pepper, salt, and the juice of a Seville orange. Pound all in a mortar, and put into skins.

VENISON OR GAME SAUSAGES.

Venison, hare, pheasant, or any kind of game is suitable. Take two pounds of the raw flesh, carefully remove every particle of skin, sinew, etc., and mince the meat with half its weight of very sound bacon fat. Season it well with salt and pepper, cloves, nutmeg, and a glass of brandy. Make them up in skins, or with the addition of egg, roll them in flour, and fry them, first dipping them into butter and bread crumbs. Capital sausages are made with the flesh of rabbits, kid, goose, or turkey.

CAKE OF VEAL OR POULTRY.

Cut rather thin slices of the uncooked meat of fowl, rabbit, veal, or turkey; add a third of cold ham. Line a plain mould or tin with well-buttered paper, season the meat with white and red pepper, and shred lemon peel; lay it in your mould, strewing amongst it minced hard-boiled eggs; mix in two raw eggs, beaten up in a glass of brandy. Cover with buttered paper, and bake slowly for three hours, Turn it into a dish, and when cold decorate it with jelly.

CALF'S LIVER CAKE.

Pound in a mortar equal quantities of bacon fat and fresh calf's liver; add a little veal fat and cold ham; season with pepper. Intersperse among it lumps of cold tongue and small mushrooms; add eight raw eggs; mix well together and put it into a stewpan lined with slices of bacon fat. Lay some of the same on the top of the cake, cover with the lid of the stewpan, and bake for three hours. Turn it out when cold by slightly heating the outside of the mould. Glaze the cake, and decorate it with crusts ornamented with jelly. Lamb's liver done in this manner is very good.

GALANTINES.

Capon, duck, goose, hare, lamb, sucking-pig, partridge, pheasant, rabbit, salmon, turkey, veal, venison, and Welsh mutton, are among the things chiefly made into galantines. Much the same mode of operation is pursued in regard to each. The piece of meat is to be carefully boned, seasoned inside, and filled with forcemeat, pieces of tongue, sausage, game, bacon fat, truffles, etc., put in layers. Sew it up, try to make it retain its original form, fasten it securely in a cloth, and do it for some hours in a rich *consommé*. Let it grow cold in the liquor, which should subsequently be reduced, clarified, and in the form of jelly used as a decoration to the galantine. Serve it upon a white napkin. The two shoulders of Welsh mutton should be employed to make a galantine; either the breast or shoulder of veal also answers for the same purpose. The heads of sucking-pigs, hares, and rabbits, should not be boned. Hard-boiled yolks of eggs, oysters, blanched sweet almonds, chesnuts, pistachio nuts, *foies gras*, veal fat, garlic, bay leaves, lemon-juice and rind, chopped pickles, anchovies, etc., enter into the composition of the stuffing. When well executed, a galantine is a very handsome dish for any kind of collation. It is invariably served cold. Rasped bread may be used to mask it with if you cannot glaze it.

GAME CAKE.

Take an undressed hare, or any other kind of game, cut the flesh from the bones, add to it the same weight of fresh calf's liver, ham, and bacon fat. Pound all in a mortar, together with the liver of the game; season it with spices, salt, and a little shalot, and a glass of rum. Mix it with half-a-dozen fresh raw eggs, and if it is a hare add the blood. Line a mould with slices of bacon fat; put in alternate layers of game paste and sliced truffles; cover with more bacon fat; place some thick paper on the top, and bake it for three hours. Let it grow cold in the mould, and slightly warm it to turn it out.

HAM CAKE.

Take cold boiled ham, cut up equal parts of the fat and lean; season well with spice; beat it to a paste in a mortar; add one-fourth of fresh butter, put it into a mould, and bake it for twenty minutes; let it become cold, and turn it out when wanted, first dipping the mould for a few moments into boiling water. A fresh egg or two may be added if approved of. Tongue cake or cold beef cake is made in the same manner. If possible it should be glazed with jelly when served.

ITALIAN CHEESE.

Chop up the liver of a young porker with two thirds the same weight of bacon fat and one-third of fresh fat pork, season it with spices and shred sage, mix with it four raw eggs, and put it into a stewpan lined with bacon fat; place some of the latter upon the top, cover it close with the lid, and bake it for three hours. Turn it out to serve cold. Glaze it, and decorate it with jelly.

MEAT, GAME, ETC., IN JELLY.

For a stylish breakfast nothing can be prettier than things served *en aspic* or in jelly. In this way may be treated small birds, pigeons, partridges, sweetbreads, chickens, lamb-cutlets, fillets of game, or the white meat of poultry, small collops of veal, poached eggs, etc. Let any of the above be nicely dressed and grown cold. Take a mould, pour into it a little melted jelly, and when this is firm place in your birds, fillets, or cutlets, which have been previously tossed in butter. Arrange them carefully, with a view to their looking well when reversed upon a dish. Fill the mould with more dissolved jelly, and when quite set immerse the mould for a few moments in boiling water, and turn the jelly upon a dish. Remark: the birds should be placed in the mould with their breast downwards, so as to be in the right position when turned out. Decorate with pieces of ornamental jelly, etc.

PIC-NIC CHEESE.

Make a raised crust as for a pasty. Boil until tender half a pound of Neapolitan macaroni—twenty minutes will do it; drain, and add to it a quarter of a pound of fresh butter, two ounces each of scraped Parmesan and Gruyére cheese, and pepper and salt. Put it over a fire in a stewpan, and stir it for five minutes. When nearly cold put it into the raised crust, add a top of paste to it, and bake for half-an-hour. When done fill it up with fresh butter sufficiently melted. Serve upon a napkin folded in a dish.

POULTRY, ETC., EN DAUBE.

Most of the things suitable for galantines, and many others, may be done *en daube*. This differs from a galantine by the meat being larded upon the outer surface, and not being stuffed inside. Braise it for a considerable time; glaze it before serving, and surround it with large lumps of jelly. If you cannot conveniently manage the braising, you may merely roll the meat and roast it. Serve it either *en aspic* or simply glazed and garnished with jelly.

POULTRY ROLLED.

Bone a fat fowl and a duck, season them plentifully with spices and salt, place them one upon the other, and let them remain for two days; then make them into a very tight roll, and fasten it in a cloth with collaring tape. Bake it in a pan with a good deal of sweet lard, oil, or fresh butter to baste it with. When done take it out, but do not uncover till cold. Either serve it as it is or put it into a preserving jar, and fill it up with clarified butter. Cut it in rather thin slices when you help it. A goose and a turkey are capital rolled in this way, and if a cold boiled tongue is enclosed inside the fowl it conduces to keep the birds, and looks exceedingly well when cut up.

ROASTED OR BRAISED GAME OR POULTRY.

When game or poultry is purposely roasted to be served hot or cold for breakfasts, great care should be taken to have it as nicely browned as possible; and as it is upon these occasions mostly served without sauce, it should be nicely garnished with herbs or cresses. Unless when braised, poultry and game are better not stuffed. Should you require to serve any left from dinner, do not send it to table partially dismembered, but cut it up nicely, and if but little, eke it out by placing a small slice of cold ham, tongue, sliced hard-boiled eggs, fillets of anchovies, dried sausage, or anything calculated to improve the appearance of the dish as well as add to its contents. Poultry and game may be larded and braised instead of roasted, then decorated with jelly or glazed sippets.

ROLLED MEAT.

Whenever necessity compels us to introduce butchers' meat cold at our breakfast table, we should prepare it beforehand by having it boned, rolled, and glazed, as it is then a more agreeable object than when presented in the form of a joint. The pieces most fitted for the purpose are ribs of beef, fore-quarter of lamb, loin of veal, leg of Welsh mutton, neck of pork, shoulder and breast of veal, loin or shoulder of mutton. These may be first larded or not. When boned, well season the meat on the inner side, and add a little game forcemeat; roll it up very tight, fasten it securely, and braise, bake, or roast it. Glaze it highly before serving.

CHAPTER VI.

COLLARED, PICKLED, AND POTTED MEAT, ETC.

BEEF À LA MODE.

Choose a piece of the round of very tender beef, lard it, and braise it in a liquor made by the addition of a calf's foot, knuckle of veal or beef bones, herbs, spices, white wine, bruised bay leaves, and a glass of brandy. Let it do slowly for six hours. Take it up. Clarify the gravy until it forms a fine jelly, and garnish your meat with it when cold. Some cooks elaborate this dish by stuffing the beef with a rich forcemeat, but this method is not correct. When wine cannot be had use a little very good ale. The jelly may be coloured red with a small quantity of cochineal. An easy way of braising is to place the meat, with the necessary adjuncts, in a pot, tie it down with thick oiled paper, and place it for some hours in a moderately heated oven.

BREAKFAST BEEF.

Take twelve pounds of tender beef, wash it and wipe it dry, rub it with half-an-ounce each of saltpetre and salprunella, and one ounce of bay salt, all finely beaten. Two hours later rub it well with half a pound of brown sugar: at the end of another two hours add more salt and bay salt. Let it lie eight-and-forty hours. Drain it, and hang it in a very dry but not warm place. In ten days it will be ready for use. Soak it in sour beer for a few hours before dressing it. Then boil or braise it like hunter's beef.

COLLARED BEEF.

Bone a good-sized piece of the flank of tender beef, remove the skin, rub it with equal parts of saltpetre, salprunella, and bay salt, half a pound of brown sugar, and a pound of common salt. Let it stay for a week, basting it daily. Wipe it, and rub it well with plenty of spices, roll it up very tight, fasten it in a cloth, and boil it for six hours. Take it up, and put it under a press until cold.

COLLARED CALF'S HEAD.

Have a head with the skin on, as for mock turtle soup; split it open, take out the bones, soak it till pretty white; then spread over it plenty of seasoning, half a pound of shred beef marrow, two dozen bearded oysters chopped small, and some sweet herbs. Lay the ears also inside the head. Make it into a compact roll. Wrap it in a cloth, and bind it tightly with tape. Boil it for two hours, and when almost cold take it up; tighten the binding, and keep the head in a collaring pickle made with salt water and vinegar. Slices of ham or tongue and hard-boiled eggs may take the place of the oysters. If the head is intended to be kept for any length of time, the collaring pickle should be re-boiled at the end of every four days.

COLLARED PIG'S HEAD.

Procure a very plump head that has been nicely scalded. Salt it for a week, boil it for an hour, bone it, cut it in half, lay the snout end of one side towards the neck end of the other, season it well with pepper, place the ears inside, and, if you please, add the boiled flesh of an ox foot or some fresh lean pork. Fasten in a cloth, tie it tightly with tape, and boil it in a seasoned liquor till perfectly tender. When cold, unbind it, and put it under a weight, and if intended to be kept, place it in a pickle until wanted.

COLLARED SUCKING PIG.

Choose a very nicely-cleaned sucking pig; bone it entirely, rub the inside with pepper, salt, and powdered herbs; roll it up as tight as possible, bind it in a cloth, tie it securely, and put it into a boiling liquor made with water, a quart of vinegar, a handful of salt, some cloves, mace, pepper-corns, and savoury herbs. Boil softly till tender. Take it out, and when nearly cold tighten the bandage; place the pig in a pan, and pour over it the cold liquor in which it was boiled. Some housekeepers put the pig into a sort of caudle made of oatmeal, white wine, and spice, but this proceeding is not absolutely necessary.

COLLARED VEAL.

Bone a large fat breast of veal; rub it over with egg, and strew upon it spices, salt, shred herbs, lemon peel, and an anchovy, or small slices of pickled tongue or ham. Add likewise, if convenient, the meat from a boiled pair of calves' feet. Roll it very tight in a cloth, and tie it securely with tape. Simmer it for three hours in salt and water. When cold put it into a pickle of vinegar, and water enough to cover it.

COLLARED VENISON.

Take the bone, sinew, and skin from part of the side of venison; lard it with fine bacon fat; season it; tie it with collaring tape when rolled tightly. Put it into a large deep pan, with some bruised bay leaves and fresh butter; cover the pan with a coarse paste, and bake it for five hours. Drain it, and place it in a large preserving-pot or wide-mouthed jar. Cover it with fresh clarified butter, and keep it close stopped. Turn it out of the pot to serve, and decorate it with branches of bay leaves or holly, etc.

FRENCH BŒUF ECARLATE.

Take part of the leg of beef; bone it, lard it, and rub it with finely-powdered spices, salt, and saltpetre. Put it into a pan with some bruised juniperberries, thyme, and a clove of garlic. Cover it down close, and let it remain six days; turn it, and leave it for six days longer. Drain it; fasten it in a cloth; put it into boiling water well seasoned with herbs, etc. Let it simmer for four hours. Allow it to grow cold in the liquor. Unbind it, and serve upon a damask napkin. Decorate it with branches of herbs, etc. You may glaze it or not, according to fancy.

GOOSE PRESERVED AS AT BAYONNE.

From some very fat geese cut the thighs and wings, retaining upon them nearly all the flesh from the bodies of the geese. Remove the principal part of the bone. Rub the meat with salt and saltpetre, and sprinkle it with shred bay leaves, thyme, etc. Leave it thus for a day and night. Melt down the apron fat of the geese; strain it. Dip the pieces of goose into water to remove the brine, etc., wipe them quite dry, put them into the fat, and simmer them slowly until they are quite tender. Drain them, and when cold pack them in pots, and pour over them the goose fat, which should be merely warm enough to run. Keep them covered in a cool place until wanted.

HAMS AND BACON.

French cooks, after drawing the juice from the meat, place it in a brine made with salt, saltpetre, and wine lees and water in equal parts, a good deal of savoury herbs being first infused in the liquor. When the hams have remained a month in this, they are drained, smoked, and subsequently rubbed over with vinegar and wine. English housekeepers frequently prefer an admixture of spices with the pickle, and likewise employ strong beer, oak chips, juniper-berries, sugar or treacle, sweet-wort, or other ingredients; but the French method is the best. Hams may be made from legs of mutton, veal, or beef; these should be properly trimmed and treated as pork hams, observing that for mutton and veal a fortnight in the pickle is sufficient. Smoke them and boil them before they are put away for keeping. Cut them in rashers, as you would an ordinary ham, and fry, toss, or broil. I shall not give any instructions about the curing of bacon. The denizens of towns invariably purchase it ready dried, and dwellers in the country mostly adhere to their own family recipes. I should observe that for forcemeat, larding, braising, etc., the bacon employed should have had no saltpetre used in its curing, or the other meat will be made hard and red by it.

HAMBOURG OR DUTCH BEEF.

Remove all the fat, and rub the beef with sugar, salt, and saltpetre; turn it daily for twelve or fifteen days; drain and wipe it, enclose it in a cloth, press it, and smoke it in the fumes of damped sweet hay for three days. When ready it may be used as a relish, cut in rashers and broiled, or tossed in butter. If dressed whole, boil it for two hours, wrapped in a cloth. Spices may be added to the pickle if approved of.

HUNTER'S BEEF.

Rub into a well-hung round of beef, first boned, salt, saltpetre, spices, and sugar, in the proportion of an ounce and a half each of saltpetre and sugar, half an ounce of spice, and four ounces of common salt, to each dozen pounds of meat. Baste and turn it in the liquor for three weeks. Before dressing it wash it in clean water. Bind it in a cloth, put it into a baking-dish with half a pint of wine or strong ale at the bottom of the dish; throw a good deal of shred suet over the meat, cover it with a coarse paste, and bake it for six hours. Do not remove the paste, etc., until the beef is cold. Serve decorated with parsley, with a white napkin under it. Beef prepared thus will keep good for a considerable time.

IMITATED BOAR'S HEAD.

Have the head of a hog cut off nearly half-way down to the shoulders, so as to retain a good part of the neck. Bone it carefully, sprinkle it, as well as the meat from the bones, with saltpetre; put it into a pan with bruised laurel-leaves, sage, cloves, thyme, crushed pepper, juniper-berries, and coriander seeds. Cover it close, and let it remain a week; drain it, and stuff it with the loose flesh, slices of ham, tongue, truffles, fat and lean pork, seasoned like the head; tie it tight in a cloth, simmer it for six hours in a liquor made rich with the bones, savoury herbs, etc. Let it become cold in this, then remove the covering, and serve the head upon a white napkin, folded in the dish. Garnish it with branches of holly, bay, or herbs. You must endeavour to keep the head as much as possible in its original form.

MARBLED VEAL.

Take some cold roasted fillet of veal, season it with spices, and beat it in a mortar. Skin a cold dried tongue, cut it up, and pound it to a paste, adding to it nearly its weight of fresh butter; put some of the veal into pots, then strew in lumps of the pounded tongue, put in another layer of veal, and again more tongue; press it down, and pour clarified butter on the top. This cuts very prettily, like veined marble. The dressed white meat of either fowl, rabbit, or turkey, will answer for the purpose as well as veal.

MOCK BRAWN.

Have a piece of the belly of pork of the size you require. Take also the head; sprinkle them well with salt and saltpetre, and let them lie four or five days. Open the head, boil it till tender, bone it, and cut up the meat. Lay the piece of pork upon a board, spread upon it the superior parts of two ox feet, add the boiled meat of the head, roll it up as tight as possible, enclose it in a sheet of tin, boil it for five hours, stand it on one end to drain, and put a heavy weight inside the tin, at the other end, to press it down firm. Next day unbind it, and keep it in water and vinegar till wanted.

PICKLED BRISKET.

Take some brisket of beef that has been salted and properly boiled, cut it into square pieces, and when quite cold put it into a deep dish with some bruised bay leaves, and pour upon it plenty of vinegar, spiced according to taste. Let it remain a fortnight. To serve it, cut it into slices rather thicker than rashers of bacon, and toss them in a pan of hot butter.

PICKLED GOOSE OR DUCK.

Pluck and singe the bird, put it for five minutes into boiling water; take it out, wipe it dry, pepper it highly inside, and put it into a large jar; fill it up with equal quantities of red wine and vinegar strongly spiced; tie it down, stand it inside a pot of water, and simmer it gently until done. While still hot, pour some melted beeswax on the top, and keep it in a cool place.

PICKLED OX PALATES.

Simmer ox palates for four hours in a liquor seasoned with salt and spices; take them up, pack them in jars, strew spices upon them, and pour over them equal quantities of white wine and strong vinegar; add a few bruised bay leaves, and cover close. Cocks' combs also are excellent pickled, but require less dressing than the ox palates.

PICKLED PARTRIDGES OR PIGEONS.

Bone them, lard them with ham or tongue on the inner side, rub plenty of spices into them; truss them in what fashion you please. Plunge them for two or three minutes into boiling water; drain and dry them. Boil together equal quantities of Madeira wine and vinegar, with some pepper, nutmeg, and bruised bay leaves. Put in the birds, simmer them for twenty minutes; take them up, boil and skim the pickle a little longer, and when all is cold put it together in stone jars; cover them down securely.

PICKLED THRUSHES OR SNIPES.

Carefully pluck the birds, cut off the heads and feet, and roast or bake them, but do not baste them. Put them into pickle-jars with some pepper and shred lemon peel; add plenty of white wine vinegar, cover them well down, and keep in a cool place.

PICKLED VEAL OR TURKEY.

Take either a fine piece of leg of veal or a large turkey, bone it, and bind it tightly in a cloth. Boil together a quart each of vinegar, white wine, and water, add a tablespoonful of salt. After skimming this liquor, put in the veal or turkey; let it simmer gently for an hour and a half; take it up, reduce and skim the pickle, and when cold pour it over the meat, which should not be taken out of the cloth till required for the table. Garnish with fennel branches. Serve a cold sauce of vinegar, sugar, Cayenne pepper, and olive oil apart. This is an admirable imitation of pickled sturgeon.

PORK CHEESE.

Boil a well-cleaned porker's head that has been previously pickled. When done, bone it, cut it up small, and immediately put it into a buttered mould. Place a weight upon it, and turn it out when wanted. Garnish with parsley leaves. Remark: the head should have been scalded, and not singed, for this purpose.

POTTED BEEF.

Cut two pounds of lean beef in slices, rub them with cochineal, salt, pepper, and put them together for four-and-twenty hours. Bake them with vinegar or ale, enough to cover them. Drain them, and when cold, beat them in a mortar; add a pound of fresh butter, and seasoning to taste. Put the paste into pots, place them in the oven until quite hot, withdraw them, and when cold cover the tops with clarified butter.

POTTED BIRDS.

Woodcocks, partridges, ortolans, grouse, pigeons, quails, and small birds are potted in much the same manner. Pluck them very carefully, singe and draw them, wipe them quite dry inside, but do not wash them. Season them, put butter to them, and bake them. When done, drain them, and next day pack them in pots and pour clarified butter over them. The heads of moor-game should not be concealed under the butter. The pinions and feet should be removed from pigeons and partridges, and the beaks of woodcocks should be skewered through the thighs, one leg being first drawn through the other. The legs of grouse, larks, and small birds are to be arranged in like manner. The larger birds may be cut up so as to pack the closer, and save butter.

POTTED CHEESE.

Pound four ounces of rich Cheshire cheese with two ounces of fresh butter, a teaspoonful of powdered loaf sugar, a bit of mace, and a glass of white wine. Press it into a deep pot, and keep it close covered.

POTTED COLD BOILED BEEF.

Separate it from skin and muscle, pound it in a mortar, together with a few boned anchovies and sufficient fresh butter; spice it according to taste, and finish in the usual way. Remark: many cooks, after putting the meat-paste into pots, place the latter for a few minutes in a hot oven, for the purpose of condensing the meat as much as possible, and thereby excluding the air.

POTTED GAME OR POULTRY.

Take the cold remains of game, poultry, or rabbits, divest the meat of bone, skin, etc., season it with salt and plenty of Cayenne pepper, pound it in a mortar, together with an equal quantity of scraped cold bacon fat and a little anchovy. Press it well down in pots, and pour clarified butter over. Keep in a cool place.

POTTED HARE.

Cut up a well-hung hare, pack it in a deep dish, with the liver, and plenty of very fresh butter; tie it down with oiled paper, and bake it till tender. Drain it, and when cold pick the meat from the bones, skin, and sinew; season it highly, and beat it to a paste, adding the cold water that you have taken off the gravy from the hare. Put it into pots, press it down well, pour clarified butter upon the tops, and tie down tight.

POTTED RABBITS.

Take the best parts of some full-grown rabbits, such as the haunches and loins; remove the superfluous bone, rub the meat well in a mixture of spices, pack it in a dish, put in plenty of sweet lard, and bake slowly for two hours. Take the pieces of rabbit out of the lard, drain them, and when cold put them into pots, and cover them with butter that has been well clarified.

POTTED TONGUE.

Take a fine ox tongue, rub it with a quarter of a pound of moist sugar and an ounce of saltpetre; let it remain for four or five days; boil it till tender in a liquor enriched with wine, spices, bruised bay leaves, etc. Skin it and cut it up; pound it in a mortar together with a pound of fresh butter, add pepper, nutmeg and mace. Put it into pots, pour clarified butter on the tops, and tie down close. A dried tongue first boiled, or cold ham, may be potted in this manner.

POTTED VENISON.

Rub the venison with vinegar. An hour after wipe it, and rub it with port wine; season it with salt and spices. Put it into a pie-dish with a pound of fresh butter and a pint of port, cover it with a coarse paste or stout oiled paper, and bake it well. If a large piece it should remain in the oven for some hours. Drain it, let it grow cold, extract the sinews, bone, etc., beat the meat in a marble mortar, together with the butter skimmed off the gravy that was rendered in baking, press it down in pots, add a top layer of clarified butter, and tie it close for keeping.

PRESERVED RABBITS.

Take some young rabbits, bone them, lard them inside with bacon fat, ham, or tongue; season them with pepper, salt, and nutmeg. Make them into rolls, tie them tightly, pack them in a stewpan with herbs, spices, a little garlic, and enough olive oil to cover them. Do them gently for an hour. Let them become cold, cut them into thick fillets, put them into pots, and cover them with fresh oil. Tie skins over them, and they will keep well for a length of time.

SMOKED GOOSE.

Open a fine fat goose down the back, wipe it dry, wash it well with vinegar, then rub in half a pound each of brown sugar and salt and an ounce of saltpetre; rub it well, and baste and turn it regularly for a fortnight. Drain it, sew it in a piece of muslin, and smoke it till dry. Cut it in slices. This is very relishing devilled for breakfast.

TO CURE A TONGUE.

A French tongue *à l'ecarlate* is done thus: Wipe the tongue quite dry, then trim off part of the root; sprinkle it with two ounces of saltpetre, put it into a pan with thyme, peppercorns, bay leaves, savoury herbs, etc.; boil two handfuls of salt in enough water to cover the tongue; when this brine is cold pour it over and let it lie six days. Blanch the tongue, and dress it in a flavoured liquor for two hours. Do not take it out till cold. When tongues are to be smoked add half a pound of brown sugar to the salt, and use no water with the pickle. Tongues are frequently enclosed within ox-guts before they are cured. Pigs', sheep's, or calves' tongues may be salted in the same manner.

VENISON BEEF.

Take six pounds of tender beef, cut it up, rub into it four ounces of brown sugar, and one of powdered saltpetre. Let it lie two days. Wipe it dry, and put it to soak for twenty-four hours in equal parts of red wine and vinegar. Drain it well and bake it, with the addition of a good deal of fresh butter, until the meat is perfectly tender. Take it up, and when cold beat it to a paste in a mortar, using with it the cold butter from the dish in which it was baked. Add pounded cloves, cayenne, and black pepper. Place it in pots in the usual way.

CHAPTER VII.

FISH.

No kind of comestible is more deservedly popular for the breakfast-table than fish, whether fresh or in a state of preservation. It is known to be easy of digestion, yet nourishing; quickly cooked, relishing, capable of being prepared in a greater number of ways than even poultry or game; and the better sorts, such as turbot, soles, salmon, lobsters, etc., are in season nearly the whole year round. The only disadvantage attending it is, that the necessary quantity of fresh fish cannot always with certainty be obtained; but as a set off against this we can generally procure some kinds dried, smoked, or kippered, and when the supply of fresh fish is abundant we can ourselves salt, pickle, collar, or pot it to a sufficient extent to ensure our being provided with a reserve for a considerable time. Sea fish is generally supposed to be preferable to river or pond fish, the first being esteemed higher and finer flavoured than fresh-water fish; yet, who would have the temerity to choose a piece of cod before a cutlet of sturgeon? or a herring or a mackerel, be it ever so good, to a Rhine carp or a Thames salmon?

FISH BOILED.

Unless it be certain sorts of shell-fish, such as oysters, etc., and those kinds of fish which are smoked or otherwise cured, almost all fish may be boiled; but for a breakfast dish it is not so relishing dressed in this manner, and is rarely so served, *relevées* being inadmissible. When, however, it is required boiled, and intended to be introduced hot, the dish should be garnished with a few fried oysters, or some slices of the same kind of fish highly seasoned, and tossed in plenty of fresh butter. If it is to appear at table cold, some red wine should be added to the liquor in which the fish is boiled, and a cold sauce of oil, etc., served apart; thus treated, fish is said to be *au bleu*. Turbot, perch, bream, bass, carp, soles, and salmon are mostly cooked in this way; and, sent to table with a folded damask napkin under them, are perfectly admissible for a breakfast dish. When you have any plain boiled fish remaining from dinner, which you purpose warming up as an omelette, curry, or other way, be careful to have it broken into flakes, and boned before it has become cold, otherwise it will become so hard and unmanageable as to need re-warming before it can be made anything of. Remember, when you can get it, to use sea water for boiling your fish in; but failing this, a little salt and a cupful of vinegar, added to a sufficiency of spring water, will answer the purpose. Fish of a slender form, other than flat-fish, should have their tails neatly skewered in their mouths, so as to keep the bodies curled round. For garnish to boiled fish, tufts of parsley, chervil, or fennel, scraped horse-radish, pickles, or sliced lemon may be placed on the rim of the dish, outside the folded napkin.

FISH BROILED.

Shad, barbel, brill, plaice, Yarmouth bloaters, mackerel (first split down the back), herrings, codsounds (first parboiled), mullet (scored across the back), haddocks (split open), soles, sprats (skewered together in rows), whiting, dace, crimped cod (previously scalded), turbot, or salmon (in slices), and eels. These are the kinds of fish usually grilled for breakfast. Simply rub them over with oil and seasoning after they have been properly cleaned, and broil them upon a well-heated gridiron over a clear fire; or they may be enclosed in oiled paper, and served in the envelopes in which they were broiled. In either way the gridiron should be thoroughly rubbed over with fresh beef suet, and made exceedingly hot. That the fish may be made firm and the skins remain unbroken, it is advisable to wet them with strong vinegar some time before they are dressed, then wipe them dry and dip them into spiced olive oil. The time required for broiling varies from five to ten minutes, according to the thickness of the fish. Remark: English cooks almost invariably dust over with flour the fish they grill. This method is not practised on the Continent; but upon the shores of the Mediterranean, where fish may be had in perfection, it is frequently broiled between branches of bay, myrtle, or any similarly fragrant shrub; by this means the fish is prevented from scorching, and a deliciously aromatic flavour is communicated to it. Grilled fish may be served either with sauce poured over or under it. Tomato, caper, anchovy, or any such sauce may be employed.

FRIED FISH.

Sprats, eels, oysters, carp, lampreys, smelts, gudgeons, herrings, whitings, perch, ling, skate, or brill (in slices), soles, plaice, dabs, trout, tench, jack, etc., may be fried. I must here remark that in England everything cooked in a frying-pan is erroneously supposed to be fried; whereas we can only correctly apply the term to such things as have been first dipped into milk, butter, beaten egg, or dusted over with flour, bread crumbs, grated cheese, or crushed vermicelli. On the contrary, when the articles we dress are simply placed in a frying-pan of hot fat, without any previous addition except being seasoned, they are said to be *sauté*, or tossed. In this manner we ordinarily cook beef-steaks, mutton-chops, bacon and eggs, etc. For things that are fried, foreign cooks use either oil or a regular friture composed of equal parts of hog's-lard, fresh veal-fat, and beefsuet melted down together, and kept in pots for use. This is greatly to be preferred to lard or butter, from the fact that lard frequently contains a large amount of water and salt, and butter a considerable proportion of curd, all of which conduce to make the frying-pan sticky, and thereby discolour whatever is cooked in it, which never happens when oil or friture is used. The fish you require to fry should be well cleaned and wiped dry, and if thick it should either be split open or scored across in the most fleshy parts; pass it through some flour and fry it in plenty of friture, if you object to oil; but be particular that the fat boils before putting in the fish. Bread-crumbs or batter, etc., may take the place of flour. Fried fish should always be served upon a white napkin folded at the bottom of the dish, and garnished with either sliced lemon or crisp parsley. Such as smelts, sprats, etc., should be arranged *en buisson,* by inserting a small basin beneath the napkin in the dish, and placing the fish to stand with their tails upwards against the support formed for them to rest against.

FISH TOSSED, OR SAUTÉ.

Fish is not often cooked whole in this manner, unless it be the smaller kinds, but fillets from the following fish may be successfully *sauté*—shad, silver eels, pike, carp, mackerel, whiting, gurnet, salmon, soles, turbot, trout, skate, conger, pressed caviare, etc. The fillets should be nicely trimmed, skinned, and in most cases seasoned and sprinkled over with finely-chopped herbs, then tossed, or as English cooks would term it, fried in oil, lard, or clarified butter. When thus dressed the fish should be well drained from the friture, and served with a gravy or a sauce apart. Slices of cold fish may be quickly warmed up in this way.

FISH AU GRATIN (WITH BREAD-CRUMBS).

Take some ready dressed fish of any kind, slice it, and, if possible, bone it; dip it into either oil, cream, or melted butter; season it; place it in a dish upon a piece of buttered toast, sift grated bread upon the top, and place it in an oven until sufficiently browned. Serve upon the toast with a garnish of sliced lemon. One-third the quantity of rasped Parmesan cheese added to the bread-crumbs is a material improvement.

BAKED FISH.

Several descriptions of fish eat well when baked; but for the breakfast table it seldom appears hot when thus treated. As for this method of serving, it should be accompanied with a forcemeat, and be baked in a deep dish with plenty of cream, oil, or white wine. Trout, carp, bream, jack, cutlets of salmon, etc., are exceedingly good done in this way. When we intend it to be eaten cold we should season it well, and simply bake it with half vinegar and half water in the dish, or baste it with olive oil, white wine, or lemon-juice. Pieces of sturgeon, shad, salmon, bass, etc., are excellent dressed thus, and will keep for some time. Serve it upon the liquor, and let there be a cold sauce apart.

FISH ROASTED.

Sturgeon, lobster, pike, eels, and lampreys, are occasionally introduced among the entrées at a breakfast, roasted. The three latter should be first stuffed with a forcemeat made with shrimps, oysters, etc.; then curled round with their tails in their mouths, and skewered securely to keep them in shape. Place them before the fire and baste with butter. Serve with a sauce piquante. Lobsters should be finely frothed.

FISH COLLARED.

After it has been cleaned, cut open the fish and bone it, whether it be salmon, carp, trout, eels, or mackerel. Cut off the head and tail, lay the fish upon its outer side flat on a board, wipe it and season it highly with a mixture of white pepper, pounded mace, grated nutmeg, and salt; rub both inside and out, then roll it very tight; put it into a collaring-cloth, fasten it securely, and boil it in two-thirds of water and one of vinegar, to which you have added some bruised bay leaves, salt, peppercorns, and mace. If it is a large piece of salmon it requires above an hour's simmering; but for mackerel, etc., twenty minutes will suffice. Take it up, reduce the liquor by boiling down, and when cold, having removed the cloth, pour it over the fish. Serve cold, decorated with branches of fennel.

ANCHOVY SANDWICHES AND CANAPÉS.

Cut some very thin slices of bread and butter, trim them properly, lay between them some slices of boned anchovies cut as thin as possible, season them with pepper and a little lemon-juice. For canapés proceed thus: chop together a small quantity of pickled gherkins, capers, shalots, and herbs, add a little vinegar, oil, and coarse pepper. Cut some slices of bread and give them what form you please, either lozenges, rounds, stars, or triangles; fry them in olive oil till well browned, spread upon them the above seasoning, and decorate them with very thin slices of Gorgona anchovies, interspersed with hard-boiled eggs chopped very fine. Sprinkle over with oil, and serve.

ANCHOVY TOAST.

Fry some thin slices of bread in fresh butter; when they are nicely browned place them in a dish, lay upon them some slices of anchovy cut exceedingly thin, add some coarse pepper and a sprinkling of salad oil.

BUTTERED CRAB.

Pick the meat from the inside of a medium-sized crab, add to it some bread-crumbs, chopped parsley, cayenne, and pieces of butter; put it again into the shell, sprinkle it with lemon-juice, strew it over with bread-crumbs, and bake it. Serve it quite hot.

BUTTERED SHRIMPS.

Put some pickled shrimps into a saucepan with a good piece of fresh butter, and enough eggs beaten up in white wine to thicken with. Carefully turn them one way while cooking them, and when quite hot serve upon sippets of toast.

BRANDADE OF COD FISH.

Take some boned meat from a previously boiled salt cod, flake it, and put it with a little cream into a saucepan upon a very gentle fire; stir it continuously with a spoon in one hand; hold an oil flask in the other, and let the oil fall in single drops while you keep stirring. When the composition forms a sort of thick cream, arrange it in a pyramid upon your dish; decorate it with sliced lemon or sippets of bread tossed in butter, and garnished with prawns or shrimps. This is a favourite dish in Provence and many parts of Spain. A bruised clove of garlic may be employed by those who like the flavour it imparts.

CASSEROLE OF FISH.

Nicely flake some previously-dressed fish, add to it a similar quantity each of hard-boiled eggs and mashed potatoes or bread-crumbs; season it with nutmeg, white pepper, and essence of anchovy. Mix it with a little cream, put it into a buttered mould, and place it for a quarter of an hour in a gentle oven. Turn out to serve. It is good cold or hot.

CROQUETTES OF FISH.

Rub a quarter of a pound of fresh butter in a dessert-spoonful of flour; melt it over the fire with a table-spoonful of cream; when it comes nearly to a boil pour it over any kind of cold fish which you have, cut into small pieces no larger than peas; highly season them with pepper and nutmeg; stir all about well, and when cold make it into cakes; dust them over with bread-crumbs, dip them into beaten egg, add more bread-crumbs, and fry them in plenty of hot friture until they are of a fine brown; arrange them in a pyramid upon a napkin folded in the dish, and garnish with fried parsley. A little grated Parmesan cheese is a considerable improvement to the flavour. Crayfish, prawns, and shrimps, first shelled, are excellent as croquettes. Halved lemons should accompany them at table.

DRESSED CRAB.

Take out the meat, mince it small, mix with it some salad mixture, and replace it in the shell; garnish with slices of lemon.

DRIED SALMON AND OTHER FISH.

Soak it over night; pull some into flakes, pepper it well; have ready some eggs, boiled hard and coarsely chopped; put both together into half a pint of cream and two ounces of fresh butter rubbed in a teaspoonful of flour; stir it until it is scalding hot, make a wall of mashed potatoes round the inner rim of a dish, and pour the fish inside. Remember, smoked fish is inapplicable for this dish.

FISH PASTE.

Yarmouth bloaters, smoked salmon, shrimps, prawns, lobsters, anchovies, are suitable for paste. Take the flesh of the already dressed fish, carefully bone it, and divest it of skin, fins, etc.; season it plentifully with spices, and pound it in a mortar; add to it a small proportion of very fresh butter, and when quite a smooth paste press it down well into pots, and cover them with a layer of clarified butter. Tie them securely from the air, if intended to keep for any length of time.

FISH WITH PARMESAN CHEESE.

If you happen to have a small quantity of cold fish at hand, bone it carefully; break it up with a spoon, season it with coarse pepper, and add to it a little grated Parmesan cheese—a dessert-spoonful to half a pound of fish will suffice. Mix it with enough white sauce to make it tolerably stiff, pile it up in a dish, smooth over the surface with yolks of egg, sift bread-crumbs on the top, and put sippets of toast round the edge. Bake it until it is thoroughly hot and looks nicely browned. The meat of any kind of white-fleshed fish eats deliciously done thus.

GALANTINE OF SALMON.

Take from a large salmon a prime piece, of at least eighteen inches in length; clean it thoroughly; open it at the stomach, bone it as perfectly as possible, and with a large needle insert upon the inner side fillets of preserved tunny fish, anchovies, and pickled gherkins; stuff it with the boned meat of any other fish you can procure, adding some pickled prawns, oysters, lobsters, etc., well seasoned. Give the piece of salmon its original form, fasten it securely together, tie it tight in a cloth, and boil it in vinegar and water until it is done. Let it grow cold in the liquor, remove the cloth, glaze the fish, decorate it with bits of jelly and sippets of toast, and serve cold. This is esteemed a very elegant dish for the breakfast-table, and is not extravagantly expensive when salmon is plentiful.

HOT CRAB.

Pick the meat from the shell, beat it in a mortar, add a few bread-crumbs, pepper, nutmeg, a spoonful each of strong gravy and cream. Warm it well, and serve it upon hot toast, with plenty of lemon-juice squeezed over it.

MAYONNAISE OF FISH.

Take some nicely cut slices of fish, previously cooked; arrange them round a dish, and pour in a mayonnaise sauce, which *see*. Any description of fish which is suitable for a salad answers very well in this way. Decorate it with tufts of tarragon leaves, pieces of jelly, capers, slices of anchovy, hard-boiled eggs, bits of beet-root, small gherkins, etc. A mayonnaise of salmon is a dish fit for the most distinguished occasion.

OMELETTES OF FISH.

There are two ways of making these: one is merely to flake some ready-cooked fish—cold salt cod is very suitable; season it with cayenne, nutmeg, and white pepper; mix it well with six beaten eggs and one dessert-spoonful of cream or milk; fry it on one side only, fold it, and serve. The other method of making an omelette is as follows: Chop up what cold fish you have, add a little parsley and shalot shred small, and a piece of fresh butter and some lemon-juice. Place this in an oven to get hot; then beat six eggs, season them, and pour them into a buttered frying-pan; put it over the fire, and as soon as the eggs begin to turn opaque lay the warm fish in the middle of them; roll in the ends of the omelette so as to enclose the contents, and capsize it upon a dish. Garnish with crisped parsley. The roes of various fish, unpressed caviare, the flesh of preserved tunny-fish, or sardines, are admirably adapted for omelettes.

OYSTER LOAVES.

Get seven halfpenny buns with tender crust; cut out a piece, the size of a crown, from the top of each, and scoop out most of the crumb; put a portion of the latter, with a good bit of butter and eight-and-twenty fresh oysters into a frying-pan, and fry all together for five minutes; add a little cream and seasoning. Then fill the loaves, allowing four oysters to each; replace the pieces of crust upon the tops, butter the outsides, and place them for a short time in an oven to get crisp. Serve hot or cold.

OYSTERS AND MACARONI.

Slowly stew some macaroni in good gravy till quite tender; then lay it in a pie-dish, put in a good layer of fresh oysters, bearded; add pepper, salt, a little grated lemon-rind, and a teaspoonful of cream. Strew bread-crumbs over, and just brown it in a tolerably brisk oven. Serve with plenty of lemon-juice, or a sauce piquante. Olive oil may replace the cream where it is preferred.

OYSTER SAUSAGES.

Beat a pound of veal in a mortar, season it; beard and cut in piece two dozen oysters, add them to the veal, as well as some bread-crumbs soaked in the oyster liquor. Put this into skins, or mix together with beaten egg, and fry as flat sausages.

PIECE OF SALMON WITH MONTPELLIER BUTTER.

Boil a handsome piece of salmon, and let it grow cold in the liquor in which it was dressed. When wanted, drain it, remove the skin, trim it neatly, glaze it well with jelly, decorate it with bits of Montpellier butter, garnish the dish with pieces of jelly, and serve as an entrée for a breakfast or cold collation of any kind.

PICKLED MACKEREL OR SALMON, ETC.

Carefully clean your fish, and boil it gently in vinegar and water until it is done. Take it up, strain the liquor in which the fish was dressed, add to it some bruised bay leaves, whole pepper, and salt to taste; boil it up, and when cold put with it one-third the quantity of fresh vinegar, and pour it upon the fish. The more vinegar you use the longer the pickle will keep. Eels and lampreys should be cut into lengths for pickling, and their heads and tails taken off.

PICKLED COCKLES AND MUSSELS.

Well wash the fish in two or three waters, and put them into a stewpan without any water; when they are opened take them out of the shells, and from the mussels cut away the unwholesome parts. Strain the liquor rendered by the fish, add to it thrice its quantity of vinegar, some salt, and spices, according to taste; give it a boil up, pour it upon the fish, and when quite cold tie down with skins.

PICKLED SMELTS.

Properly wipe and draw half a gallon of fresh smelts, salt them in layers in a deep dish, with the following ingredients: half an ounce each of pepper and ginger, a little beaten mace and nutmeg, half a dozen chopped bay leaves, and a quarter of a pound of bay salt. Pour over them a boiling-hot pickle, made with an ounce of saltpetre, a little cochineal, and a pint each of red wine and strong vinegar. When perfectly cold cover them down close. These are considerably superior to anchovies.

PICKLED OYSTERS.

Shell and trim the beards from the oysters; put them, with their own liquor, into a stewpan, simmer them for about a quarter of an hour; then take out the oysters, strain the liquor, and add to it twice its measure of strong vinegar, some salt, peppercorns, and mace; boil this up, and when quite cold pour it upon the oysters, and tie them down in jars.

POTTED FISH.

Clean and wipe your fish dry, but do not wash it; cut off the head, tail, and fins, and, if you prefer it, extract the bones. Cut the fish into lengths, and season with a sufficiency of powdered cloves, mace, nutmeg, pepper, and salt; pack the pieces in pots, cover with a coarse paste, and bake slowly till done. Remove the paste, drain the fish from the gravy, and next day pour clarified butter upon it. Some cooks bake the fish with some butter with it, or a little strong vinegar is sometimes added in the baking, and afterwards poured off; but the foregoing method succeeds equally well. Eels and lampreys should be skinned before being potted; carp, trout, tench, salmon, herrings, mackerel, pike, smelts, char, and perch are most usually potted, as well as the flesh of lobsters, prawns, and shrimps.

POTTED OYSTERS.

Beard some nice plump oysters; drain them from their liquor; rub them in a little beaten mace, grated lemon-peel, and Cayenne pepper. Put them into a jar, with enough lemon-juice to cover them, place them in a hot oven for a quarter of an hour; then drain them thoroughly, and when cold arrange them in small pots, and pour over them sufficient Italian olive-oil to cover them. Keep them tied down with skins.

SALAD OF FISH.

Besides lobster, pike, salmon, soles, turbot, crayfish, and crab are capable of forming delicious salads. Cut the ready dressed, but cold fish, into thin slices, free from bone or skin, mix them with a composition of chopped herbs, four dessert-spoonfuls of strong vinegar, two ditto of melted jelly, six of olive-oil, and some coarse pepper. Arrange the meat in your salad bowl, pour in all the mixture, and decorate with the hearts of white lettuce quartered, hard-boiled eggs cut into four, anchovies in slices, pickles, etc.

SCALLOPED FISH.

Take thin slices of any kind of cold fish; season them according to taste; dip them into cream or melted butter, roll them in bread crumbs, and place one upon another in scallop shells, until the shells are filled. Brown them in a quick oven, and serve them in the shells. Oysters, or the roes of any kind of fresh fish, such as herrings, cod, carp, or mackerel, make delicious scallops. Oysters do not need to be previously cooked, as is necessary in other cases; there should be about four oysters put into each shell, and plenty of butter added.

SCOTCH WOODCOCK.

Mince the flesh of a dozen Gorgona anchovies, lay them between slices of hot buttered toast, and mask them with some scalding hot cream, thickened with the beaten yolks of eggs. Sprinkle with Cayenne pepper and rasped lemon-peel, and serve quite hot.

SMELTS IN JELLY.

Wipe some very fresh smelts, but do not wash them; season them with a little beaten mace, and put them in a deep dish, cover them with butter, and tie them down with paper. Place them in a moderately hot oven, and let them bake for half an hour; take them out, and as they cool sufficiently, lay them upon a cloth to drain. When cold arrange them in a deep glass mould, and cover them with a clear jelly that has been just melted enough to allow it to run. When this is well set, it may be either introduced in the glass or turned out upon a dish. Perch, trout, etc., may be similarly treated.

SMOKED SALMON.

Cut the fish into rather thin slices, place them in a frying-pan of boiling olive oil, and directly they feel firm, when pressed with the blade of a knife, take them up and squeeze lemon-juice over them. Serve with toast.

PRAWN OR SHRIMP PUDDING.

Pick the flesh from a sufficiency of fish, mince it pretty small. Dry and pound the shells in a mortar, together with some fresh butter; add to this the mince, with an equal quantity of cold chicken, veal, or sweetbread chopped small. Mix with the yolks of raw eggs, add a few bread-crumbs, a little gravy, or cream, and white pepper to taste; put it into skins, prick them with a needle, and fry in butter when wanted. The flesh of lobster, crayfish, sardines, anchovies, or tunny fish is equally good done thus.

SPANISH PICKLE.

Take any sort of fish that is fit for pickling, such as salmon, mackerel, red mullet, tunny fish, etc., clean it thoroughly, and cut it into good thick slices. For about three pounds of fish, beat together one ounce of fine white pepper, a saltspoonful of cayenne, three pounded nutmegs, a tablespoonful of salt, half an ounce of saltpetre, a clove of garlic, a small piece of mace, and a teaspoonful of pimienta (not *pimento*). Make holes in the fish with your finger, and charge them well with the mixture; rub it also on the outside. Heat some olive oil in a frying-pan, fry the fish of a fine brown; then put it into pots, just cover them with strong vinegar, and fill up with fresh oil; tie them down with skins, and the pickle will keep a long time and be found an excellent relish for breakfast.

TO CURE SALMON.

Draw and split open a fine fresh salmon; wipe it well inside and out, but on no account wash it. Sprinkle it plentifully with brown sugar, and let it remain a day or two; then rub it over with a small quantity of salt and pounded saltpetre. When this has become pretty well absorbed, wipe the fish, hang it up for a short time in an airy place, and afterwards smoke it slowly.

CHAPTER VIII.

Fish Pies.

These being exceedingly convenient, as affording to housekeepers the means of, for a time, preserving fish in a fresh state, I have given particular directions for making them; but I must here remark that the gravy used in their composition should, if possible, be also made from fish, as an indiscriminate use of meat and fish together is most objectionable; when, however, it cannot be avoided, veal gravy is the best adapted for the purpose.

CARP PIE.

Clean, draw, and wipe a good-sized carp. Make a forcemeat of the following ingredients:—The minced flesh from a boiled eel, a few savoury herbs, some finely-shred lemon-peel, pepper, grated nutmeg, salt, a dozen oysters chopped small, an anchovy, the hard-boiled yolks of six eggs cut fine, and a handful of bread-crumbs. Mix these together with a quarter of a pound of fresh butter; add a little strong gravy and white wine; stuff some of this into the carp, and with the remainder make balls. Cover the dish with a light pie-crust, put in the fish and forcemeat, add some pieces of butter, and a squeeze of lemon. Put on a lid of crust, and bake it for an hour. Serve cold.

COD PIE.

Take a handsome piece of fresh cod; wipe it dry, rub it over with lemon-juice, and let it remain for an hour or two; then cut it into slices, season them well with spices, toss them in plenty of fresh butter until they are pretty firm. Line a pie-dish with a good crust, and when cold place in the fish; add some finely-shred lemon-peel, a cup of fish jelly, some oysters, the hard-boiled yolks of eggs, and some slices of fresh butter. Cover with a top crust, and bake for an hour or more, according to size. When made into a raised pie the fish should be boned, and the jelly poured in after the pie is baked.

EEL PIE.

Dry a few sage leaves and powder them; skin and wipe your eels; take off their heads and tails, and cut them into pieces about two inches long; season them with salt and plenty of pepper, and rub them in the sage leaves; then take some light paste, lay some round a pie-dish, put in the eels with some bits of fresh butter, and cover with a lid of paste. Bake in a moderately quick oven.

FISH PATTIES.

Boil the fish, bone it, mince the flesh with chopped herbs and an onion, or some shred lemon-peel; stew it in a little butter, add the juice of a lemon, and a small quantity of essence of shrimps; when cold, mix up with beaten raw eggs. Put portions into puff-paste, and bake until the crust is done. For fried patties the fish should be simply sliced very thin and seasoned.

FLOUNDER, OR FLAT FISH PIE.

Clean and draw the fish, toss it in butter, take the meat from the bones, cut it into rather large-sized pieces, and lay them in your pie-dish, which you have first lined with paste and slices of butter; strew some pepper over; add a little minced anchovy. Boil down the bones, skin, etc., with some horse-radish, parsley, lemon-peel, and a piece of toast; reduce this gravy to a breakfast-cupful, pour it upon the fish, lay a lid of crust upon the top and bake slowly.

HERRING PIE.

After having scaled, drawn, and wiped the herrings, cut off their heads, tails, and fins. Line a dish with a light crust, put some butter at the bottom; season the fish with plenty of pepper, nutmeg, and a little salt; lay them in the dish; add a sprinkling of lemon-juice; put on a top crust, and bake rather slowly. Some cooks toss the fish quickly in butter before putting them into the pie, and add a little shred shalot.

LOBSTER PIE.

Cover the inside of a pie-dish with a rich paste. Take the flesh from the tails of two boiled lobsters; cut it into lengths. Pick the meat out of the claws, etc., and pound it in a mortar, adding pepper, essence of anchovy, a little lemon-juice, some grated bread, the yolks of two eggs, and half a pound of fresh butter, first slightly melted. Put the lobster into your dish and lay the forcemeat upon it; cover with a top crust, and bake in a gentle oven. Crab or crayfish likewise makes a very good pie.

LOBSTER PATTIES.

Take some of the flesh from the tail of a lobster, chop it tolerably small; add a little nutmeg and pepper, some anchovy butter or essence of anchovy; warm it, together with some cream and the beaten yolk of eggs, to give it the requisite consistency. Place portions of this in patty-pans, which you have previously lined with puff-paste; cover with the same, and bake for about twenty minutes. In a similar manner shrimp, prawn, or crayfish patties may be prepared.

MACKEREL PIE.

Clean the fish, divest it of the heads and tails, etc., and cut each mackerel into four pieces, rub them in a mixture of chopped fennel, pepper, and salt; toss them slightly in butter; let them grow cold; sprinkle them with pounded loaf sugar; lay them in your dish upon slices of fresh butter; add some forcemeat balls made with chopped oysters, bread-crumbs, spice, and eggs; cover with a top crust, and bake gently for half-an-hour.

MIXED FISH PIE.

By the sea-coast, where different kinds of fish are sold at twopence a pound, such as gurnets, tomlins, thornback, plaice, shad, etc., they can be converted into very delicious pies, which if properly seasoned will keep for a week or ten days. Boil the fish for a quarter of an hour, take it up, cut the flesh free from bone, put the latter again into the water, as well as the inferior parts, skin, etc., and boil it down until it forms a jelly; strain it, season it with plenty of pepper and some salt. Put the fish into a pie-dish, add some fresh butter, the flesh of two anchovies, pour the jelly over, and put a rim and lid of crust. Very little baking will suffice, so long as the crust is nicely browned. If you should not immediately require the pie you may re-bake it in the course of a few days, which will conduce to its keeping its flavour unimpaired.

SALMON PIE.

Clean a good piece of salmon, season it with nutmeg, salt, and pepper. Line a pie-dish with a good crust, put in some pieces of butter, then lay in the fish. Take the flesh from the tail of a large boiled lobster, chop it roughly, bruise the remainder of the lobster in a mortar, mix with it a sufficient quantity of rich melted butter, pour it in with the salmon, add a little shred lemon rind. Cover the pie with a top crust, and bake it well.

SALT FISH PIE.

Take your fish after it has been properly soaked and cleaned; parboil it; flake it nicely, and remove all bone, skin, etc. Boil a pint of new milk, and pour it upon the grated crumb of a penny loaf; add cinnamon and shred lemon-peel. Put this with the fish, place it in a dish between layers of fresh oysters and pieces of butter, put a rim of paste round, and cover with a lid of crust. Hard-boiled yolks of egg may be added, if approved of.

SHRIMP PIE.

Make a very thin pie crust, and with it line your dish; lay upon it a good slice of butter, and fill it with some picked shrimps, to which you have added a little beaten cloves, the chopped flesh of four anchovies, a gill of white wine, and some slices of hard-boiled eggs. Place more butter on the top, put on a lid of crust, and bake in a pretty quick oven for twenty minutes.

SOLE PIE.

Cut the flesh from a pair of large soles; boil a couple of pounds of silver eels, pick the meat free from the bones, and return the latter to the liquor in which the eels were dressed; add the bones, skin, etc., of the soles, and boil down until the gravy is reduced to little more than half a pint. Make a forcemeat of the eels with a few crumbs of bread, some butter, a little lemon-peel, an anchovy, chopped parsley, some spices, and two hard-boiled eggs; put this at the bottom of the dish, lay the pieces of sole upon the top, pour in the gravy, put an edge and top of paste, and bake for an hour. The sole may be first tossed in butter or not, as preferred.

TENCH PIE.

Take the fish as soon as they come out of the water, and either rub them well with salt or dip them for a moment or two in boiling water, so as to make them easier to clean.

Draw them, and lay them in a pie-dish, with a layer of butter under them, strew pepper and salt over them, pour in a little wine or tarragon vinegar, place some butter on the top, and finish with a lid and rim of crust. A few fresh or pickled mushrooms are a great improvement.

TROUT OR GRAYLING PIE.

Make a forcemeat with hard-boiled eggs, anchovy, spices, mushrooms, yolk of egg, and fresh butter; stuff your fish with part of it, and make the rest into balls. Prepare your crust, place in the fish, etc., and fill up with pieces of silver eel boned; cover with slices of butter and a top of crust. It may be made into a raised pie, if preferred. Bream also makes a capital pie in this manner. Bake for an hour.

TURBOT OR BRILL PIE.

Cut the flesh of your fish free from bone, and divide it into good-sized pieces; rub them in pepper, salt, and savoury herbs shred fine; then toss them in a pan of butter until they are three parts done. Let them grow cold. Get ready the paste in your dish; lay in the fish with hard-boiled eggs, some balls of rich forcemeat, some pieces of butter, and half-a-pint of fish jelly. Place a crust upon the top, and bake for half-an-hour or more, according to size. Essence of anchovy or unpressed caviare may be employed at discretion.

OYSTER OR MUSSEL PIE.

If your pie is to be of oysters, they require to be simply taken out of their shells and bearded; mussels should be washed until their shells are perfectly clean, then put them into a saucepan without water, and when they are all open take them out of their shells, observing, at the same time, to divest the fish of the objectionable parts. Put your fish into a stewpan, with enough of their strained liquor to cover them; add a few blades of mace, some bread-crumbs, a large piece of butter, and simmer them for a few minutes. Let them grow cold. Cover your dish with a good puff-paste. Place in the fish, add a lid of paste, and bake for half-an-hour.

OYSTER PATTIES.

There seems to be a conventional feeling in favour of oyster patties; so much so, that anything of a stylish breakfast or light repast can scarcely be considered complete without them. Beard the oysters, and, if large, halve them; put them into a saucepan with a piece of butter rolled in flour, some finely-shred lemon rind, and a little white pepper, cream, and a portion of the liquor from the fish; stir all well together, let it simmer for a few minutes, and put it into your patty-pans, which you have already prepared with a puff-paste in the usual way. Serve hot or cold.

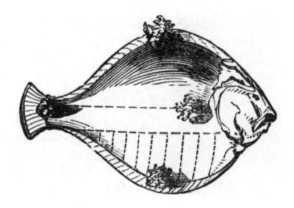

CHAPTER IX.

Bills of Fare for Breakfasts throughout the Year.

Spring Quarter.

Breakfast for 8 or 10 Persons.

Middle of the Table.
Ox-Tongue, glazed.

---

4 By-dishes, Cold.

Prawns.	Potted Birds.
Potted Oysters.	Preserved Sardines.

---

2 By-dishes Hot.

Sausages, tossed.	Sweetbreads, grilled.

---

2 Entrées.

Rump Steaks, broiled.	Fillets of Soles, tossed.

Marmalades, Creams, Dried Fruits, Biscuits or Bonbons at discretion.

Spring Quarter.

BREAKFAST FOR 10 OR 12 PERSONS.

Middle of the Table.

Ribs of Beef, rolled.

----

4 By-dishes, Cold.

Pickled Oysters.	Shrimps.
Radishes.	Plovers' Eggs, *à la coque.*

----

2 Dishes of Cold Meat.

A piece of Salmon, *au bleu.*   A Bayonne Ham, glazed.

----

4 By-dishes, Hot.

Russian Caviare, tossed.	Croquettes of Fish.
Sheep's Kidneys, grilled.	Small patties of Chicken.

----

4 Entrées

Mayonnaise of Turbot.	Blanquette of Lamb.
Raised Pie of Pigeons.	Fillets of Mackerel, broiled.

Accessories as usual.

Spring Quarter.

Breakfast for 12 or more Persons.

Middle of the Table.

Target of Lamb.

---

6 By-dishes, Cold.

Pickled Gherkins.   Preserved Tunny Fish.
Fillets of Anchovies.   Bayonne Goose.
Potted Hare.   Pickled Ox Palates.

---

6 By-dishes, Hot.
Small Patties of Shrimps.
Haunches of Rabbits, *en papillotes.*
Smoked Salmon, tossed.
Lambs' Tongues, with Parmesan.
Trout Cutlets, broiled.
White Puddings, tossed.

---

4 Entrées.

Veal Cutlets, tossed.   Curried Chicken.
Smelts, in case.   Duck Pie.

---

2 Entremets.
Omelette of Veal Kidney.   Young Potatoes, *au naturel.*

Cream Cheese, Candied Fruit, etc., according to fancy.

Summer Quarter.

Breakfast for 8 or 10 Persons.

Middle of the Table.
Collared Calf's Head.

---

4 *By-dishes, Cold.*

Fish Paste.   Small Patties of Eel.
Potted Beef.   Italian Cheese.

---

2 *By-dishes, Hot.*
Mutton Cutlets, *au naturel.*
Cervelas, or Smoked Sausage, tossed.

Entrées.
Piece of Salmon, with Montpellier Butter.
Raised Pie of Chickens.

Fresh Fruits, Brioche Cakes, and Dishes of Dessert, etc.

Summer Quarter.

Breakfast for 10 or 12 Persons.

Middle of the Table.
A Cray Fish.

---

4 By-dishes, Cold.

Potted Tongue.   Sliced Cucumbers.
Oysters, *au naturel.*   Pickled Partridges.

---

2 Dishes of Cold Meat.

Veal Cake.   Lamb Pie.

---

4 By-dishes, Hot.

Meat Rolls.   Sheep's Tongues, *au gratin.*
Rabbit Puddings, *à la Richelien.*   Devilled Duck.

---

4 Entrées.

Mayonnaise of Soles.   Capilotade of Chicken.
Leveret, *à la minute.*   Civet of Venison.

Preserves, Jellies, and Bonbons, according to fancy.

Summer Quarter.

Breakfast for 12 or more Persons.

Middle of the Table.
Galantine of Veal.

---

6 *By-dishes, Cold.*

Cold Meat, *en vinaigrette.* Potted Venison.
Pickled Turkey. Oyster Loaves.
Lobster Patties. Preserved Rabbit.

---

6 *By-dishes, Hot.*

Calf's Liver, tossed. Pigeons, broiled.
Kippered Mackerel. Croquettes of Prawns.
Coquilles of Fowl. Poached Eggs and Spinach.

---

4 *Entrées.*

Perch, tossed. Poulet, *à la chipolata.*
Raised Pie of Ham. Salad of Pike.

---

2 *Entremets.*

Oysters and Macaroni. Artichokes, with Gravy.

Candied and Fresh Fruits, Biscuits, etc.

Autumn Quarter.

BREAKFAST FOR 8 OR 10 PERSONS.

———————————

Middle of the Table.
Collared Sucking Pig.

———————

4 *By-dishes, Cold.*

Anchovy Canapés.   Pressed Caviare.
Potted Cheese.   Pickled Mussels.

———————

2 *By-dishes, Hot.*

Brain Cakes.   Dried Sprats, tossed.

———————

2 *Entrées.*

Salmi of Partridges.   Pork Cutlets and Poached eggs.

———————

Compotes of Fruit, Cheese, Breakfast Cakes, etc.

Autumn Quarter.

Breakfast for 10 or 12 Persons.

Middle of the Table.
Grouse, in Jelly.

---

4 By-dishes, Cold.

Spanish Pickle.   Pickled Smelts.
Potted Rabbit.   Anchovy Fillets.

---

2 Dishes of Cold Meat.

Galantine of Pheasant.   Hunter's Beef.

---

4 By-dishes, Hot.

Rissoles of Hare.   Partridges, *en papillotes.*
Truffle Sasuages, tossed.   Strasbourg Puddings.

---

4 Entrées.

Raised Pie of Pork.   Fillets of Carp, tossed.
Sportsman's Salmi of Snipes.   Pâté de Pithiviers.

Jellies, Sweets, and Cold *Entremets,* if approved of.

Autumn Quarter.

Breakfast for 12 or more Persons.

Middle of the Table.
Partridges, roasted and glazed.

---

6 By-dishes, Cold.

Lyons Sausage.   Pheasant Patties.
Pickled Cockles.   Marbled Veal.
Potted cold boiled Beef.   Canapés of Sardines.

---

6 By-dishes, Hot.

Oyster Sausages.   Game Puddings.
Devilled Turkey.   Dolpettes of cold Meat.
Ham Toast.   Bloaters, tossed.

---

4 Entrées.

Tench Pie.   Rolled Goose.
Grouse, *à la minute.*   Terrine of Hare.

---

2 Entremets.

Truffles, *à la serviette.*   Omelette of Mushrooms.

Biscuits, Marmalades, Bonbons, and the usual accessories.

Winter Quarter.

BREAKFAST FOR 8 OR 10 PERSONS.

Middle of the Table.
Guinea Fowl, glazed.

---

4 By-dishes, Cold.

Pickled Thrushes.   Olives.
Venison Beef, potted.   Small Patties of Truffles.

---

2 By-dishes, Hot.

Oysters, fried.   Scotch Woodcock.

---

2 Entrées.

Beef, *à la Mode.*   Kidney Raised Pie.

Brioche Cakes, Honey, Dried Fruits, and other adjuncts.

Winter Quarter.

Breakfast for 10 or 12 Persons.

Middle of the Table.
Galantine of Lamb.

———

4 By-dishes, Cold.

Slices of Cold Tongue.   Slices of Game Cake.
Potted Lobster.   Pickled Snipes.

———

2 Dishes of Cold Meat.

French Bœuf, *écarlate.*   Woodcock Pie.

———

4 By-dishes, Hot.

Shrimp Puddings.   Anchovy Toast.
Curried Rabbit.   Marinade of Chicken.

———

4 Entrées.

Fillets of Salmon, tossed.   Lobster Salad.
Civet of Hare.   Sweetbreads, *en caisse.*

———

Creams, Candies, Cakes, etc., according to taste.

Winter Quarter.

Breakfast for 12 or more Persons.

Middle of the Table.
Imitated Boar's Head.

---

6 By-dishes, Cold.

Slices of cold Ham.   Oyster Patties.
Pickled Salmon.   Cresses.
Pork Cheese.   *Petits Pâtes* of Trout.

---

6 By-dishes, Hot.
Marinade of Turkey.
Sweetbreads, *en caisse.*
Game Toast.
Devilled Rabbit.
Dressed Crab.
Mayonnaise of Turbot or Salmon.

---

4 Entrées.

Yorkshire Pie.   Perigord Pie.
Blanquette of Veal.   Curried Mutton.

---

2 Entremets.
Omelette of Gruyère Cheese.   Truffles, tossed.

Accessories as usual.

FISH.

1—Oyster Patties.   2—Fried Whiting.   3—Boiled Turbot.   4—Fried Whitebait.
5—Mackerel.   6—Mayonnaise of Salmon.   7—Lobster.   8—Crab.

CHAPTER SEVEN

Breakfast Dishes for Every Morning of Three Months

Miss M. L. Allen

Miss M. L. Allen's (1884) *Breakfast Dishes for Every Morning of Three Months* is aimed at housekeepers of establishments in which—even though the author describes the work as intended for houses of the upper middle class—economy was a prime consideration. The three months she concentrates on—January, February and March—were purposely chosen because, at the time in which she wrote, these were the months when it was possible to get more variety of fresh food than any other consecutive three months of the year, a limitation that no longer affects us. Of the three cookbooks, this is the most representative of English plain cookery.

Breakfast Dishes was an extremely popular book and these are among the appreciative reviews it received:

> 'The question "what shall we have for breakfast?" is here answered in a practical way.'—*The Queen*

> 'A housewife armed with this little manual need never be at a loss to know what to order for the first meal of the day.'—*The Literary World*

> 'The housekeeper must be hard to please who does not find something to suit both her taste and her purse'—*Dundee Advertiser*

Breakfast Dishes

FOR EVERY MORNING OF THREE MONTHS

By Miss Allen (Mrs. A. Macaire)

TWENTIETH EDITION

Author's Note: Breakfast Dishes ran to several editions over many years with no changes to the recipes, and only three minor revisions to the text. First, the menus, originally at the front, were moved to the back of the book. Second, an index of recipes was added. The twentieth edition of 1900 is reproduced here because the index will be an aid to the reader. Third, the following passage, originally the last paragraph in the *Preface* through at least the second edition of 1884, was dropped:

If the writer is in any way the means of varying the terrible monotony of the breakfasts that are to be met with in most houses, especially those of the upper middle class, she will congratulate herself that her trouble has not been in vain.

Preface.

This little work has been undertaken with a view to supplying a want long acknowledged by housekeepers both of small and large establishments.

Almost every one complains of the monotony of breakfast dishes, which consist for the most part of boiled eggs, bacon, dried fish, or sausages.

It has been, therefore, the writer's aim not so much to provide new receipts, as to collect and arrange those that appear suitable for the purpose in hand from manuscripts lent her by friends chiefly, and from other sources; but any ordinary cookery-book will be found to contain a good many of them. The compiler does not aspire to offer the public anything startlingly fresh, but she believes that her arrangement of breakfasts will greatly facilitate a housekeeper's efforts to vary the usual monotonous routine.

It may appear at first sight that some of the dishes recommended are of too costly a character to be obtainable except by the very rich; but a farther examination will serve to show that such a variety of receipts are given for each breakfast, that if *some* are not suitable there are others which are eminently so.

For instance, on January 1st pheasant rissoles are recommended, but as well there are receipts for kidneys à la maître d'hôtel, potted shrimps, buttered eggs, and quince marmalade, surely *some* of which dishes would not be beyond the most limited means.

It will be found that some things, such as sweet-breads, for instance, are very expensive in London; but on the other hand the writer knows places in the country where they are so little thought of as to be given away by the butcher with other meat that may be bought of him.

Oysters, which are largely used in the breakfast dishes of this little book, can be bought at a cheap rate in tins, as well as lobster, and it will be found that the dishes prepared from them are almost as delicious as if made with the more costly article. If anyone has a prejudice against tinned food, as some have, let them, if they cannot manage the fresh article, pass that dish over, and content themselves with others they feel able to afford.

Again, it may be contended that some of the dishes are too heavy and substantial for breakfast. Let it be pointed out that tastes differ in *that* respect, as in all others; and, moreover, what is a sufficient breakfast for a man whose occupation is sedentary, would be a very inadequate one for another whose days are spent in the open air, whether riding, shooting, fishing, or walking.

The compiler of this little book has selected January, February, and March, the three first months of the year, because in them it is possible to get more variety of food than in any other three consecutive months, *i.e.* game, spring poultry, lamb, trout, salmon, &c. Mushrooms and tomatoes can be bought pickled, forced, or in tins; all the other things given will be found to be in season during the months named. At the same time, the dishes given will be found, with the exception of pork in the summer months, and oysters in May, June, and July, to be obtainable at any other time of the year, excepting, of course, game.

To an intelligent cook the receipts given, and the daily arrangement of breakfasts for three months, will suggest other dishes that will be equally suitable, or she will observe that other material prepared in the same way, when that given is out of season, will answer her purpose.

M. L. A.

FRUIT.

1—Apricots.   2—White Cherries.   3—Black Cherries.   4, 5 & 6—White,
Black, and Red Currants.   7—Melon.   8—Strawberries.   9—Raspberries.
10—Black Diamond Plums.   11—Greengages.   12—Victoria Plums.

Receipts

FOR PREPARING DISHES FOR BREAKFAST.

Buttered Eggs.

Put into a stew-pan two ounces of butter; break four fresh eggs, and add half a tablespoonful of salt, and pepper; stir it on the fire continually. Have ready some slices of buttered toast, on a hot dish; pour the eggs on the toast and serve hot.

To Boil a Ham.

Soak your ham for twenty-four hours. After the ham has been scraped or brushed as clean as possible, pare away lightly any part which disfigures it, lay it in a ham kettle, and cover it plentifully with cold water; bring it very slowly to boil, and clear off carefully the scum, which will be thrown up in great abundance. So soon as the water has been cleared from this, draw back the pan quite to the edge of the stove, that the ham may be simmered softly but steadily until it is tender. On no account allow it to boil fast. Put into the water in which it is to be boiled either a quart of old cider or a pint of vinegar, or better still, a pint of champagne, a large bunch of sweet herbs, and a bay-leaf. When it is two-thirds done, skin, cover it with raspings, and set it in an oven until it is done enough. It will prove incomparably superior to a ham boiled in the usual way.

To Bake a Ham.

A ham for baking should be well soaked; then wipe it dry, then trim away any rusty places underneath, and cover it with a common crust, taking care that this is of sufficient thickness all over to keep the gravy in. Place it in a moderately-heated oven, and bake for nearly four hours. Take off the crust and skin, and cover with raspings, the same as for boiled ham, and garnish the knuckle with a paper frill. This method of cooking a ham is, by many persons, considered far superior to boiling it, as it cuts fuller of gravy, and has a finer flavour, besides keeping a much longer time good.

Duck Olives.

Cut into two joints the legs of a cold duck or chicken; take off the drumsticks; mix half a teaspoonful of pepper with five or six teaspoonfuls of breadcrumbs, some mixed herbs, a very finely chopped onion, and two teaspoonfuls of chopped parsley. Cut four thin slices of bacon, sprinkle with the crumbs, roll up each joint of fowl in the bacon, tie securely; make hot in a frying-pan or before the fire. Serve on a piece of fried toast.

Breakfast Cakes.

One pound of flour, three ounces of butter, one gill of new milk, one tablespoonful of brewers' yeast, (or German yeast), a piece of butter the size of a walnut; baked in a hot oven.

Sausages and Chestnuts.

Roast and take the husk and skin from twelve Spanish chestnuts; fry gently in a morsel of butter six small flat oval cakes of fine sausage-meat, and when they are well browned lift them out, and pour into a saucepan, which should be bright in the inside, the greater part of the fat in which they have been fried; mix with it a large teaspoonful of flour, and stir these over the fire till they are well and equally browned. Then pour in by degrees nearly one pint of strong beef or veal broth or gravy, and one glass of good white wine; add a *small* bunch of savoury herbs, and as much salt and pepper, or cayenne, as will season the whole properly. Give it a boil; lay in the sausages round the pan, and the chestnuts in the centre. Stew them *very* softly for nearly an hour, take out the herbs, dish the sausages neatly, and heap the chestnuts in the centre; strain the sauce over them, and serve them very hot. There should be no sage mixed with the pork to dress thus.

French Cold Meat Pudding.

FOWL, PHEASANT, OR TURKEY PUDDING.

Two ounces of suet, three-quarters of a pound of meat chopped fine, two ounces of bacon or ham, two ounces of grated breadcrumbs soaked in boiling milk, two eggs, lemon peel, onion, pepper, a teaspoonful of sauce, parsley, and any kind of herb, some chopped mushrooms, salt. Bake in a basin for an hour; turn out and serve with some gravy or without.

Breakfast Rolls.

Crumble down very small indeed, an ounce of butter into a couple of pounds of the best flour, and mix with them a large saltspoonful of salt. Put into a basin a dessertspoonful of solid, well-purified yeast, and half a teaspoonful of pounded sugar; mix these with half a pint of warm new milk; hollow the centre of the flour, pour in the yeast, gradually stirring to it sufficient of the surrounding flour to make a thick batter; strew more flour on the top, cover a thick double cloth over the pan, and let it stand in a warm kitchen to rise. In winter it must be placed within a few feet of the fire. In about an hour, should the leaven have broken through the flour on the top and have risen considerably in height, mix one lightly whisked egg, or the yolks of two, with nearly half a pint more of quite warm new milk, and wet up the mass into a very smooth dough. Cover it as before, and in from half to three-quarters of an hour, turn it on to a paste-board, and divide it into twenty-four portions of equal size. Knead these up as lightly as possible into small round or olive-shaped rolls; make a slight incision round them, and cut them once or twice across the top, placing them as they are done on slightly floured baking-sheets an inch or two apart. Let them remain for fifteen or twenty minutes to prove, then wash the tops with yolk of egg mixed with a little milk, and bake them in a rather brisk oven from ten to fifteen minutes. Turn them upside down upon a dish to cool after they are taken from the tins.

Broiled Mutton Kidneys.

Split them open lengthwise without dividing them; strip off the skin and fat, run a fine skewer through the points and across the back of the kidneys to keep them flat while broiling; season them with pepper, or cayenne, lay them over a clear brisk fire, with the cut sides towards it; turn them in from four to five minutes, and in as many more; dish and serve them quickly with or without a cold maître d'hôtel butter on them. Season them with pepper and fine salt, and brush a very small quantity of oil, or clarified butter, over them before they are broiled.

Oysters on Toast.

Cut some pieces of bread the size of half-a-crown, barely a quarter of an inch thick. After they are fried, cut out bacon the same size; very thinly fry. Put on bread anchovy and cayenne, then bacon, then a roasted oyster, a few grains of cayenne, and a little oyster liquor. N.B. Roasted oysters are really only made hot through.

Buttered Scones.

Beat two eggs a little, put them in nearly a pint of milk (new) warmed, with two or three spoonfuls of yeast to rise; then put in a quart of flour, mix it with a spoon, and lay in eight cakes; roll them the size of muffins, and put them before the fire to rise, with a cloth to cover them; then put them in the oven.

Sausages in Mashed Potatoes.

Mash smoothly with some milk and a little piece of butter or dripping, about one pound and a half of potatoes; have ready broiled one pound of sausages (sausages take about fifteen minutes to broil); mould round each sausage some of the mashed potatoes to give it the appearance of a roll, put a piece of dripping on each, and bake in the oven, or before the fire, till of a nice brown colour. These rolls can be fried, but require great care taking them out, or the potatoes will fall away from the sausages.

Dried Haddock.

Boil it in a frying-pan, with just enough water to cover it; put it on a drainer to drain, then put it before the fire, with a large piece of butter on it.

Savoury French Omelette.

Beat the yolks of four eggs slightly, and beat the whites also separately, then beat both together for a minute; add a dessertspoonful of finely chopped mushroom, a teaspoonful of finely chopped parsley, white pepper and salt to taste. Heat two ounces of butter in an omelette pan, and put in it an onion cut in four pieces; let the fat boil up, then take out the onion and pour in omelette mixture, which stir about with a spoon until it sets, then tilt the pan towards the handle and shape the omelette, turn out on a very hot dish and serve before it quite sets.

Fleed Cakes.

Fleed is to be bought from any pork butcher. Two pounds of flour, one and a quarter pounds of fleed; six ounces of butter; baked ten to fifteen minutes.

Potted Pheasant, Lobster, or Liver.

Roast the birds as for table, but let them be thoroughly done, for if the gravy be left in, the meat will not keep half so well. Raise the flesh of the breast, wings, and merrythought quite clear from the bones; take off the skin; mince, and then pound it very smoothly with about one-third of its weight of fresh butter, or something less, if the meat should appear of a proper consistence without the full quantity; season it with salt, mace, and cayenne only, and add these in small portions until the meat is rather highly flavoured with both the last. Proceed with it as with other potted meats.

Kedgeree.

Half a pound of dried haddock, quarter of a pound of rice, two eggs, two ounces of butter, white pepper, and anchovy sauce. Throw the well washed rice into boiling water, and allow to boil for twenty minutes, then put into a sieve and turn a tap of cold water on it for two minutes to separate the grains, drain and put in a saucepan before the fire (without a lid) to dry. Melt two ounces of butter in a saucepan, stir in one ounce of fine flour, add three quarters of a pint of milk, stir till smooth; add a teaspoonful of anchovy sauce, the whites of two eggs chopped into large slices. Cut up the fish, add it, also the rice, season with white pepper; stir over the fire till hot, pile on a dish, and garnish with the yolks of two eggs grated over the top of the pile, and tufts of green fried parsley round the base.

Anchovy Toast.

Toast some thin dry bread, which must be cut in oblongs about the length and breadth of a sardine; cut it before the toast becomes brittle, and again place in the oven to become brittle and thoroughly crisp; spread with anchovy butter made by just cleaning three anchovies, pound them in a mortar with one ounce of butter, cayenne pepper, a little nutmeg, and a teaspoonful of anchovy sauce; rub through a hair sieve, and use as directed. Wash your anchovies, wipe with a cloth; divide the fillets by splitting down the back with the finger and thumb of both hands. The fillets must then be placed on the toast like lattice-work. Garnish with hard-boiled egg chopped.

To Poach Eggs.

Take for this purpose a wide, delicately clean pan, about half filled with the clearest spring-water; throw in a small saltspoonful of salt, and place it over a fire quite free from smoke. Break some new-laid eggs into separate cups, and do this with care, that the yolks may not be injured. When the water boils, draw back the pan, glide the eggs gently into it, and let them stand until the whites appear almost set, which will be in about a minute; then, without shaking them, move the pan over the fire, and just simmer them from two minutes and a half to three minutes. Lift them out separately with a slice, trim quickly off the ragged edges, and serve them upon toasted bread freed from crust and buttered.

Roman Pie.

Well oil a plain tin mould, sprinkle well with vermicelli broken small, then line it with a *very* thin paste. Have ready some boiled macaroni, which cut in pieces half an inch long; take a sprinkling of grated cheese, cut your meat up into small dice, mix all together and season with pepper and salt, and add sufficient gravy to moisten the whole (if the meat is white, the sauce must also be white and made with milk). Then put all into a lined mould, cover with thin paste, and bake in a moderate oven half an hour. Then turn it out, with a rich brown sauce round it in the dish.

Ham Toast.

Take of cooked ham finely chopped two tablespoonfuls, one of white breadcrumbs, two of veal gravy, two of cream, a little chopped parsley, a little pepper and mustard; heat up all together, then make a good buttered toast, and sprinkle the above upon it. Fry crumbs of bread and a little parsley on the top of it; when served cut it into long square pieces.

N.B. One anchovy chopped is considered a great improvement.

Œufs au Tomato.

Hard boil and shell two eggs, cut them in two lengthwise, cut up the whites in strips, heat them in tomato sauce; put this on a dish with fried bread round it; chop the yolks fine, and put a layer on the tomato and eggs, two or three layers of each; end with the yolks. Serve very hot.

Golden Eggs.

Hard boil three or four eggs, shell and sprinkle them with flour. Beat up one or more raw eggs, and dip the hard ones in this; roll them in breadcrumbs (to which add some salt), and fry a good golden brown colour. Serve in rich white sauce.

Bombay Toast.

One ounce of anchovies, wash, bone, and pound in a mortar with one ounce of fresh butter, till reduced to a smooth paste. Melt the anchovy butter in a saucepan, and as it melts add the beaten-up yolks of two eggs; stir till of the consistency of cream, add cayenne to taste, and spread on some slices of fried bread.

Winchester Cutlets.

Take any cold cooked meat, mince and pound it; add an equal quantity of breadcrumbs, one ounce of butter, pepper, salt, cayenne, and a little ketchup. Make this into a stiff paste with a raw egg, and shape into small cutlets with a little flour; egg, breadcrumb, and fry in hot fat. Put a small piece of uncooked macaroni into the end of each to represent the bone.

Tea-Cakes.

Flour, sixteen ounces; butter, four to eight ounces; add sufficient milk, and roll the cakes thin. Bake in a pan or on tins in an oven.

Sausage-Meat Cake.

Season very highly from two to three pounds of good sausage-meat, both with spices and with sage, or with thyme and parsley, if these be preferred; press the mixture into a pan, and proceed exactly as for veal cake. A few minced eschalots can be mixed with the meat for those who like their flavour. Make into cakes and fry. Serve on hot fried toast.

Scotch Woodcock.

Four slices of bread toasted and buttered both sides; cover one side thickly with anchovy paste, put the toasts one on the top of the other, and cut in four pieces. Have ready the yolks of four eggs well beaten, with half a pint of good milk, which set over the fire to thicken but not to boil; then pour it over the toast and send it to table as hot as possible. Half the above is sufficient for three persons.

Macaroni and Kidneys (Mutton or Ox).

Cook two ounces of macaroni in boiling water; skin three mutton kidneys, and remove the fat, cut them into slices, season with salt, cayenne, and finely mixed herbs; fry them on both sides in butter; then stir in half a pint of gravy well flavoured with tomatoes. Dish with a layer of macaroni over them, the gravy poured over; add pepper, salt, and chopped hard-boiled eggs and some grated Parmesan cheese.

Fried Bacon à l'Armstrong.

Take slices of raw bacon and place them between slices of thinly cut bread slightly soaked in milk, then fry all togother in batter.

Des Œufs sur le Plat.

Well butter a tin or china baking dish, break four eggs into it; place a lump of butter, some salt, and a little cayenne on the top. Fry over a slow bright fire, and serve in the dish in which they are cooked as hot as possible.

Broiled Mushrooms (forced).

Allow three or four mushrooms for each person. Cleanse mushrooms by wiping them with a piece of flannel and a little salt. Peel the tops, broil them over a clear fire, turning them once, and arrange on very hot dish. Put a piece of butter on each, season with pepper and salt, and squeeze a few drops of lemon-juice over each. Place dish before fire till the butter is quite melted and serve very hot.

Stewed Mushrooms (bottled).

Five or six buttons for each person. Pare a pint of mushroom buttons neatly, put them in a basin of water with a little lemon-juice as they are done. Take them from the water, avoiding the sediment; put them in a stew-pan with fresh butter, salt, and juice of half a lemon; cover the pan closely, and stew gently for twenty-five minutes, or longer if they are not tender. Thicken the butter with one teaspoonful of flour, cream or milk, and a very little mace added for flavouring.

Hot Buttered Toast.

Bakers' bread a day or two days old. Cut slices rather more than a quarter of an inch in thickness, toast before a very bright fire; when a light brown colour both sides, place it on a hot dish, put a good piece of butter on each piece, and set it before the fire. When the butter melts spread it over the toast, trim off the crust and ragged edges, and send the toast quickly to table. Pile the slices one on the top of the other and cut them into quarters.

Fried Patties, Brains, Chicken, or Oysters.

Mince some calf's brains previously boiled; add an egg boiled hard and chopped, and a little parsley, a tiny piece of pounded mace, salt, pepper, a little lemon-peel; moisten with a gravy and cream. Make a good puff-paste, roll rather thin, and cut it into round pieces, put the mixture into them, and fry a light brown (or bake in patty-pans, and brush them over with the yolk of an egg). Fry for fifteen minutes.

Scotch Collops.

Cut veal the same thickness as for cutlets; flour it well, and fry a light brown in butter, sprinkle with flour and add half a pint of water, pouring it in gradually; set it on the fire, and when it boils add an onion and a tiny piece of mace (pounded). Simmer gently for three quarters of an hour, flavour gravy with two tablespoonfuls of sherry, one tablespoonful of mushroom ketchup. Give one boil up and serve.

Veal Cake.

Cut all the brown off some slices of cold veal, and cut two hard-boiled eggs into slices. Get a pretty mould, lay ham, veal, and eggs in layers, and some chopped parsley and a little pepper between each, and when the mould is full get some strong stock and fill up the shape. Bake half an hour, and when cold turn out.

Curried Crab, Sardines, or Lobster.

Take all the meat out of a boiled crab, mix it with a little curry-powder and cream, a few drops of lemon-juice, and a little sugar; stew gently until hot, and serve with an edging of boiled rice. The curry may be ornamented with capsicums on top. An onion and a large acid apple previously fried is an improvement.

To Boil Rice for a Curry.

Take a teacupfull of rice, wash it well; take another cup of the same size and measure it twice with boiling water, add a pinch of salt; make the water boil quickly, throw in the rice, and after it boils reckon twenty minutes. There will be no water to draw off. Stir up rice with a fork; then turn it into a dish, and let it dry before the fire a few minutes.

Pheasant Rissoles, Chicken or Lobster.

(Half a pound.) Mince the white meat of a pheasant, mix a few breadcrumbs, pepper and salt to taste, a few chopped herbs, half a teaspoonful of minced lemon-peel, and some chopped bottled mushrooms or truffles; add a little milk and some white stock, and then put all together in a saucepan and stir over a bright fire (a wooden spoon) for ten minutes. Then turn out into a plate; mix in one raw egg and leave it six hours to cool, when the mixture will be quite hard. Make into balls, egg and breadcrumb, and fry in boiling fat sufficient to cover the rissoles. Garnish with fried parsley. After taking the ris soles out of the frying pan, place them on kitchen paper to drain off all grease.

To Boil Eggs.

Place a saucepan on a bright fire, half full of water, put in eggs, and allow them to remain in five and a half minutes, so that they are cooked gradually all through.

Potted Shrimps.

Pick shrimps, and then tightly fill earthenware pots with them; add cayenne pepper and salt to taste, then pour over them boiling butter till the pot is quite full. Set it to cool, and then pour over the top, to exclude all air, a mixture of boiling lard and butter.

Honey.

Either in jars or in the comb, ten pence to one shilling a pound.

Curried Eggs.

Make a curry sauce as on page 38; hard boil some eggs, shell them, cut a piece off one end and enable them to stand on end; place eggs in sauce, and surround with rice.

Quince Marmalade.

Pare, core, and quarter some inferior quinces, and boil them in as much water as will almost cover them, until they begin to break; strain the juice from them, and for the marmalade put half a pint of it to each pound of fresh quinces. In preparing these be careful to cut out the hard stony part round the cores. Simmer them gently until they are tender, and then press them through a coarse sieve; put them into a clean pan and boil them till they form a dry paste; add for each pound of quinces and half-pint of juice, three-quarters of a pound of finely-powdered sugar, boil the marmalade for half an hour, stirring it gently all the time. It will be firm and bright in colour. Four pounds of quinces, one quart juice, four pounds sugar, makes rather a richer marmalade. Boil fast from twenty to forty minutes.

Partridge Pudding.

OR BEEF CAN BE USED INSTEAD OF THE BIRDS.

Skin a brace of partridges, and cut them into joints; line a basin with suet crust, lay the birds on the crust, first highly seasoning them with cayenne pepper and some salt; pour in water for gravy, a little pounded mace for seasoning, layers of button mushrooms (bottled) between the layers of meat; fill up the pudding with crust, and boil three and a half hours.

N.B. The crust not to be eaten unless particularly liked. If beefsteak be used, cut up two kidneys also.

Deviled Pheasants' or Chickens' Legs.

Cut off legs from cold pheasants, score them with a sharp knife, put pepper and mustard and a little salt into the cuts; broil them with a piece of cold butter on each. Serve *very* hot.

Fried Soles or Fried Slices of Cod.

Cleanse the fish, and, two hours before they are wanted, rub them inside and out with salt; wash and rub them very dry, dip them into egg, and sprinkle over with breadcrumbs; fry them in boiling lard, dish on a hot napkin, and garnish with crisped parsley.

Fried Bacon, Ham, or Sausages.

Cut the bacon into thin slices, trim away the rusty parts, and cut off the rind. Put it into a cold frying-pan, turn it two or three times, and dish it on a very hot dish. Fry sausages in the same way till deue.

Sausages and Mashed Potatoes.

Prick the sausages with a fork, and put them into a frying-pan with a small piece of butter. Keep moving the pan about and turn the sausages two or three times. In twelve minutes they will be cooked. Have ready some smoothly mashed potatoes, and place the sausages on it and serve very hot.

Strawberry Jam or Apricot.

Strip the stalks from some strawberries, weigh and boil them for *thirty-five* minutes, keeping them very constantly stirred; throw in eight ounces of good sugar beaten small, to a pound of fruit; mix them well before putting on the fire again, and then boil quickly for twenty-five minutes.

Scones.

Mix into a smooth paste with half a pint of milk one pound of flour, half an ounce of cream of tartar, a quarter of an ounce of carbonate of soda, and one ounce of sugar. Rub three ounces of butter into the flour with the hands. Roll the mixture to insure the butter being well mixed with the flour. Roll the paste out to a sheet of one third of an inch in thickness. Cut the paste into triangular pieces, each side about four inches long. Flour a tin and put the scones into it and bake them directly in an oven (240°) for forty minutes.

Snipe on Toast.

Do not draw a snipe, but wipe it with a soft cloth, and truss it with the head under the wing. Suspend the bird with the feet downwards to a bird-spit, flour it well and baste it with butter, which should be ready dissolved in a pan. Lay a thick round of slightly toasted bread buttered on both sides in the pan for the trail to drop on. The birds will be done in twenty minutes. Lay the toasts in a very hot dish and dress the birds upon them (one piece of toast to each bird).

Orange Marmalade.

Three pounds oranges, six pounds sugar, three quarts water.
Take some bitter oranges and double their weight in sugar, peel off the rind. Cut chips as thin as possible about an inch long. Put the chips and pulp in a dish of boiling water, let them thus remain for fourteen hours, then turn the whole into a preserving-pan and boil till the chips are perfectly tender. Then add pounded sugar and boil it until it jellies.

Oysters or Shrimps Curried Dry.

Heat some shrimps or flesh of a boiled lobster slowly through, and serve in the following curry sauce. Dissolve a good slice of butter in a deep, well-lined saucepan, and shake it over a brisk fire till it begins to colour, then put in the lobster or shrimps, and brown them well and equally. The pan must be well shaken, and the shrimps turned in it frequently. When this is done lift them out, and throw into the saucepan three large onions finely minced; add a morsel of butter, and fry until they begin to soften. Then add a quarter of a pint of soup and a large acid apple, or a tablespoonful of lemon-juice, with the hearts of two or three lettuces and a heart of a cabbage shred quite small, a few small pickled gherkins, and two tomatoes (freed from seeds). Stew the whole till it resembles a thick pulp, and add any liquid it may require should it become too dry; put in the lobster or shrimps with two teaspoonfuls of flour, one of salt, and three of curry-powder. Simmer softly till the whole is done, which will be in three quarters of an hour to an hour. Surround the curry with well-boiled and drained rice, and serve on a hot dish.

If preferred, the shrimps might be simply warmed through and added to the curry sauce after it is entirely cooked, before surrounding it with the rice.

Brain Cakes.

Boil the brains in a little veal gravy very gently for ten minutes, drain them on a sieve, and when cold cut them into thick dice; dip them into beaten yolk of egg and very fine breadcrumbs mixed with salt and chopped herbs, pepper, &c.; fry them a light brown and dry them well. Serve on a very hot dish with fried parsley to garnish them.

Stewed Potatoes.

Put in a saucepan on the fire a piece of butter the size of an egg, one chopped onion, two spoonfuls of parsley, half a teaspoonful of celery and common salt mixed. Cut half a pound of potatoes into pieces, put them in a saucepan with three tablespoonfuls of water, when soft add a quarter of a pint of milk, a tablespoonful of vinegar and flour; stir and boil up.

Sausage Cakes of Tinned Meat.

Pound up in a mortar one pound of Australian meat, with a tablespoonful of salt, ditto of pepper, a quarter ditto of ground cloves, and two ounces of butter. Make into cakes and fry.

To Cook Rhubarb.

Cut two pounds of rhubarb about an inch in length. To this is added one pound of sugar and the rind of a lemon grated; mix the two together, and leave it until the rhubarb is cooked. Have a large tin saucepan full of boiling water, and put the rhubarb in and stir it with a wooden spoon; the cover is put on, and for five minutes it may be left. When the cover is taken off, the rhubarb must not be left till it is done. It must be quickly turned with the spoon so as not to break the rhubarb. The moment it boils it softens; in about three minutes this happens, according as to whether the rhubarb is old or young. Strain it off quickly, only leaving a little juice to serve with it. Put it into a glass dish and leave it to cool; gently scatter the sugar and lemon over it.

Pheasant Broiled, or Partridge, or Chicken.

Split a young and well-kept partridge, and wipe it with a clean cloth inside and out, but do not wash it Broil it delicately over a very clear fire, sprinkling it with a little salt and plenty of cayenne; rub a good piece of butter over the bird the moment it leaves the fire, and send it quickly to table in a very hot dish.

Devonshire Omelette.

Beat the yolks of four eggs till almost white. Beat the whites of four eggs for same time. Beat the two together for five minutes after adding a teacup full of milk, and a dessertspoonful of flour, finely chopped parsley, pepper, salt, a few drops of lemon-juice, and an onion cut into four pieces. Beat well; boil enough fat in a frying-pan to cover the bottom, and when it is just on the boil, take out the pieces of onion, and pour the mixture into the pan and hold it over a good clear fire.

Salmon or Lobster Cutlets.

Pound the coral with half an ounce of butter, and rub through a hair sieve. Make a panada (one ounce of butter, one ounce of flour, and a gill of milk, stir on the fire until it comes away from the sides of the saucepan), and add the coral butter, lobster, pepper, salt, cayenne, and a few drops of lemon-juice. Fry in boiling fat, having brushed them with egged breadcrumbs.

Scalloped Oysters.

Plump and beard oysters, after having rinsed them well in their own strained liquor; add to this an equal quantity of very rich white sauce, and thicken it, if needful, with a teaspoonful of flour mixed with a slice of butter; put in the oysters, and keep them at the point of simmering for three or four minutes; lay them into the shells and cover the tops thickly with crumbs fried a delicate brown and well dried; or heap over them instead a layer of fine crumbs; pour clarified butter on them, and brown them with a salamander.

Angels, or Oysters, on Horseback.

Cut some pieces of bread the size of half a crown, barely a quarter of an inch thick; after they are fried cut out bacon the same size very thinly; fry. Put on bread, anchovy and cayenne, and a little oyster liquor.

N .B. Roasted oysters are really only made hot through.

Grenadines of Veal.

Remove all skin and fat, and cut veal into nice shapes; then lard. Put a small quantity of dripping or butter in frying-pan; then put in fillets round the pan; in the centre chopped carrot, turnip and small onion, and a bouquet garni (sprig of marjoram, thyme, and parsley, tied in a bay-leaf), pepper, salt, and not quite enough stock to cover the fillets. Put a piece of buttered kitchen paper on the top to prevent browning, put in an oven for three-quarters of an hour; put round a dish in which are cut vegetables. Boil stock till glazy and pour over.

Kromeskies.

Three ounces of flour, pinch of salt, dessertspoonful of salad oil, about one gill of tepid water, white of one egg well beaten. Oysters to be soaked a short time in cream with a little cayenne and a few drops of lemon-juice. Take a piece of cooked bacon, all fat (cold boiled), wrap each oyster in a slice of bacon, and fry in batter. Serve oyster in bacon.

Sweetbread.

Soak and scald, simmer gently in milk for half an hour; egg, crumb, and fry, and serve with a little good gravy and button mushrooms.

Fish Pudding.

Take any boiled fish, or fowl, or veal, pound it in a mortar, take an equal quantity of bread soaked in milk; put these into a pan, and stir over a fire till it becomes thick as dough; then add one ounce of butter, two yolks of two whisked whites of eggs, a little chopped parsley, a small onion chopped fine, a tiny little nutmeg, cayenne, and salt. Put into a buttered mould, steam one hour. Serve with white sauce poured over.

Cold Meat or Oyster Fritters.

Make a light batter, dip each seasoned oyster one by one into the batter, and toss from a spoon into hot fat. It will immediately assume a grotesque shape. Serve on a hot d'oyley.

Potato Patties.

Chop up six ounces of cold meat, mix it with two teaspoonfuls of anchovy sauce, one teaspoonful of finely chopped onion, ditto parsley, and five tablespoonfuls of milk; make one pound of mashed potatoes, grease six large patty-pans, line them with the potatoes, making them very much raised in the middle; put in a piece of butter on top of each, bake for three-quarters of an hour, turn out of the patty-pans, and serve very hot.

Eggs and Anchovy Sauce.

Boil four eggs hard, take off the shells, mince the eggs; put a piece of butter into a saucepan the size of a walnut, melt it, and add one teaspoonful of flour, ditto of anchovy sauce, a quart of milk, a teaspoonful of vinegar, a quarter of a teaspoonful of pepper. Stir it over the fire till it boils, add the chopped eggs, stir well, and pour it over three rounds of buttered toast. Put into the oven till required.

Russian Gallimaufry.

Cut a pound of cold meat into moderate-sized pieces; cut up any cold vegetables, ham, bacon, batter or suet pudding into small pieces, fry all together in a little dripping, add half a teaspoonful of pepper and salt to taste, a tablespoonful each of finely chopped onion, parsley, flour, and vinegar, and a teaspoonful of sugar. Stir it all up over the fire, and serve very hot.

Savoury Rice Pudding.

Boil slowly four large tablespoonfuls of rice in a pint of water, with half a tablespoonful each of pepper, salt, mixed herbs, chopped parsley and onion, and a little celery seed; chop up four ounces of cold meat, beat up with a quarter of a pint of milk, two eggs; mix the minced meat with it, and a tablespoonful of ketchup; add to it the rice when it is well cooked; pour all into a well-greased pie dish, and bake for three-quarters of an hour. Serve hot or cold.

Shrimp, Crab, or Bacon Omelette.

Cut up half a pound of lean bacon into small dice, put them in a shallow baking-tin in the oven for a few minutes; beat up the yolks of four eggs with one tablespoonful of flour, one tablespoonful of very finely chopped onion, two ditto of parsley, quarter of a teaspoonful each of pepper and mixed herbs, and half a pint of milk; beat up into a stiff froth the whites of four eggs, and add quickly to the batter, which must be poured over the hot bacon and the whole put into the oven for twenty minutes. A frying-pan will cook this omelette just as well. To be served at once.

German Dumplings and Gravy.

Chop small three ounces of suet, three ounces of any cold meat, a small onion, five leaves of parsley; mix with these half a pound of flour, half a teaspoonful each of pepper, salt, herbs, and two eggs well beaten, with enough milk to make a stiff dough. Divide into dumplings and throw into boiling stock. Serve in a good brown gravy.

Liver and Bacon in Paper Cases.

Boil some calf's or sheep's liver tender, cut it into thin slices. Cut some bacon into very thin slices; take a sheet of common note-paper, lay on one half of it a slice of bacon, sprinkle it with a teaspoonful of the following mixture: to a tablespoonful of breadcrumbs add half a teaspoonful each of pepper, herbs, parsley, and onion. Lay the liver over the bacon, sprinkle the liver with another teaspoonful of the crumbs, put the other piece of bacon on, and turn the other half of the paper over, and turn up the edges round the three open sides. Fry for fifteen minutes, turning them once over.

Curry Balls.

Boil half a pound of rice with one pint of water and a large tablespoonful of curry-powder, half a tablespoonful of salt, and one of sugar, an acid apple chopped fine, a large onion chopped fine. Chop up six or eight ounces of cold meat, with some parsley; while the rice is hot mix the meat with it, add an egg, and form into balls (rolling them in flour every now and then), put them in a frying-pan with some grease, or bake them in a baking-tin well greased.

Cold Sheep's Head Shape.

Take a sheep's head, boil it with salt and some peppercorns till the meat falls from the bones. Cut the meat into small pieces and place them in an earthenware shape. Cut four hard-boiled eggs and place them in the shape before putting in the meat, which must be well seasoned with cayenne pepper and a few drops of lemon juice, and salt to taste, a chopped onion, and some chopped parsley, and some ham cut into small pieces. Bake in an oven for twenty minutes; then while hot pour in the liquor that the sheep's head was boiled in (mixed with a little dissolved gelatine) over the shape, leave to get cold, and turn out of shape when perfectly firm, and send to table on dish.

Italian Puffs.

Mix up in a basin six ounces of finely chopped cold meat, two ounces of breadcrumbs, two teaspoonfuls *of* vinegar, ditto chopped parsley, half a teaspoonful each of chopped onion, mixed herbs, pepper, salt, and sugar, and a teacup of milk. Make a teaspoonful of baking-powder and a pound of flour into a dough, and three ounces of lard or dripping and a little water; roll it out thin, and cut out fourteen or sixteen round pieces, lay some of the mixture on each piece, wet it all round, and double the paste over, pressing it down well. Place them in a baking-tin with some lard or dripping, and place in the oven. While they are cooking, baste three or four times with the grease in the tin. When done, drain them and serve very hot.

Calf's Liver, Potted.

Boil some calf's liver quite tender, cut it into small pieces, and put through a mincing-machine; then add butter, pepper, and powdered cloves. Pound in a mortar. One pound of liver requires two ounces of butter, half ditto of salt, and a small pinch of powdered cloves. Put into a pot and pour melted butter on the top.

Tomatoes and Maccaroni.

Cook half a pound of maccaroni in a pint and a half of water and a quart of milk, boil until tender; dissolve gently ten ounces of rich white cheese in a pint of good cream, add a little salt, a good deal of cayenne, and two ounces of fresh butter. The cream should be boiled before the cheese is melted into it. The maccaroni is to be arranged round a hot-dish, and the cheese mixture to be poured lightly on it. In the centre of the dish should be four or five large baked tomatoes. The whole should be sent to table *very* hot.

Stewed Kidney.

A kidney cut into four pieces, well floured all over, and put into a pan with mushrooms and a rich gravy. Parsley and fine herbs, pepper and salt to taste must be added; the whole carefully browned.

Maccaroni and Salmon.

Cook half a pound of maccaroni by boiling it in a pint and a half of water and a quart of milk, adding the liquor out of the tin of American salmon; put the pieces of salmon in a well-greased pie-dish, pour the maccaroni over, sprinkle breadcrumbs over and a few pieces of butter; bake for twenty minutes.

Salmon en Papillote.

Take a small salmon steak, sprinkle it with pepper, salt, and lemon juice. Butter the inside of a large sheet of letter-paper and place the steak upon it, fold the paper over, cut it round, roll up the edges, lay in a greased baking-tin, and bake twenty minutes. When dished cut the paper open at the top.

Shrimps and Boiled Rice.

Shell a pint of shrimps, make a thick white sauce with a little cream, butter, some flour and milk, nicely flavoured with cayenne, salt, and a little mace. Heat together in a saucepan, and pour into the middle of a very hot dish. Have ready some boiled rice, arrange it nicely round the dish, and send to table.

(Receipt for boiling rice on page 25.)

Broiled Cod's Sounds.

Lay them a few minutes in hot water. If fresh, rub with some salt, clean, till they look white, and give them a gentle boil. Take up, dry, flour, sprinkle with salt and pepper; broil them. Serve with melted butter and mustard.

Fried Potatoes.

Fry a good quantity of fat, and when boiling place chips of potatoes in a frying-basket and stand it in the boiling fat; shake it frequently. When done stand the chips on paper to drain.

Beef or Pork and Apple Pasties (hot).

Roll out some good butter crust. Season with pepper very highly, and some salt, a tender beef-steak previously cut into pieces about half an inch square. Have ready the paste rolled out thin, about six inches long by three broad; place the meat on the crust and place another piece over it, pinching down the edges together. Brush over with egg, and bake. If pork is used, put a previously baked apple, minus core and skin, into each pasty with the cut-up meat.

Salmon Cutlets.

Cut slices one inch thick and season very highly with pepper and salt (fresh ground pepper); butter a sheet of white paper, and lay each in a separate piece, with their ends twisted, and broil gently over a clear fire, and serve with caper sauce.

Fried Smelts.

Smelts should be very fresh. Do not wash them, but dry in a cloth, flour lightly, dip them in egg, sprinkle with very fine crumbs of bread, and put them in boiling lard for five minutes. Fry a pale brown. Dry them before the fire on a drainer.

Crimped Skate.

Clean, skin, and cut the fish into slices; have ready some highly salted water, in which boil the fish till it is done (about twenty minutes). The slices of fish should be rolled and tied with string previously to being boiled. Drain well, remove the string, and serve with anchovy sauce poured over it.

Kidney Balls.

Chop a veal kidney and some of the fat, some leek or onion, black pepper and salt to taste; roll it up with an egg into balls and fry them.

Potato aux Boulettes.

Boil some large potatoes very dry, mash a pound very smooth; mix with them while yet warm, two ounces of fresh butter, three tablespoonfuls of fresh cream, a teaspoonful of salt, one and a half of black pepper, the beaten and strained yolks of four eggs, and last of all the white thoroughly whisked; add some finely minced ham and a little chopped parsley. Mould the mixture with a teaspoon and drop it into a small pan of boiling butter; fry the boulettes for five minutes over a moderate fire. Drain them well, and dish them on a hot napkin.

Salmi of Game.

Half roast the birds, carve them very neatly, and strip every bit of skin from the legs, wings, and breasts; bruise the bodies well, and put them, with the skin and other trimmings, into a very clean saucepan with the following mixture: cut down into dice four ounces of lean and unboiled ham, and put it, with two ounces of butter, into a thick, well-tinned saucepan; add four minced eschalots, two ounces of sliced carrot, and two dozen button mushrooms, four cloves, a dozen and a half peppercorns, a bay leaf, two sprigs of thyme, a good bit of parsley. Stew these over a gentle fire, stirring and shaking them often; then mix well with them a dessertspoonful of flour and let it take a little colour. Next add by degrees three-quarters of a pint of veal stock, and half a pint of sherry or Madeira. When this is done put in the *bodies* of the birds and boil for an hour and a quarter. Strain and clear the sauce quite from fat, pour it on the joints of game, heat them in it slowly, and when they are on the point of boiling dish them immediately, with delicately fried sippets round the dish.

Bloaters in Batter.

Cut the heads and tails off two bloaters, split them open, and remove the backbones. Make half a pint of French batter, pour half of it into a greased frying-pan, lay in the bloaters with a little mustard rubbed over them, pour in the rest of the batter, and fry.

Broiled Mackerel, whole.

Empty and cleanse a large fresh mackerel, opening it as little as possible; hang it in a cool air till stiff. Make an incision with a sharp knife the whole length of the fish on either side of the backbone, and with a feather put in some cayenne and fine salt mixed with a few drops of pure salad oil. Lay the fish, wrapped in thickly buttered writing-paper, over a moderate fire on a well-heated gridiron which has been rubbed with suet; loose it gently should it stick, and when done equally on both sides turn the back to the fire. Half an hour will broil it well.

Beef Olives.

Cut the beef into thin slices. Mix four tablespoonfuls of breadcrumbs with half a teaspoonful of pepper, half ditto of mixed herbs, a finely chopped onion, two teaspoonfuls of chopped parsley; finely chop some fat bacon; roll up the mixture in the slices of beef and tie securely, then make hot in the oven or in a frying-pan. Serve olives on fried toast.

Calf's Head.

Scald the skin off a large head, clean it nicely, and take out the brains. Boil it tender enough to remove the bones; then have ready a good quantity of chopped parsley, salt, and a good quantity of pepper; mix well, season it highly with these, lay the parsley in a thick layer, then some thick slices of fine ham, then the yolks of six nice yellow eggs stuck here and there about. Roll the head quite close, and tie it as close as possible; boil it, and lay a weight upon it.

Stewed Eels.

Clean and skin the eels, season with salt, cloves, pepper, and mace; put into a small stew-pan with very strong beef gravy, port, and an equal quantity of Madeira. It must be covered close; stew till quite tender, take out the eels and keep hot while you boil up the liquor with one or two chopped anchovies and some flour and butter; strain the gravy through a sieve and add lemon juice. Serve with sippets of bread and horseradish if liked.

Fried Herrings.

Serve them a light brown with fried sliced onions.

Hot Crab.

Pick the meat out of a crab, clear the shell from the head; then put the meat, with a tiny pinch of nutmeg, salt, a good bit of pepper, three spoonfuls of vinegar, some breadcrumbs, and a good bit of butter, into the shell again, set it before the fire, and brown with a salamander. Serve dry toast to eat it on.

Scalloped Cod or Lobster.

The remains of boiled cod must be cleared of bones and mixed with a cup of milk, one dessertspoonful of flour, some anchovy sauce, one teaspoonful of vinegar, a very little mustard, a little cayenne, a little black pepper, and some pieces of butter. Grease some scallop-shells, put in the mixture, grate breadcrumbs over and bake a nice brown for three-quarters of an hour.

Bloaters and Crumbs.

Cut off the head and tail of a bloater, split it open, and take out the backbone; sprinkle it with two spoonfuls of breadcrumbs, half a teaspoonful each of dry mustard and chopped parsley, a little onion, a few drops of Yorkshire relish. Put four pieces of butter on the top of bloater, and cook in an oven or before the fire.

Egg Kromeskies.

Boil hard four eggs, take off the shells, cut four thin slices of lean bacon eight inches long and three wide. Take two tablespoonfuls of breadcrumbs mixed with one ditto of chopped parsley, one of finely chopped onion, some pepper, and a teaspoonful of mixed herbs; sprinkle this mixture on the four slices of bacon, place an egg in each, and roll up; tie with a piece of string, or put a little skewer through each. Put in an oven for three-quarters of an hour.

Sausages and Artichokes or Vegetable Marrow.

Wash and boil two pounds of Jerusalem artichokes the same as potatoes, peel them; put one pound of sausages in boiling water and let them cook fifteen minutes. Lay the sausages in a *very* hot dish, and put the artichokes round them. Put a piece of butter the size of an egg into a saucepan; when it is melted add two tablespoonfuls of flour, stir well, and then pour in slowly a pint of milk, a finely chopped onion, and some salt. Pour over sausages and artichokes.

Oatmeal Porridge and Hominy.

Have the water boiling over a good fire with some salt in it, take a handful of meal and sprinkle it in boiling water, stirring well with a large spoon. Then let it boil, for oatmeal three hours, and for hominy twenty minutes to half an hour (if coarse, longer). It should be now thick enough to serve, that is, just so stiff as not to run. In two or three minutes it may be turned into a dish and served without a cover. It is best eaten with cold milk or cream poured on it by degrees, and a little salt.

Muffins or Tea-Cakes.

Half a teaspoonful of tartaric acid, half a teaspoonful of bicarbonate of soda rubbed into a pound of flour, two ounces of butter worked into the flour, one egg well beaten, half a pint of cold new milk poured into a hole made in the flour; add salt, and bake in a tin for twenty minutes.

Shrimp Pie.

Pick a quart of shrimps; if they are very salt season them with only mace and a clove or two. Mince three anchovies, mix these with the spice and some black pepper, and then season the shrimps. Put some butter at the bottom of the dish and over the shrimps, with a glass of sharp white wine and a few drops of lemon juice. The paste must be light and thin. Very little time serves to make this dish.

Eggs en Caisse.

Make some small paper boxes, butter the bottom, half fill with following mixture: stale breadcrumbs, butter, minced parsley, salt, and cayenne; break an egg into each box, cover with breadcrumbs till the box is quite full. Put them on a gridiron for three minutes or in an oven. Servo very hot.

Indian Pillau.

Boil rice in plenty of water for twenty minutes, so that the water drains off easily, leaving the grains whole and with some degree of hardness; then stir in some butter to make the grains separate easily; add pepper and salt. Garnish the pillau with hard-boiled eggs cut in quarters, and with a fringe of onions fried very dry.

Curried Macaroni.

Cut up two onions, fry them in some fat, add a tablespoonful of curry-powder, ditto vinegar, ditto sugar, one chopped apple, a teaspoonful of salt; add one pint and three-quarters of water and boil in it slowly half a pound of macaroni till quite tender, and serve very hot.

Corn-flour Cakes.

Beat two ounces of butter into a cream, add a teaspoonful of salt. Beat two eggs well, and stir into the mixture a quarter of a pound of corn-flour and a tablespoonful of flour. Pour the mixture into a well-greased cake-tin, or on a flat baking-tin divided into small cakes. Bake from fifteen to twenty minutes in a hot oven. When the cakes are taken out slant them against a plate to prevent them from getting heavy.

Pigs' Trotters.

Take some pigs' trotters, wash them well, and put them in a stew-pan with enough cold water to cover them, and when it boils take the stew-pan off, strain off the water, and put the trotters into a basin of cold water. Put the trotters into two quarts of water in the stew-pan, with a tablespoonful of vinegar and a tablespoonful of salt, and stir in some smoothly mixed flour and water (an ounce of flour and a tablespoonful of cold water). Put the stew-pan over the fire till it just boils, and then set it on one side to simmer once for four hours. Serve the trotters on a hot dish with a good white sauce.

Cheese Trifles.

Put some very thin puff-paste in patty-pans, mix one ounce of grated Parmesan cheese, pepper, cayenne, the yolk of an egg, and one tablespoonful of cream; whisk the white, stir in, place in the patty-pans, and bake in a quick oven for ten minutes.

Stuffed Tomatoes.

Take four large tomatoes wipe them, put them on a plate, and cut off a small round from the top with a sharp knife and as much of the inside as can be got at, leaving the sides of the tomato, entire. Chop some ham, the inside of the tomato, some red and black pepper, a little salt, some vinegar, a teaspoonful of sugar, three onions chopped very fine, and a sprig of thyme. Put all these into a sauté-pan over the fire and stir the contents with a spoon until they are reduced (about ten minutes). Pass it all through a hair sieve, and fill the tomato walls with the mixture. Put them into a hot oven on a dish in which they can be served, with a piece of butter on each tomato, and slightly cook. Serve very hot.

Hard-boiled Eggs and White Sauce.

Hard-boil six fresh eggs, quarter, and place them on a dish. Make a white sauce by putting half all ounce of butter into a stew-pan, and when it is melted put in one ounce of flour, stirring it well for ten minutes; then add one gill of cream and half a teacupful of milk. Take one dozen button mushrooms and peel them and wash them, put them in a stew-pan with a piece of butter the size of a nut, squeeze over them a teaspoonful of lemon juice and a tablespoonful of cold water; put it on the fire and just bring it to a boil, first adding minced parsley and salt to taste. The sauce is then strained over the hard-boiled eggs, and the dish is served very hot. If more sauce is needed, use a little white stock to mix with the other.

Sardines on Toast.

Cut some toast into long pieces the length of a sardine and a trifle wider; butter, spread with anchovy paste; split a sardine and take out the backbone, lay a half on each piece of toast, and heat through.

Oatmeal Cakes.

Melt three ounces of lard in a saucepan. Take seven ounces of flour and three ounces of oatmenl, a tablespoonful of salt, and a quarter of a teaspoonful of carbonate of soda; mix with a spoon, stir in the melted lard. Break an egg into a tablespoonful of water and beat together. Pour this into the flour mixture and stir well together. Turn the paste on a board. Roll out the paste as thin as required; put on to a greased baking-tin. Bake for twenty minutes in a hot oven (240° at oven door).

Pork Cutlets and Anchovy Sauce.

Grill six delicately cut pork cutlets and serve in a not dish, with anchovy sauce in the midst of them.

Stewed Jack.

Well wash the jack in salt and water, cut it into thick slices. Boil half a pint of stock, and when it boils put the jack in, and then let it boil for ten minutes; add a teacupful of claret, one large tablespoonful of anchovy sauce, a lump of butter the size of an egg, two teaspoonfuls of ketchup, one of lemon juice, one small lump of sugar. Thicken with a little flour, and keep the stew-pan well shaken for five or seven minutes.

Hot Scones.

One pound of flour, one saltspoon of carbonate of soda, one ounce of salt, and enough buttermilk or sour milk to make a dough. This makes eight scones. Cook them in a frying-pan or on a griddle *over* the fire.

Maître d'Hôtel Kidneys.

Plunge some kidneys in boiling water, open them down the middle without dividing them altogether, and peel. Pass a skewer through them to keep them open, pepper well, salt, and dip them in melted butter. Broil them over a clear fire, cooking the cut side first; remove the skewers, put a little piece of maître d'hôtel butter into the hollow of each kidney, and serve very hot.

Maître d'Hôtel Butter.

Chopped parsley beaten up in butter, a little lemon juice and salt, and plenty of black pepper.

Breakfast Cake (Anchovy).

One cup of rice boiled quite soft in water. When cold stir a tablespoonful of flour into rice, and a lump of butter, two eggs, and some anchovy sauce. Well mix, and bake a light brown in a tin plate.

Spatchcock.

Split a fowl in halves through the middle of the breast and back; pepper and salt it, rub it over with butter; grease a gridiron, and broil it over a clear, bright fire. Put a lump of butter on a hot dish before the fire, let it dissolve; lay the fowl on a round of toasted bread, pepper and salt it, and serve very hot.

Curried Mincemeat.

Slice an onion and fry it in butter. Soak a slice of bread in milk, and grate eight sweet almonds; beat two eggs into half a cupful of milk, and mix the whole well together, with half a pound of minced meat, a small lump of butter, and a tablespoonful of curry-powder. Rub a pie-dish with butter and the juice of a lemon. Bake in a not too hot oven for half an hour.

Stewed Ducks' Giblets.

Well wash the giblets, divide the pinions and the neck, head and gizzard, put them into a stew-pan, with a bunch of savoury herbs, one onion, two cloves, fourteen peppercorns, some ketchup, a piece of butter as big as an egg, and half a pint of stock. Set the pan over a gentle fire to stew till the giblets are tender, then thicken the gravy with a piece of butter rolled in flour; add a glassful of white wine just before serving, boil it up and pour over the giblets.

Broiled Pheasant.

Cut the legs off at the first joint, cut up the bird. Put the pieces into a frying-pan with a little lard; when browned on both sides and half done through, take them up and drain them, brush them over with egg, dip them in breadcrumbs well seasoned with salt and cayenne, broil for ten minutes, and serve with mushroom sauce.

Beef and Onion Fried in Slices.

Cut some slices of cold roast beef and one large onion, fry them a nice brown in a quarter of a pound of butter; turn the pan round frequently to prevent the meat from burning. Then boil up half a pint of beef broth, well seasoned with pepper, salt, and a little mustard. Pour over the meat and serve as hot as possible.

Croquettes of Brains.

Blanch a calf's brains, and beat them well together with a spoonful of sage-leaves chopped very fine, seasoned with pepper and salt. Mix them with bread-crumbs soaked in a little milk and a well-beaten egg. Make into balls and fry for ten minutes in butter.

Veal Rolls.

Cut some thin slices off a fillet of veal, hack them with a knife, rub them over with the yolks of eggs, lay some veal forcemeat over them, roll each up tight, and tie it with a thread. Brush them over with the beaten yolks of eggs and sprinkle with breadcrumbs; lay them in a buttered dish, and bake in a quick oven half an hour. Boil up a pint of brown gravy with some pickled mushrooms in it, pour round the rolls, and serve very hot.

Pig's Cheek.

Boil a pig's cheek for three-quarters of an hour, cover it with breadcrumbs, and brown them or glaze it.

Rice Bread.

Boil half a pound of rice in three pints of water till the whole is quite thick; mix yeast as well as six pounds of flour to form the dough. Bake one and a half to two hours.

American Breakfast Bread.

Heat one third of a quart of milk, and scald it with half a pint of flour. When the batter thus made is cool, add the rest of the quart of milk, a teacupful of yeast, a dessertspoonful of salt, and flour enough to make a stiff paste. Knead it on a paste-board till it is very fine and smooth. Let it rise all night. Bake in the morning half an hour.

Potato Bread.

Boil two and a half pounds of nice mealy potatoes till floury; rub and mash them smooth; then mix them with sufficient cold water to let them pass through a coarse sieve. Mix this paste with yeast and then add it to the flour. Set it to rise, well knead it, and make it into a stiff, tough dough.

Breakfast Rolls.

Take half a pound of flour and rub two ounces of butter into it, add one ounce of salt and mix it with one beaten egg. Bake for three-quarters of an hour.

Water Cakes (Breakfast).

Mix two ounces of butter with one pound of flour, a pinch of salt, and a pint of cold water. Bake for fifteen minutes.

Birds' Nests.

Four eggs, boil for ten minutes; warm half a pint of rich brown gravy. Take off the eggshells and brush the eggs over thickly with a forcemeat preparation; put a little butter in a stewpan and fry them, pour gravy over them, and serve very hot. Forcemeat to be made of breadcrumbs, beef suet chopped *very* fine, parsley, grated lemon peel, pepper and salt, and bound with the beaten yolk of an egg.

Scalloped Mussels or Cockles.

Clean the shells well with repeated washings, but do not keep them long in water. Stew them in a small quantity of boiling water; when the shells open they are done. The saucepan should be covered and shaken continually. In boiling mussels put a silver spoon in with them, and if it turns black do not eat them. Pick them out of their shells and save the liquor that runs from them; pick out the hairy appendage to be found at the root of the tongue. To the pint of mussels put half a pint of the saved liquor; put in a blade of mace, thicken with butter rolled in flour, let them stew gently a few minutes. Serve in scallop-shells *very* hot, with browned crumbs on the top.

Bread and Milk.

Cut the bread into dice, put them into a basin; boil the milk, and when boiling pour it over the bread. Cover the cup up for five minutes, and then stand it before the fire for five more. Sugar to taste.

Egg Toast.

Put the yolks and whites of four eggs with four ounces of clarified butter; beat them well together, then stir it over the fire in the same direction till mixed. Make a round of thin, delicate toast, well butter it, and salt and pepper it. Put the mixture on it and serve very hot.

Turbot Loaves (or American Oyster Loaves).

Take four round breakfast rolls, four ounces of butter; take a circular piece out of the top of each roll and extract the crumb. Then put half a dozen oysters and some cold turbot (with the oysters' liquor) into a stew-pan with two ounces of butter, a teaspoonful of pepper, salt to taste, a teaspoonful of anchovy paste, and half the crumb from the loaves. Let them simmer for six minutes, and stir in a tablespoonful of cream. Fill directly the holes in the loaves. Fit the tops on again, and put them in an oven to crisp. Serve on a napkin.

Fried Beef Kidney and Onion.

Take a beef kidney, cut it in slices, not too thick, and let them soak in warm water for two hours and a half, changing the water twice to thoroughly cleanse them. Dredge a very little flour over these slices, and fry a nice brown in three ounces of butter; add some slices of onion or not, as preferred, seasoning them well with pepper, salt, and mustard. Arrange them in a circle round a dish, and stir a teaspoonful of tomato sauce into a quarter of a pint of good gravy with a lump of sugar in it.

Fillets de Bœuf aux Truffles.

Cut out the inside of a sirloin of beef, beat it well to make it tender, cut it in slices, trimming them neatly; lay them in oil and let them soak for ten minutes, then fry in butter. Chop up some parsley, lemon thyme, half a shallot, and slice some truffles (that have been previously cleaned and brushed, boiled for twenty minutes in some good stock, quarter of a pint and half a pint of white wine, pepper and salt), and add fifteen drops of vinegar. Lay the herbs in the middle of the dish and the fillets round, and the truffles round the fillets.

Broiled Beef Palates.

They take one hour to simmer (which can be done overnight); *five* minutes to broil. Wash and soak three palates and boil them until tender, removing the skin; then put them in a stewpan with a pint and a half of new milk, pepper, salt, clove, shallot, a bunch of thyme and parsley, and a lump of butter rolled in flour. Let the whole simmer slowly for one hour; then take them out, brush the palates over with the yolk of a beaten egg, dip them into breadcrumbs and boil them lightly. Place them on a very hot dish, and serve with a piquant sauce.

Bombay Ducks, or Mummalon Fish.

To be bought in tins at two shillings and three pence a tin, imported by Dickinson Brothers & Co., London. The fish are toasted very crisp and served on pieces of hot buttered toast about two and a half inches wide and one and a half square. Served very hot.

Fried Trout.

Thoroughly clean and remove the gills, brush them over with the yolk of a well-beaten egg, dip them into breadcrumbs, and fry in hot fat till a fine brown. Garnish with sliced lemon.

Lamb's Fry.

Take one pound of lamb's fry, boil it for about a quarter of an hour, then drain it dry. Brush it over with the yolk of a beaten egg, then cover with breadcrumbs, seasoned with minced parsley, pepper, and salt. Fry it till it is a nice colour, *i.e.* five minutes, and serve with fried parsley on a folded napkin.

Grilled Kidneys and Lemon Juice.

Cut four kidneys *nearly* in halves, grill them on a well-greased gridiron. When done, put on each some chopped onion, parsley, butter, and lemon juice, pepper and salt.

Apple Fool.

Put your apples into a stew-pan with half the measure of water. When they are quite soft drain the water from them and press them with the back of a spoon through a colander; sweeten, and flavour with a little lemon juce. Put a quart of milk over the fire beaten up with the yolks of four eggs, stir it over the fire till it begins to simmer; then let it cool a little, and add half a pint of cream; stir it gradually into the cold apples. Let it stand till cold, and serve it.

Strawberry or Apricot Fool.

Press the fruit (whether tinned or jam) through a hair sieve, simmer some milk with the yolk of one egg beaten up in it; add the cream when cooling, and stir it all gradually into the cold fruit.

Salsify.

Scrape the salisfy quite white, and throw it into a pan of boiling water, with a good lump of salt and some lemon juice. When it is tender put it to drain; then cut it into pieces and dip it in batter and fry a light brown. Serve fried parsley with it. Make the batter of one egg, a little flour, pepper, salt, mace, and nutmeg.

Reindeer's Tongues.

Soak them for three hours in cold water, and then expose them to the air. This must be done three times. Then scrape them very clean and put them into a stew-pan of cold water and bring them gradually to a boil. Let them simmer slowly, skimming them carefully all the time. Serve on a table napkin.

Red Mullet Baked.

Fold each mullet in well-oiled paper, tie the ends, pass the string over them, and bake in a small dish in a moderate oven twenty-five minutes. Make a sauce of the gravy that comes from the fish, a piece of butter, a little flour, a glass of port or sherry, a teaspoonful of anchovy sauce, and the juice of half a lemon. Boil it and serve separately from the fish, which are to be served in their paper cases.

Broiled Trout.

When the fish is thoroughly cleaned, wipe it dry in a cloth and tie it round with thread (to preserve its shape). Melt a quarter of a pound of butter with a tablespoonful of salt, and pour it over the trout till quite covered; let it remain in it for five minutes, then take it out and place on a gridiron over a clear fire, and let it cook gradually for fifteen minutes.

Sheep's Tongues Stewed.

Put the tongues into cold water and let them boil till tender enough to remove the skins. Then split them and lay them in a stew-pan with enough *good* gravy to cover them. Chop some parsley, some mushrooms, and onion finely, work a lump of butter with it, and season with pepper and salt to taste; add it to the gravy and stew till tender, then lay them in a dish, strain the gravy, pour it *very* hot over the tongues, and serve.

Veal and Potato Rissoles.

A few mashed potatoes, some cold veal or chicken, hard-boiled eggs. Chop as much meat as you require and mix it with three-quarters of a pound of mashed potatoes, two hard-boiled eggs minced fine. Add chopped parsley, a little lemon juice, pepper, and salt. Mix with the yolk and white of an egg beaten separately, the white to a stiff froth. Make into balls, roll in the yolk of an egg, and brown in a Dutch oven before the fire.

Cow's Heel Fried.

Cow's heel to be thoroughly washed, cleaned, and scalded; cut it into pieces about two inches long and one wide; dip them into the yolk of a beaten egg, cover them with fine breadcrumbs mixed with chopped parsley, cayenne pepper, and salt. Fry in boiling butter, and arrange prettily on a hot dish.

Beef Fritters.

Mix to a smooth batter ten ounces of flour with a teacupful of water; warm two ounces of butter and stir into the flour, with the whites of two eggs whisked to a stiff froth. Shred the well-seasoned beef as thin and small as possible, and add it to the batter. Mix all well together, and drop it into a pan of boiling lard. Fry on both sides.

Ox Tails.

The upper half of two ox tails. Cut the tails in pieces about three inches long; stew them for a long time till they *are very* tender. Skim the gravy well, stand the pieces of tail upon a dish, and pour the gravy over them. (For a breakfast dish the tails must be stewed overnight and warmed up in the morning.) Time, three hours and a half.

Potted Hare.

Hang up a hare for about a week, then case it and cut it in quarters. Put it into a stone jar, season it with cloves, mace, pepper, and salt, put a pound of butter over it, and bake it four hours in a slow oven. When done, pick meat from the bones, pound it in a mortar with the butter it was baked in (skimmed clean from the gravy). Pound it till it becomes a smooth paste; season it to taste. Press it down in the pot and pour clarified butter over it.

Grilled Kippered Salmon.

Cut some dried salmon into narrow pieces about two inches wide and four long, broil them over a clear fire; then rub them over with fresh butter. seasoned with lemon juice and cayenne. Serve *very* hot.

Deviled Oysters.

Open enough oysters for the dish required, leaving them in their deep shells and their liquor; add a little lemon juice, pepper, salt, and cayenne; put a small piece of butter in each, and place the shell on a gridiron over a clear fire and broil for three minutes. Serve on a napkin with bread and butter.

Deviled Hot Meat.

Cut some cold meat in slices and then rub it with the following mixture: a tablespoonful of ketchup, one of vinegar, two of made mustard, one of salt, and two of butter, four table spoonfuls of cold gravy, one of currypaste; mix all as smooth as possible. When rubbed with the mixture put it to the grill before a good fire. Take what is left of the sauce and make it warm, and pour over the grill before sending it to table.

Filleted Soles.

One pair of large soles filleted. Put them to boil in a little salt and water for a few minutes; keep them quite straight. Make a sauce consisting of melted butter, twelve oysters, a few shrimps, one large spoonful of anchovy sauce, and two of capers chopped. Stew them in the sauce for five minutes, and serve with the sauce *over* them.

Breakfast Cakes.

Take three ounces of butter and rub it into one pound of flour; take a small cupful of new milk, one teaspoonful of brewers' yeast, a small piece of butter. Bake in a hot oven.

Mushrooms in Cream.

Put some cream in a white-lined saucepan, season it with salt and pepper, and let it just boil. Prepare some mushrooms, and when the cream boils rub salt over them and some pepper, and put them into the saucepan with the cream. Boil all together for four minutes. Serve very hot.

Deviled Biscuits.

Take some milk biscuits, soak them in clarified butter or oil. Then rub them with a little curry-powder, ketchup, some salt and pepper. Toast them on a gridiron over a clear fire. Serve very hot.

Tomatoes Scalloped.

Put six tomatoes through a sieve, add one cup of breadcrumbs, one teaspoonful of sugar, one of salt, one of pepper, a piece of butter the size of an egg. Butter a scallop-dish and bake in a quick oven.

American Waffles.

Boil one cup of rice quite soft. Take two tablespoonfuls of flour, two eggs, two tablespoonfuls of milk; beat to a smooth paste; keep till cold. Well grease the waffle-irons, pour in some of the mixture, and when done on both sides put on a warm plate and butter. Serve them very hot.

A Potato Soufflé.

Mix into a smooth paste four dessertspoonfuls of well-boiled potato and one of flour with milk; then pour in the rest of the pint, salt and pepper it, and then put it into a *very* clean stew-pan with an ounce and a half of fresh butter. Stir it over a clear fire until it is of the consistency of cream, then add the yolks of six well-beaten eggs, and then stir in the whites. When whisked stiff enough to bear the weight of an egg, pour it into the soufflé-dish, and bake it in a moderate oven. When done, hold a salamander over it for a few minutes, and serve with a napkin pinned round the mould.

Broiled Lobster.

After the lobster is boiled split it from head to tail. Take out the uneatable part, lay it open, put pieces of butter over the meat, sprinkle it with pepper, salt, and cayenne, and a spoonful of thin melted butter to moisten it. Set the shells on a gridiron over bright coals until nicely heated through. Serve in the shells on a napkin.

Fried Skate.

Brush some pieces of skate over with the yolk of an egg, season it with salt, cover it with breadcrumbs, and fry a nice brown. Serve on a hot table napkin with shrimp sauce.

Mackerel Stewed.

Take two mackerels, raise each fillet from the mackerel in two, and lay them in a stew-pan with two ounces of butter previously melted with a little flour, cayenne, salt, black pepper, and the rind of half a lemon. Shake the stew-pan over the fire for a few minutes, turning the fillets. Then pour in slowly nearly half a pint of port wine, with a tablespoonful of Worcester sauce and a little mace; boil up and pour over the fish.

Lobster Scallops.

The flesh of a boiled lobster must be cut in neat pieces. A white sauce made of milk, butter, and flour, with a dessertspoonful of anchovy sauce stirred in, some nepaul and black pepper, a teaspoonful of vinegar. Put this sauce on the fire till it boils, then off the fire add the beaten yolk of an egg and half a pint of cream. Put in the pieces of lobster. Heat altogether over the fire, but do not allow the mixture to boil, stirring gently all the time. Put in some scallop shells or the empty lobster shells of the tail and head; cover with breadcrumbs and place a minute or two in an oven, or brown the crumbs with a salamander. Serve very hot, on a napkin, with fried parsley.

Veal and Potato Rissoles.

Chop your cold veal very fine, and mix about two-thirds of the quantity of mashed potatoes and one or two hard-boiled eggs minced fine; season with pepper, salt, and a little lemon juice. Mix together with the yolk and the white of an egg beaten separately, the white to a stiff froth; make into balls, and brown them in a Dutch oven before the fire for eight minutes.

Madras Anchovy Toast.

Put a piece of butter upon a very hot plate; add the well-beaten yolks of two eggs, cayenne pepper to taste, a teaspoonful of sherry or champagne, a teaspoonful of anchovy paste; mix well, soak hot toast in it, and serve very hot. Toast ought to be rather thick.

Cold Duck Stewed with Peas.

Cut the duck into neat pieces and season with cayenne pepper and salt, with the peel of half a lemon minced *very* fine. Put it in a stewpan, pour over it three-quarters of a pint of good gravy, and place it over a clear fire to become very hot but *not* boil. Boil a tinful of green peas in boiling water, drain them on a sieve, stir in a large piece of butter mixed with flour; just warm the stew-pan over the fire, pile the peas in the centre of a dish, and arrange the pieces of duck round.

Lamb Chops.

Cut chops from a loin of lamb, let them be three-quarters of an inch thick. Broil over a clear fire when done season with pepper and salt. Serve in a dish garnished with fried parsley.

Apple Jelly.

Take a peck of apples, quarter them, and take out the cores; put them into a preserving-pan with one gallon of water, and let them boil moderately till the pulp will run. Then run the pulp through a jelly-bag or cloth; weigh the juice, and boil it rapidly for fifteen minutes. Draw it from the fire and stir into it until entirely dissolved an equal weight of finely sifted sugar. Then boil for twenty minutes longer, until it jellies strongly in the spoon. It must be *perfectly* clear from scum. Then pour it into glass jars. It ought to be pale and transparent.

Suet Pudding.

Put one pound of flour and half a pound of beef suet into a basin, a teaspoonful of salt, and one dessertspoonful of Goodall's baking-powder, and sufficient milk or water to make the materials into a thick paste. Mix all well together, tie up the paste in a floured cloth, and put into boiling water, and keep boiling for two hours. When the pudding is cold, cut it in slices and brown in a frying-pan. Serve in a hot dish for breakfast.

Normandy Pippins.

Take eight Normandy pippins, strew a hall-pound of moist sugar over them, and pour enough cider (or water) to cover them completely. Set them in the oven the last thing at night. Add a little more water and sugar, and bake for half an hour.

Baked Pears.

Take twelve pears, peel them, and cut them in halves; cut a lemon in thin slices, and lay the pears and lemon in layers in a bright block tin, with a cover to it, putting a clove here and there, and strewing the sugar over each layer. Pour enough water to cover the pears completely, set the cake tin in a slow oven, and bake about five hours.

Tea-Cakes.

Mix two and a half pounds of very fine dry breadcrumbs, with four ounces of melted butter, and the beaten yolks of five or six eggs, two teaspoonfuls of sugar, and a teaspoonful of salt. Chop a few blanched almonds, and add. Lastly stir in the beaten whites of the eggs. Bake in patty-pans. If less quantity is required, use everything in like proportion.

Anchovy Paste.

That made by C. Osborne of London, "Patum Piperium, or Anchovy Paste," recommended by author as the very best made, and sold in earthenware pots. To be got of J. A. Bovill & Co.

Paté de foie Gras.

In china pots, "Paté de foie Gras" made by J. G. Hummel, Strasbourg, to be bought in London of J. A. Bovill & Co., 29A, Upper Gloucester Place, N.W.

Fresh Herrings Stuffed.

Take six fresh herrings and open them down the back; take out the bone and take off the head. Put a little piece of veal stuffing in each, and roll them up. Lay small pieces of butter over them, and bake in a quick oven fifteen minutes,

Pheasant or Chicken Soufflé.

Mince the meat by putting it through a sausage-machine twice. Take a cupful of breadcrumbs, half a pint of good strong stock, put into a stew-pan, and boil until it leaves the pan clean; then stir in the yolks of three eggs, pepper and salt six finely chopped mushrooms, two finely chopped truffles, and a large spoonful of chopped parsley. Whip up the whites to a stiff froth, and when the mixture is cold stir them lightly into it. Line the mould with buttered paper before you put the mixture into it.

Potted Eggs and Anchovy.

Boil five eggs hard, run the yolks through a sieve, mix anchovy sauce to taste, and pound it in a mortar. Put it in a shape and decorate with parsley.

Toasted or Grilled Kippered Salmon.

Toast or grill the salmon; place it in a basin with the outside downwards, pour boiling water over it; repeat the process if very salt. Place it on a dish the right side uppermost, and spread butter on it. Put the dish in front of the fire and serve *very* hot. Altogether it takes ten minutes to cook.

Curried Sweetbreads (excellent).

Have ready some good white stock, add one fried onion, a tablespoonful of vinegar, salt and sugar to taste, and a tablespoonful of curry powder. Rub two ounces of butter into this gravy (about three-quarters of a pint) rolled in flour sufficient to make it nice and thick; cut up your sweetbreads into pieces two inches square, and stew in the gravy for about thirty-five minutes.

Baked Tomatoes.

Take eight tomatoes, scald them in boiling water, cut them in thick slices without removing the stem; rub the sides of a pie-dish with butter and lay in the slices of tomato; season well with pepper and salt, add two teaspoonfuls of Goodall's Yorkshire Relish, cover with breadcrumbs and scatter some lumps of butter over the top, and bake for thirty minutes.

Periwinkle Patties.

Mince some perriwinkles previously simmered, not boiled, and taken out of their shells, add a little lemon juice, some pepper and salt to taste, moisten with a little stock, and a tablespoonful of cream. Make a good puff-paste, roll thin and cut into round pieces, put the paste in patty-pans, the mixture on it, and cover again with paste. Brush with the yolk of an egg.

Hot Cross Buns.

Mix with two pounds of fine flour half an ounce of allspice and half a pound of fine moist sugar. Make a hole in the centre and stir in half a gill of yeast and half a pint of lukewarm milk. Cover the pan and let it rise two hours. Then dissolve half a pound of butter, stir it into the other ingredients, and add some more warm milk if necessary to make a soft paste. Set to rise for an hour more. Then shape the buns and place on a buttered tin, and put in a warm place till they have risen double their original size. Make a cross on each with a knife, bake in a hot oven, and when done brush them over with milk when taken out.

Brawn.

Clean and wash a pig's head of six or seven pounds, and put it into a stew-pan with two pounds of lean beef; cover with cold water and boil until the bones are easily removed, skimming often. Mince the beef and head as fine as possible, but don't let it get cold, season with five cloves, a lot of pepper, salt, and cayenne. Stir briskly together, and put into a cake-mould, with a heavy weight on the top. Let it stand for six hours. Dip the mould in boiling water when required, and turn the brawn out on a dish. Decorate with green parsley, and serve cold.

Graham Cakes.

One pint of sour milk, one beaten egg, one teaspoonful of soda, one of salt, and enough Graham flour to make a batter. Bake in gem tins or patty-pans.

Rice and Meat Balls.

One cupful of cooked rice, one cupful of finely chopped pork, one apple finely chopped, a little sage chopped, some salt and pepper, half a cupful of milk, one egg, and two tablespoonfuls of butter. Boil milk before adding meat, rice, and seasoning; add the egg last of all when almost cold. Shape into balls and fry.

Aspic Jelly.

Stew two pounds of knuckle veal or mutton, put the meat into a stew-pan that shuts very closely, with two slices of ham, a bunch of sweet herbs, a blade of mace, one onion, the peel of half a lemon, a teaspoonful of bruised Jamaica pepper, the same of whole pepper, salt to taste, and three pints of water. As soon as it boils skim it clean and let it simmer till quite strong and rich; dissolve one ounce of isinglass in it when boiling. Strain it, and when cold take off the fat with a spoon. Then lay over it a clean piece of blotting-paper, and remove all particles of grease. When cold boil it a few minutes with the whites of two well-beaten eggs and their shells. Take it off the fire, let it stand to settle, and pour it through a jelly-bag into a plain mould or basin that has first been dipped in water. Let it stand all night, and next morning turn it out of the mould by dipping the bottom in cold water. Ornament with green parsley and serve on a dish.

Cold Mutton Sliced and Fried with Bacon.

Cut some cold mutton in slices, dredge a little flour over each slice, seasoning each slice with mushroom ketchup, pepper, and salt. Fry some bacon, and the slices of mutton in the bacon fat. Arrange alternately round a dish.

Baked Haddock.

Thoroughly dry and clean the haddock, fill the inside with veal stuffing, sew it up, and curl the tail into its mouth. Brush it over with egg, and strew breadcrumbs over it. Set it in a warm oven to bake for about half an hour; but a Dublin Bay haddock will require double that time.

Shortbread.

Add four ounces of sugar to one pound of flour, and into it rub one pound of butter. Roll out thick and bake thirty minutes.

Baked Mackerel.

Clean the fish well, stuff it with breadcrumbs, oysters or shrimps, chopped onions, and parsley; mix well together with butter, stuff the fish, putting some stuffing over the outside. Bake in a warm oven.

Stewed Macaroni.

Put half a pound of macaroni into a stew-pan with some salt, and well cover it with water; simmer till *quite* tender, taking care to preserve the form, and when done strain it through a sieve. Mince the white meat of a cold fowl and some slices of ham very fine, season with pepper and salt and finely grated Parmesan cheese. Well beat the yolks of five and the whites of two eggs; add them to minced fowl. Mix with half a pint of cream. Mix all together, and put into a buttered mould. Steam for an hour, and serve with some good gravy.

Norfolk Dumplings.

Take some bread dough after it has risen, and throw into boiling water; boil till done. Serve at once, very hot, or they will get heavy. Eat them with butter or brown gravy.

Fowl or Fish Quenelles.

Soak a cupful of bread crumbs in cream. Mix half a cupful of pounded fish or fowl, mix well with the foregoing, and also an ounce of fresh butter. Mix a well-beaten egg with this (the white and yolk beaten separately), add pepper and salt, and convert the whole into a paste. Roll the quenelles into the shape of an egg, and poach them in a stewpan of white stock for fourteen minutes. The same mixture is good put into a buttered mould.

Cauliflower in Batter.

Boil a cauliflower till not quite soft. Divide it into pieces, dip in a well-seasoned batter, and fry in butter. Batter should be served dry without gravy.

Breakfast Dishes

FOR THREE MONTHS FOR SIX PERSONS.

Receipt on Page	**JANUARY 1ST, SUNDAY.**
10.	Pheasant rissoles.
27.	Kidneys à la maître d'hôtel.
2.	Buttered eggs.
11.	Potted shrimps.
28.	Hot breakfast cakes (anchovy).
11.	Quince marmalade.

	JANUARY 2ND, MONDAY.
3.	Duck olives.
18.	Shrimp omelette.
20.	Fried potato chips.
2.	Cold boiled ham.
4.	Milk rolls.
11.	Honey.

	JANUARY 3RD, TUESDAY.
4.	Oysters on toast.
5.	Sausages in mashed potatoes.
12.	Deviled pheasants' legs.
3.	Cold French meat pudding.
5.	Buttered scones.
13.	Strawberry jam.

Receipt on Page	
	JANUARY 4TH, WEDNESDAY.
5.	Savoury omelette.
6.	Kedgeree.
6.	Potted pheasant.
2.	Cold ham.
13.	Scones.
13.	Marmalade (orange).
	JANUARY 5TH, THURSDAY.
7.	Golden eggs.
8.	Bombay toast.
7.	Roman pie.
5.	Breakfast scones.
11.	Honey.
	JANUARY 6TH, FRIDAY.
27.	Stewed jack (pike).
7.	Ham toast.
7.	Œufs au tomato.
	Cold ox tongue bought in tins.
27.	Hot scones.
38.	Apple jelly.
	JANUARY 7TH, SATURDAY.
27.	Pork cutlets grilled, with anchovy sauce.
10.	Rissoles of chicken.
6.	Potted lobster.
27.	Oatmeal cakes.
	Sardines and watercress.
39.	Stewed prunes or baked pears.
	JANUARY 8TH, SUNDAY.
23.	Scalloped cod.
19.	Tomatoes and maccaroni,
2.	Buttered eggs.
3.	Breakfast cakes.
6.	Potted tongue.
11.	Quince marmalade.

Receipt on Page	
	JANUARY 9TH, MONDAY.
24.	Oatmeal porridge.
15.	Broiled partridge.
8.	Winchester cutlets.
6.	Poached eggs and bacon.
2.	Grated ham on toast.
13.	Strawberry jam.
	JANUARY 10TH, TUESDAY.
5.	Dried haddocks.
5.	Savoury omelette.
3.	Sausages boiled with chestnuts.
6.	Potted pheasant.
13.	Scones.
	Stewed fruit (or bottled gooseberries).
	JANUARY 11TH, WEDNESDAY.
12.	Fried slices of cod.
11.	Boiled eggs.
25.	Curried macaroni.
4.	Breakfast rolls.
6.	Anchovy toast.
13.	Orange marmalade.
	JANUARY 12TH, THURSDAY.
17.	Cooked meat fritters.
22.	Calf's head rolled and stuffed (cold).
25.	Corn-flour cakes.
9.	Mushrooms (broiled).
32.	Bombay ducks.
11.	Honey.
	JANUARY 13TH, FRIDAY.
	Rasher of ham and fried eggs.
36.	Potato soufflé.
23.	Hot crab.
24.	Oatmeal porridge.
26.	Sardines on toast.
11.	Quince marmalade.

BREAKFAST DISHES 47

Receipt
on Page

JANUARY 14TH, SATURDAY.

25.	Indian pillau.
24.	Shrimp pie.
25.	Pigs' trotters.
24.	Muffins or tea-cakes.
38.	Stewed apples (pippins).

JANUARY 15TH, SUNDAY.

25.	Eggs en caisse.
24.	Boiled hominy.
24.	Sausages and artichokes (or vegetable marrow).
23.	Bloaters and crumbs.
13.	Orange marmalade.

JANUARY 16TH, MONDAY.

13.	Snipe on toast.
13.	Oysters curried dry.
14.	Stewed potatoes.
14.	Sausage-cakes of meat (*tinned* will do).
14.	Stewed rhubarb.
9.	Hot buttered toast.

JANUARY 17TH, TUESDAY.

15.	Spatchcock of partridge or chicken.
15.	Devonshire omelette.
15.	Scalloped oysters.
12.	Fried bacon.
13.	Strawberry jam.

JANUARY 18TH, WEDNESDAY.

43.	Fowl or fish quenelles.
14.	Brain cakes.
15.	Lobster cutlets.
18.	German dumplings and gravy.
13.	Apricot jam.
13.	Scones.

Receipt   **JANUARY 19TH, THURSDAY.**
on Page
18.   Bacon omelette.
19.   Italian puffs.
19.   Potted calf's liver.
20.   Boiled cods' sounds.
 3.   Breakfast cakes.

JANUARY 20TH, FRIDAY.

20.   Beef pasties (hot).
 8.   Winchester cutlets.
21.   Salmi of game.
11.   Boiled eggs.
 9.   Hot buttered toast.
14.   Stewed rhubarb.

JANUARY 21ST, SATURDAY.

22.   Broiled mackerel.
22.   Beef olives.
26.   Hard-boiled eggs and white sauce.
27.   Oatmeal cakes.
                           Stewed or bottled fruit.

JANUARY 22ND, SUNDAY.

16.   Angels on horseback (oysters).
16.   Grenadines of veal.
16.   Fish puddings.
 3.   Breakfast cakes.
13.   Strawberry jam.

JANUARY 23RD, MONDAY.

17.   Oyster fritters.
16.   Sweetbreads and mushrooms.
17.   Savoury rice pudding.
19.   Calf's liver potted.
13.   Scones.

Receipt on Page	
	JANUARY 24TH, TUESDAY.
24.	Oatmeal porridge.
15.	Lobster cutlets.
21.	Crimped skate.
26.	Stuffed tomatoes.
	Preserved apricots, bought in tins.
28.	Breakfast cake (anchovy).
	JANUARY 25TH, WEDNESDAY.
20.	Shrimps and boiled rice.
19.	Stewed kidney.
17.	Potato patties.
6.	Potted pheasant.
24.	Boiled hominy.
	JANUARY 26TH, THURSDAY.
12.	Fried bacon.
15.	Scalloped oysters.
17.	Eggs and anchovy sauce.
34.	Potted hare.
13.	Scones.
	Baked apples.
	JANUARY 27TH, FRIDAY.
12.	Fried pork sausages.
12.	Partridge pudding.
10.	Curried sardines.
9.	Stewed mushrooms (forced or tinned).
9, 39.	Hot buttered toast or tea-cakes.
	JANUARY 28TH, SATURDAY.
9.	Baked eggs.
8.	Macaroni and kidneys.
9.	Fried bacon à l'Armstrong.
8.	Scotch woodcock
8.	Tea-cakes (hot).
13.	Orange marmalade.

Receipt
on Page

JANUARY 29TH, SUNDAY.

8.	Sausage-meat cakes.
8.	Bombay toast.
6.	Poached eggs.
6.	Kedgeree.
13.	Scones.
39.	Stewed pears.

JANUARY 30TH, MONDAY.

5.	Dried haddock.
5.	Fleed cakes.
10.	Fried patties (calf's brains).
6.	Potted lobster.
10.	Scotch collops.

JANUARY 31ST, TUESDAY.

12.	Fried bacon.
10.	Veal cake.
11.	Curried eggs.
13.	Apricot jam.
5.	Scones (buttered).

FEBRUARY 1ST, WEDNESDAY.

15.	Devonshire omelette.
15.	Lobster cutlets.
14.	Stewed potatoes.
24.	Oatmeal porridge.
4.	Milk rolls.
	Stewed gooseberries (bottled fruit).

FEBRUARY 2ND, THURSDAY.

17.	Russian gallimaufray.
21.	Salmi of game.
20.	Salmon and maccaroni.
4.	Hot milk rolls.
	Tinned apricots.

Receipt
on Page

FEBRUARY 3RD, FRIDAY.

22.	Beef olives.
22.	Bloaters in butter.
22.	Rolled calf's head.
28.	Anchovy breakfast cakes.
13.	Orange marmalade.

FEBRUARY 4TH, SATURDAY.

16.	Grenadines of veal.
14.	Stewed potatoes.
17.	Cold meat fritters (hot).
24.	Boiled hominy.
	Boiled bacon (cold).
13.	Strawberry jam.

FEBRUARY 5TH, SUNDAY.

16.	Kromeskies.
16.	Sweetbreads.
16.	Fish puddings.
17.	Potato patties.
14.	Stewed rhubarb.

FEBRUARY 6TH, MONDAY.

18.	Shrimp omelette.
27.	Kidneys à la maitre d'hôtel.
18.	Liver and bacon in paper cases.
27.	Oatmeal cakes.
38.	Normandy pippins.

FEBRUARY 7TH, TUESDAY.

24.	Egg kromeskies.
23.	Fried herrings.
23.	Scalloped lobster.
21.	Potato aux boulettes.
	Stewed gooseberries (bottled).

Receipt on Page	**FEBRUARY 8TH, WEDNESDAY.**
10.	Fried patties.
8.	Scotch woodcock.
9.	Fried bacon à l'Armstrong.
9.	Stewed mushrooms.
9.	Hot buttered toast.
11.	Quince marmalade.

FEBRUARY 9TH, THURSDAY.

3.	Sausages and chestnuts.
4.	Broiled mutton kidneys.
6.	Potted pheasant.
5.	Fleed cakes.
5.	Dried haddock.
	Jam.

FEBRUARY 10TH, FRIDAY.

9.	Baked eggs.
7.	Roman pie.
6.	Potted liver.
10.	Scotch collops.
9.	Hot buttered toast.
39.	Baked pears.

FEBRUARY 11TH, SATURDAY.

27.	Stewed jack.
34.	Rice and veal rissoles.
39.	Pheasant soufflé.
40.	Potted eggs with anchovy.
29.	Potato bread.

FEBRUARY 12TH, SUNDAY.

12.	Fried soles.
26.	Cheese trifles.
10.	Chicken rissoles au truffles.
32.	Bombay ducks.
39.	Anchovy paste.

Receipt on Page	
	FEBRUARY 13TH, MONDAY.
12.	Pork sausages.
11.	Eggs plain boiled.
38.	Suet pudding cut in slices and fried.
	Stewed apricots (bottled or tinned).
36.	Tomatoes scalloped.
11.	Potted shrimps.
	FEBRUARY 14TH, TUESDAY.
21.	Salmon cutlets.
35.	Hot deviled meat.
35.	Mushrooms in cream.
36.	American waffles.
14.	Stewed rhubarb and Devonshire cream.
	FEBRUARY 15TH, WEDNESDAY.
39.	Fresh herrings rolled and stuffed.
36.	Tomatoes scalloped.
8.	Scotch woodcock.
35.	Breakfast cakes.
13.	Orange marmalade.
	FEBRUARY 16TH, THURSDAY.
35.	Filleted soles.
35.	Grilled kippered salmon.
35.	Deviled oysters.
33.	Sheeps' tongues stewed.
13.	Scones.
	Bottled or tinned apricots.
	FEBRUARY 17TH, FRIDAY.
11.	Boiled eggs.
37.	Veal and potato rissoles.
34.	Potted hare.
36.	Deviled biscuits.
34.	Ox tails stewed.
9.	Hot buttered toast.

54   BREAKFAST DISHES

Receipt   **FEBRUARY 18TH, SATURDAY.**
on Page
33.   Fried salsify in batter.
33.   Reindeers' tongues.
34.   Cow heel fried.
 6.   Poached eggs and bacon.
28.   Breakfast cakes with anchovy.
13.   Strawberry jam.

                           FEBRUARY 19TH, SUNDAY.

34.   Beef fritters.
33.   Sheep's fry.
16.   Fish pudding.
24.   Oatmeal porridge.
                           Stewed bottled gooseberries.

                           FEBRUARY 20TH, MONDAY.

21.   Kidney balls.
21.   Fried smelts.
20.   Shrimps and boiled rice.
20.   Fried potatoes.
35.   Breakfast cakes.
                           Jam.

                           FEBRUARY 21ST, TUESDAY.

18.   Shrimp omelette.
16.   Sweetbreads.
16.   Fish pudding.
35.   Grilled kippered salmon.
                           Stewed fruit (apple).

                           FEBRUARY 22ND, WEDNESDAY.

20.   Salmon en papillote.
20.   Broiled cods' sounds.
20.   Hot beef pasties.
24.   Boiled hominy.
24.   Muffins.
39.   Stewed pears.

Receipt on Page	**FEBRUARY 23RD, THURSDAY.**
25.	Eggs en caisse.
24.	Shrimp pie.
25.	Corn-flour cakes.
25.	Pigs' trotters.
11.	Honey.

FEBRUARY 24TH, FRIDAY.

6.	Sardines on anchovy toast.
8.	Fried pork sausages on toast.
	Broiled slices of cod.
27.	Oatmeal cakes.
13.	Orange marmalade.
	Dry toast.

FEBRUARY 25TH, SATURDAY.

31.	Fillets de bœuf aux truffles.
11.	Boiled eggs.
6.	Potted lobster.
4.	Milk rolls.
	Bottled fruit (apricot).

FEBRUARY 26TH, SUNDAY.

31.	Boiled beef palates.
32.	Bombay ducks or mummalon fish.
31.	Kidney and onion.
12.	Fried bacon and eggs.
4.	Breakfast rolls.
38.	Stewed apple (Normandy pippins).

FEBRUARY 27TH, MONDAY.

31.	American oyster loaves.
35.	Kippered salmon.
9.	Broiled mushrooms.
34.	Beef fritters.
35.	Breakfast cakes.
14.	Stewed rhubarb.

Receipt on Page	
	FEBRUARY 28TH, TUESDAY.
28.	Broiled pheasant.
30.	Scalloped mussels.
8.	Pork sausage-meat cakes.
39.	Paté de foie gras.
35.	Breakfast cakes.
32.	Apple fool.
	FEBRUARY 29TH, WEDNESDAY.
30.	Birds' nests.
28.	Spatchcock.
28.	Stewed ducks' giblets.
24.	Oatmeal porridge.
29.	American breakfast bread.
13.	Strawberry jam.
	MARCH 1ST, THURSDAY.
29.	Veal rolls.
29.	Pig's cheek.
29.	Potato bread.
11.	Boiled eggs.
11.	Honey.
	MARCH 2ND, FRIDAY.
28.	Beef and onion fried in slices.
29.	Croquettes of brains.
28.	Curried mincemeat.
29.	Rice bread.
38.	Stewed apples (pippins).
	MARCH 3RD, SATURDAY.
30.	Bread and milk.
30.	Egg toast.
31.	Turbot and oyster loaves.
2.	Cold ham (baked).
27.	Oatmeal cakes.
13.	Marmalade.

BREAKFAST DISHES   57

Receipt on Page	MARCH 4TH, SUNDAY.
31.	Fried beef kidney.
10.	Patties.
25.	Egg en caisse.
13.	Strawberry jam.
13.	Scones.

MARCH 5TH, MONDAY.

26.	Hard-boiled eggs, sliced, with white sauce.
9.	Mushrooms on toast.
40.	Curried bullock's sweetbreads.
24.	Oatmeal porridge.
11.	Quince marmalade.

MARCH 6TH, TUESDAY.

33.	Red mullet.
8.	Chopped ox kidney, eggs, and maccaroni.
12.	Grilled chickens' legs.
32.	Apple fool.
18.	Cold sheep's head shape.

MARCH 7TH, WEDNESDAY.

19.	Stewed kidney.
20.	Salmon and maccaroni.
20.	Fried potatoes.
32.	Apricot fool.
39.	Paté de foie gras.

MARCH 8TH, THURSDAY.

33.	Broiled trout.
	Split and grilled pork sausages.
16.	Grenadines of veal.
30.	Breakfast rolls.
13.	Strawberry jam.

Receipt
on Page

March 9th, Friday.

24.	Oatmeal porridge.
20.	Hot beef pasties.
9.	Fried bacon à l'Armstrong.
21.	Salmon cutlets.
32.	Strawberry fool.

March 10th, Saturday.

10.	Scotch collops.
36.	Broiled lobsters.
11.	Curried eggs.
35.	Breakfast cakes.
	Stewed (bottled) gooseberries.

March 11th, Sunday.

37.	Fried skate and shrimp sauce.
25.	Curried pigs' feet.
4.	Breakfast cakes.
40.	Potted anchovy.
35.	Deviled hot meat.
9.	Hot buttered toast.
13.	Jam.

March 12th, Monday.

37.	Mackerel, stewed.
3.	Fowl pudding.
17.	Oyster fritters.
29.	Little hot loaves (American bread).
13.	Marmalade.

March 13th, Tuesday.

37.	Lobster scallops.
9.	Broiled mushrooms.
9.	Fried bacon à l'Armstrong.
10.	Veal cake.
14.	Stewed rhubarb.

Receipt on Page	**MARCH 14TH, WEDNESDAY.**
26.	Hard-boiled eggs, white sauce, and parsley.
40.	Tomatoes baked.
7.	Ham toast.
40.	Periwinkle patties.
13.	Scones.
11.	Honey.

MARCH 15TH, THURSDAY.

9.	Baked eggs.
10.	Curried sardines.
32.	Fried trout.
30.	Breakfast rolls.
38.	Stewed apples (pippins).

MARCH 16TH, FRIDAY.

23.	Stewed eels.
29.	Potato cakes.
39.	Paté de foie gras.
12.	Beefsteak pudding.
27.	Breakfast scones.

MARCH 17TH, SATURDAY.

18.	Crab omelette.
11.	Curried eggs.
19.	Stewed kidney.
39.	Anchovy paste.
24.	Hominy boiled.

MARCH 18TH, SUNDAY.

13.	Scones.
2.	Buttered eggs.
23.	Scallops of cod and oysters.
20.	Shrimps and boiled rice.
43.	Cauliflower in batter.

Receipt on Page	
	MARCH 19TH, MONDAY.
41.	Hot cross buns.
8.	Scotch woodcock.
21.	Salmon cutlets.
9.	Broiled mushrooms.
10.	Oyster patties.
	MARCH 20TH, TUESDAY.
18.	Liver and bacon in paper cases.
17.	Savoury rice pudding.
17.	Hard-boiled eggs and anchovy sauce.
14.	Stewed potatoes.
32.	Apple fool.
	MARCH 21ST, WEDNESDAY.
2.	Boiled rasher of ham.
10.	Curried tinned lobster.
11.	Plain boiled eggs.
19.	Italian puffs.
35.	Breakfast cakes.
11.	Quince marmalade.
	MARCH 22ND, THURSDAY.
36.	Omelette soufflé.
43.	Norfolk dumplings.
42.	Cold mutton sliced and fried with bacon.
42.	Stewed macaroni.
18.	Sheep's head shape.
13.	Jam.
	MARCH 23RD, FRIDAY.
20.	Pork and apple pasty.
42.	Baked stuffed haddock.
6.	Kedgeree.
42.	Shortbread.
	Stewed apricots (tinned).

BREAKFAST DISHES 61

Receipt on Page	**MARCH 24TH, SATURDAY.**
10.	Fried rissoles.
10.	Chicken patties.
25.	Corn-flour cake.
41.	Aspic jelly (very savoury).
32.	Strawberry fool.
41.	Brawn (cold).

MARCH 25TH, SUNDAY.

42.	Pressed calf's head and eggs.
42.	Baked mackerel.
12.	Boiled meat pudding (beefsteak).
7.	Golden eggs.
27.	Oatmeal cakes.

MARCH 26TH, MONDAY.

18.	Curry balls.
10.	Brain patties.
23.	Bloaters and crumbs.
13.	Scones.
32.	Apple fool.

MARCH 27TH, TUESDAY.

6.	Sardines on anchovy toast.
26.	Stuffed tomatoes.
10.	Lobster rissoles and fried parsley.
35.	Breakfast cakes.
39.	Paté de foie gras
	Bottled gooseberries.

MARCH 28TH, WEDNESDAY.

6.	Poached eggs on buttered toast.
23.	Fried herrings and onions.
41.	Rice and meat balls (pork).
11.	Potted shrimps.
39.	Tea-cakes.

Receipt
on Page

MARCH 29TH, THURSDAY.

38.	Cold duck stewed with peas.
32.	Lamb's fry.
24.	Oatmeal porridge.
41.	Graham cakes.
34.	Veal rissoles.
6.	Potted pheasant.

MARCH 30TH, FRIDAY.

38.	Lamb chops.
24.	Egg kromeskies.
32.	Grilled kidneys and lemon juice.
13.	Scones.
32.	Strawberry jam fool.
12.	Fried bacon.
39.	Fresh herrings stuffed.

MARCH 31ST, SATURDAY.

37.	Veal and potato rissoles.
16.	Angels on horseback (oysters).
37.	Madras anchovy toast.
34.	Cows' heel fried.
3.	Breakfast cakes.
32.	Apple fool.
22.	Bloaters in batter.

Index.

KITCHEN WARFARE

Fifty Breakfasts

Colonel Arthur Robert Kenney Herbert

Redolent with the taste of Empire, *pukka* Colonel Kenney Herbert's bracing book is the epitome of the manly, no-nonsense approach to cookery. He writes with aplomb and inclines to the kinds of offerings once described as 'dishes men like' such as Irish stew, along with recipes for colonial delicacies like Indian crumpets. A colourful figure, Colonel Kenney Herbert served as Military Secretary to the Governor of Madras and was a friend of the spiritualist Madame Blavatsky, whom he met at Ootacamund during a performance at which she turned one sapphire ring into two, as a demonstration of the power of Theosophy.

Colonel Kenney Herbert was the author of two classic works on colonial cookery, *Culinary Jottings for Madras* and *Wyvern's Indian Cookery Book*. On returning from India, he founded and directed the School of Common Sense Cookery in London.

Fifty Breakfasts

By
A. Kenney Herbert)
(*"Wyvern"*)
"CORDON ROUGE," AUTHOR OF "COMMONSENSE COOKERY," ETC.

FOURTH IMPRESSION

Introduction.

These little breakfast *menus* are designed for a family or party of six: each will be found to contain a dish of fish, a meat dish, and a dish of eggs, any two of which can be selected if three be considered too many. Seven of them are composed for days of abstinence. A plate of fancy bread is suggested for every *menu* to facilitate choice, recipes for which will be found in the Appendix.

The dishes that have been described will be found practicable by a large section of the community; for while many of the recipes as they stand may be suited to those with whom a very careful consideration of kitchen economy is unnecessary, by the exercise of a little discretion expensive adjuncts such as chopped ham, tongue, mushrooms, &c., can of course be very easily omitted without sacrificing much of the general tastiness of the dishes themselves, and thus bring them within the reach of all readers of the treatise.

It will be seen that I have propounded to a great extent tasty *réchauffés* of fish and meat rather than dishes requiring fresh ingredients. At first sight some of these may be considered troublesome, but I would here point out that, in order to provide nice little dishes for breakfast, it is absolutely necessary that the cook should effect some portion of their preparation on the evening of the previous day. She rarely has sufficient time in the morning for much delicate work of course, yet with a little forethought this can be combated, and the whole category of *croquettes, rissoles, pettis caises*, &c., be brought into play without difficulty. If the meat or fish required for such dishes be prepared and set in the sauce overnight the process the next morning is both simple and expeditious. In the same way hashes, stews, *ragoûts*, &c., can be re-heated in the *bain-marie*, and will be found all the better for having marinaded all night in their well-flavoured sauces. The "stitch in time" accomplished during the afternoon, or before the kitchen fire is let down at night, "saves nine" at the busy hour before breakfast the next day. Indeed the ding-dong monotony of "bacon and eggs" alternated with "eggs and bacon" of many English breakfast tables is wholly inexcusable, so easy is it to provide variety with the exercise of a little consideration.

For the "warming-up" process there is nothing so safe as the *bain-marie*. This is a utensil which it is to be hoped every one possesses. Stews, curries, hashes, &c., can thus be re-heated without deterioration, or fear of burning, boiling, or other mishap.

As another most capital thing for the preparation of breakfast dishes, I strongly advocate the use of the Dutch oven. This is an old-fashioned contrivance, no doubt, but cheap, and especially handy for the fast cooking of fish and heating *gratins*. It can be placed in front of the fire closely or at a slight distance according to the degree of heat required, and the cook can see how things placed within it are getting on. This alone gives it an advantage over the ordinary oven, while the food half-baked half-roasted by its means seems crisper and more appetising.

Baking dishes in sizes, *caisses,* and scallop shells of white fire-proof, Limoges ware are to be recommended for use in connection with breakfast. They can be set without risk in the Dutch or common oven, and afford a method of serving minces, re-cooked fish, eggs, and "remains," at once tasteful and inviting.

Fried fish is, as a rule, a popular thing for breakfast, and if the cook bear in mind that *second* frying by no means spoils fillets, &c., that may have been so cooked the evening before, she will readily fall back on this method of re-cooking them. A plunge of two or three minutes' duration into very hot fat is all that is required, followed by draining, drying carefully, and service on a hot napkin. Soles should be cross-cut in pieces two and a half inches wide, or filleted, and whitings are much nicer when not curled round in the manner so invariably adopted by London fishmongers.

A propos of frying, I take it for granted that in all well-regulated kitchens a supply of good, stale, oven-dried, and finely sifted white crumbs, as well as a bottle of well-rasped light-brown crust, is always kept ready for use. Fresh spongy crumbs are wholly unfit for "breading" cutlets, *croquettes*, fish, and so on. Finely grated, hard, dry, mild cheese—not necessarily Parmesan or Gruyére—should always be similarly stored.

An almost essentially necessary article in this branch of cookery is a *wire drainer*—such as confectioners use. Upon this *croquettes, rissoles,* fried fillets, even a fried sole, can be set to dry thoroughly after draining, for which purpose the drainer should either be placed in the mouth of the oven—the door ajar—or in front of the fire. For little *fritures* such as whitebait a wire frying basket is of course indispensable.

In composing the recipes given in this little series I have done my best to avoid perplexing generalities: "some" of this, "a little" of that, and so on. The quantity of each thing, either by weight or measure of capacity, has been put down as accurately as possible. Still it often happens that very small allotments such as the exact proportions of a seasoning must be given in conventional terms, as, for instance, "a pinch" of pepper. This quantity, to be very particular, might be counted as one-eighth of an ounce. Then a breakfast cup should hold half a pint, an afternoon tea-cup one gill and a half, a coffee-cup one gill.

I frequently mention "spiced pepper." This is a kind of herbaceous mixture which I strongly advise every cook to make for herself in the autumn each year when the herbs are finally gathered. It comes in most handily for seasonings in pies, forcemeats, stuffings, and in the flavouring of nearly every *réchauffé*. Mine, adapted from that of Gouffé, is made as follows:

DOMESTIC SPICED PEPPER.

One ounce of mixed thyme, marjoram, rosemary, and bay-leaf, carefully picked and thoroughly dried, pounded, and sifted, the mixture being allotted in these proportions, two thirds thyme and bay-leaf to one third marjoram and rosemary. Half an ounce of powdered mace, the same of nutmeg, a quarter of an ounce of finely ground black pepper, and one-eighth of an ounce of Nepaul pepper. Mix after carefully sifting each ingredient, and put the mixture into a well-dried bottle. This can obviously be doubled or increased to any extent.

One ounce of the above with four ounces of salt gives a useful "spiced salt."

A little wine is occasionally recommended in flavouring sauces, &c.; for this I have chosen Marsala, which, if of a reliable quality, is the best that can be used for domestic cookery, and, if the truth be told, the equivalent of Madeira at many a pretentious restaurant.

Cream is a very excellent thing—so excellent, indeed, that in the cookery of the present day its use is far too indiscriminate. In breakfast dishes it is to my mind quite out of place, while in the course of a dinner the less often it is introduced the better. Those who like it can of course direct their cooks accordingly.

The most wholesome and handy way of boiling eggs for the breakfast table may be thus described:—

Put a small saucepan over a methylated spirit lamp, which can be placed on a side table. When the water boils put in the eggs, and in ten seconds put out the lamp, covering the saucepan closely. In eight minutes an ordinary hen's egg will be ready, the albumen soft, and the yolk nicely formed. The common method of boiling eggs at a gallop for three minutes has the effect of over-cooking the albumen and rendering it indigestible, while the yolk is scarcely done at all.

Good tea and coffee are, it need scarcely be said, important elements of a good English breakfast. To secure them it is really necessary, after having chosen the tea and coffee that suit you best, to be liberal in dispensing them. A proper cup of either is out of the question if the allowance be too narrowly curtailed. The practice of doling out tea by carefully measured teaspoonfuls (handed down to us by our elderly maiden aunts) was perhaps necessary in the days when the only leaf in the market came from China and cost from four to five shillings a pound. The required strength was then obtained by the pernicious system of setting the tea "to draw." People now, however, have come to understand that to be wholesome tea must be produced by rapid infusion, not by a long process of steeping, and in order to get this at its best a good allowance of the leaf is necessary. Teapots are to be got with perforated cylinders to hold the tea, which can be withdrawn after an infusion of five minutes.

In this way a capital and quite harmless cup of tea can easily be produced.

For coffee-making there are numerous inventions more or less ingenious, but after all for really satisfactory, easy, and rapid action nothing surpasses the percolator—"Hutchinson's patent" for choice. A tablespoonful of coffee powder per breakfastcupful of coffee is a fair allowance.

Lastly, I would advise all who like things *hot* at breakfast to invest in one of Messrs. Wolff and Co's "universal heaters," sold at 119, New Bond Street, an excellent contrivance for keeping dishes, milk, coffee, &c., hot in the breakfast-room without deterioration, superseding the somewhat cumbersome practice of placing dishes before the fire, and of course a boon during the months when fires are dispensed with.

WYVERN.

LONDON, *Feb.* 5, 1894.

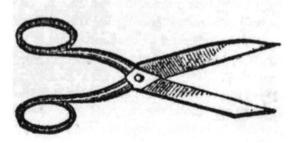

MENU I.

Baked fish in scallop shells.
Kidneys à la brochette.
Buttered eggs with vegetables.
Muffins.

This is to be composed of any cold fish and sauce left the previous evening. Pick the fish from the bones; measure the quantity (a pound will be enough for six nice scallops), add one third of its bulk of white crumbs; season with a **1. *Baked fish*** saltspoonful of spiced pepper and one of salt; let this rest awhile. Put ***in scallop*** the bones, skin, and especially the head, into a small saucepan, with ***shells.*** an onion sliced, a teaspoonful of salt, and six black peppercorns; cover this with milk and water (half-and-half), and stir into it a teaspoonful of anchovy sauce; set to boil, then simmer fifteen minutes; strain; thicken slightly, using half an ounce of butter and half an ounce of flour to a full breakfastcup of the broth; mix smoothly, stirring in any sauce that may have been left the previous evening. Now butter six scallop shells, or one medium-sized fire-proof baking dish; arrange the picked fish and crumbs therein, scattering a layer of finely minced parsley over it; moisten thoroughly with the sauce, strew a layer of crust raspings over the surface, heat up in the Dutch oven, and send up on a folded napkin.

N.B.—If the fish was boiled the previous evening, use the gelatinous water in which it was cooked instead of milk and water in preparing the sauce. Fish-boilings should never be thrown away.

The kidneys in this instance are broiled on skewers (*brochettes*—*i.e.*, little spits), which are *not* to be removed. Take six kidneys; cut six thin slices of bacon two

2. Kidneys inches long and an inch and a half wide; select three skewers (plated or
à la wooden) about seven inches long; mince a tablespoonful of parsley as
brochette. finely as possible; place an ounce of butter ready. See that the gridiron is
clean; warm, and oil it. Now cut open each kidney in the usual manner
without quite dividing the halves, peel off the skin, and pass the skewers through
them, two kidneys on each skewer, with a piece of bacon, threaded by the skewer,
over each kidney. Broil over a brisk fire, cooking the *cut* side of the kidneys first three
minutes, then the other side for three minutes. When done put the impaled kidneys
and bacon on a hot silver dish; melt the butter, stir in the minced parsley, add the juice
of half a lemon, and pour this over them. Serve as hot as possible.

Vegetables, such as greens, spinach, flower of cauliflowers, beans, peas, &c., that may
have been left the previous evening come in most usefully for breakfast. This is too
often overlooked. One ince way of serving them is on toast with a surface dressing
3. Buttered of buttered eggs. Melt half an ounce of butter, or put a coffeeecupful
eggs with of broth or milk into a saucepan, stir into it the vegetables, which, if
vegetables. greens, French beans, or cauliflowers, should be cut up rather small.
Season with papper, salt, and a dust of nutmeg, put into the *bain-marie*,
and when steaming hot turn them out neatly over six neat squares of fried bread laid
upon a hot dish, spreading the buttered eggs over them. A dusting of finely grated
cheese over the surface is an improvement.

Buttered eggs for six people:—Required six eggs, three ounces of butter, a small
coffeecupful of milk or good white sauce, a small saltspoonful of salt and the same of
white pepper. Melt half the butter in a roomy stewpan; break the eggs, mix, season,
and stir them into the butter over a low fire; whisk well with a whisk until *beginning*
to set, then add the other half of the butter and, changing the whisk for a wooden
spoon, continue stirring for two minutes longer, add the milk or sauce, when the
consistency will be correct. The addition of the second half of the butter should be
effected by degrees, to facilitate which it should be cut into small pieces beforehand.
The stirring must on no account be relaxed during the cookery of buttered eggs, and
the dish should not be kept waiting when ready. A spoonful of *Béchamel* sauce, if
available, may be used instead of the milk, or ordinary white sauce.

MENU II.

Fresh herrings au gratin.
Hashed mutton with fried bacon.
Omelette with herbs.
Scones.

Butter a flat *gratin* dish, sprinkle a layer of chopped parsley over its surface; lay four nice fresh herrings (trimmed and cleaned) upon this, season well with pepper and salt, shake a canopy a raspings and pour a few drops of melted butter over the upper sides of the herrings; put the dish thus prepared into the Dutch-oven, place this at a moderate distance from the fire, and watch the fish narrowly for a minute or two; baste with a little more melted butter, push nearer to the fire for the last minute, and serve the dish, as it is, on a folded napkin.

4. *Fresh herrings au gratin.*

For mustard sauce (if liked):—melt an ounce of butter in a saucepan; stir into it an ounce of flour; when thoroughly mixed add slowly, off the fire, a dessertspoonful of French mustard, incorporating it with the *roux* thoroughly; next add half a pint of water or broth, let it come to the boil, and pass through the pointed strainer into a hot sauce boat.

The hash ought to be prepared—partly—overnight, viz.:—cut up as much cold mutton in slices as will suffice for the party; trim off all skin and superfluous fat, dredge a layer of flour over the slices, and leave them for the present; next prepare the best sauce you can for your hash by boiling together the bones and trimmings of the mutton, an onion, a piece of celery, half a carrot, and a teaspoonful of dried sweet herbs, with half an ounce of glaze, or a teaspoonful of bovril, and sufficient water to cover all ingredients.

5. *Hashed mutton with fried bacon.*

When the best broth possible has been thus obtained, strain, thicken, and flavour it with one teaspoonful of red-currant jelly melted, a tablespoonful of vinegar from the walnut pickle, half a sherry-glass of Harvey sauce, half one of mushroom ketchup, and half one of *Marsala*. Put the sliced mutton into the sauce in a china vegetable dish, cover it from the dust, and set it in a cold larder till morning, when it will only require gentle heating up over a low fire, or in the *bain-marie*. It must on no account boil. Serve in a hot *entrée* dish with curls of crisply fried bacon and fried bread sippets as garnish.

I follow two methods of making an *omelette*. One I explain now, the other later on. This recipe is for an *omelette* "by the first intention"—a rapidly made and very digestible one. For six persons I recommend two small, rather than one large one, as being more manageable—especially at first. Nothing is more likely to produce a failure than an over-full pan. Break three eggs into one bowl, and three into another, put a saltspoonful of salt to each, with a dessertspoonful of chopped parsley, a teaspoonful of finely minced chives or shallot, one of chervil, and a pinch of pepper. Do not add milk, or cream, or water. Stir the eggs, and seasoning well together, and beat only sufficiently to effect mixture. Choose a roomy *omelette* pan not less than ten inches in diameter; see that it is dry and perfectly clean. Set it over a fast, clear fire, and put a lump of butter into it the size of a small hen's egg. Let this melt, and throw off all water; as soon as bubbling ceases the pan is hot enough; pour the contents of one of the bowls over its surface. At the moment of contact the part of the mixture nearest to the pan will set, gently lift this with a spoon, tip the pan over a little and let the unformed liquid run under it; this will also form; now give a few good shakes, and with your spoon coax the *omelette* to slide out of the *omelette* pan into the hot *entrée* dish ready for it. If carefully done the *omelette* will roll over, enveloping within it the partly formed mixture that remained on its surface, and on reaching the dish will spread itself rather, retaining no specially oval or bolsterlike shape, with a little of the juicy golden mixture escaping from its edges. *Omelettes* that are presented in neat crescent or elongated oval shapes are as a rule *puddings* in their consistency, over-cooked, and heavy.

6. Omelette with herbs.

After turning out the first *omelette,* wipe the pan, do not wash it, and repeat the same process with the second basin of mixture, sending the *omelettes* to table "hot and hot," so to speak. A small pat of butter, and chopped parsley should be put into the dish before the *omelette* is turned into it. Timed by the seconds-hand of a watch this *omelette* takes forty-five seconds from the moment of being poured into the pan to that of its being turned into the dish. Be sure that the pan is hot enough to receive the mixture in the first instance, and that the fire is brisk beneath it while frying; a powerful gas boiling-stove, circular in shape like the "Regina," is suitable for this work.

N.B.—If the chives and chervil were omitted this would be an *omelette au persil*. An *omelette aux fines herbes* is made with a totally different garniture.

MENU III.

Fried whitings; maître d'hôtel butter.
Devilled fowl; chutney sauce (Indian).
Ham toast, with poached eggs.
Hot rolls.

———————————

Bread-crumb and fry the whitings—four nice ones enough—using plenty of very hot fat, in a deep pan; dish them on a neat fish-paper, accompanied by plainly melted *maître d'hôtel* butter served in a hot boat.

For the butter, take two ounces of fresh Brittany, mix into it the juice of half a good lemon, and a dessertspoonful of finely chopped parsley, a pinch of white pepper, and half a saltspoonful of salt; form the pat with the butter-bat, and use as required; excellent with cutlets, &c.

7. Fried whitings; maître d'hôtel butter.

Assuming that the remains of a pair of fowls used at dinner the night previously are available, the following may be done: cut the birds up, neatly separating the thighs from the drumsticks, and dividing the backs in the usual manner. Shred an onion very finely; melt half an ounce of butter in a frying-pan, and fry the former till brown. Having meanwhile sprinkled the pieces of fowl with curry powder, and a dust of fine salt, put them into the pan with the butter and onions, turning them about to prevent burning. When the butter seems almost absorbed, turn the fowl and the onions with it into a hot dish. The operation after the pieces of fowl are put in should be conducted over a low fire, the object being to heat the meat thoroughly, and to serve it and the onions as dry as possible without burning. The onions can be brushed off if objected to before serving.

8. Devilled fowl; chutney sauce (Indian).

For the sauce: melt a quarter of an ounce of butter in a small saucepan, stir in a quarter of an ounce of flour; when blended well add a teacupful of gravy, or broth, mix, and put in a dessertspoonful of Harvey sauce, the same of mushroom ketchup, a teaspoonful of chilli vinegar, and a dessertspoonful of good chutney. For additional heat, a teaspoonful of finely chopped skin of green chillies may be added, carefully omitting the seeds. Boil, strain, and serve with the fowl as hot as possible.

Cut six squares of bread a quarter of an inch thick and large enough to hold a poached egg each. Fry these crisply and brown, and keep them hot. Pass sufficient lean ham through the mincing machine to yield a top-dressing for each "toast"; warm the mince in a small saucepan over a low fire, with half an ounce of butter, and moisten

9. Ham toast, with poached eggs. it with a spoonful of gravy or melted glaze. Keep this in the hot saucepan in the *bain-marie* while you poach six eggs; when they are ready, spread the mince on the fried bread, and place a poached egg on the surface of each, having trimmed the edges of the whites neatly all round. Send in quite hot.

MENU IV.

Fresh haddock, anchovy butter.
Mutton cutlets with broiled mushrooms.
Buttered eggs with tomatoes.
Bannocks.

Having procured a nice haddock the previous day, stuff it with veal stuffing, and keep it in a cold place during the night. In the morning, when wanted for breakfast, egg, and strew a thin layer of raspings over the fish, butter a fire-proof dish large enough to hold it, sprinkle a layer of chopped parsley over the bottom of the dish, and lay the fish upon it. Now set the Dutch oven in front of the fire, slip the dish into it, pour a few drops of butter-melted over, and watch the fish for a few minutes; try with a skewer if tender, and draw the dish back as soon as that occurs. Serve the fish steaming hot in the dish in which it was dressed with a pat of anchovy butter melting over it.

10. Fresh haddock, anchovy butter.

For anchovy butter *see* No. 7, and proceed in the same manner, mixing into the butter two pounded anchovies instead of the parsley and lemon juice. In a hurry, a good substitute may be made by melting an ounce of butter, and stirring into it a dessertspoonful of Moir's *anchovy vinegar,* an excellent preparation too little known and used.

11. *Mutton cutlets with broiled mushrooms.* For breakfast it will be found very time-saving if, for these cutlets, part of the best end of a neck of mutton were *slightly* roasted the previous day. On the morning required, with a sharp knife and meat-saw each little chop can easily be detached, trimmed, and then be either broiled, or breaded and fried, as may be desired. Serve the cutlets on a hot dish, accompanied by broiled mushrooms in a hot *entrée* dish.

Prepare the buttered eggs as described in No. 3, and serve them hot from the stewpan upon a bed of tomatoes dressed as follows:—

12. *Buttered eggs with tomatoes.* Choose six moderately sized tomatoes; blanch them in scalding water for three minutes to facilitate the removal of the skin, which having been done, take a small stewpan, put half an ounce of butter into it with one finely sliced half-ounce shallot; fry till beginning to turn golden, then empty into the pan the whole of the tomatoes sliced thinly; stir round, and add a teaspoonful of coarsely ground black pepper (fresh from a table-mill for choice), a saltspoonful of powdered dry *basil,* and one of salt. Continue the stirring for ten minutes over a fairly brisk fire to prevent catching, and the tomatoes will be ready. A tablespoonful of white sauce, or the yolk of a raw egg should be stirred in—off the fire—before final dishing up. It is quite unnecessary to pass this through the sieve. People fond of Continental cookery can direct that one clove of garlic be stewed with the tomatoes, uncut, to be picked out before serving.

MENU V.

Molé of brill (Indian).
Minced beef, with macaroni.
Eggs à la maître d'hôtel.
Brown flour scones.

This is a sort of fricassee. I presume that half (say a pound) a nice-sized brill has been left the previous evening. Detach all the meat from the bones, take the latter, and put them, with the skin and trimmings, an onion sliced, salt, six peppercorns, and a little mace, into a small stewpan, cover with the "boilings" (saved when the fish was first dressed), and boil, then simmer for a quarter of an hour; drain; put the broth thus obtained in a bowl handy. Meanwhile, when this was simmering, slice a shallot in thin rings, also a bit of garlic the size of a pea, fry these till yellow in an ounce of butter, dredge in an ounce of rice flour and teaspoonful of grated green ginger; slowly now add the warm fish-broth by degrees, and a tablespoonful of desiccated cocoanut (as sold for puddings) with a teaspoonful of lemon juice; let the sauce come to the boil, simmer for five minutes, colour it with a teaspoonful of turmeric, and then strain it through the block-tin strainer over the pieces of fish, which should have been placed ready in a stewpan to receive the moistening. Now gently warm up over a slow fire, garnish with strips of finely cut green skin of chilli, dish upon a hot dish, and serve steaming.

13. Molé of brill (Indian).

Boiled rice, if liked, may accompany the *Molé,* as it does in India *(see* No. 20).

14. *Minced*   This should be almost wholly prepared overnight. Pass as much
beef, with   cold beef as will yield ten tablespoonfuls of mince through the mincer.
macaroni.   Take one ounce of macaroni, or better still, the remains of a dish of
                 macaroni *au gratin* or *à l'Italienne* left from dinner. If the former,
it must of course be boiled. Take half a pint of broth, thicken and flavour it as
recommended in No. 5. Put the mince into it, and set it in a cold larder; also put
away the cooked macaroni. In the morning all you have to do is to butter a fire-proof
baking dish, and fill it with mince and cut-up macaroni, diluting the whole with a
little more gravy or broth, and shaking over the surface a layer of finely powdered
crumbs and grated cheese in half-and-half proportions. Heat this thoroughly and
send it up, in its own dish, upon a folded napkin.

15. *Eggs à*   Arrange six nicely poached eggs upon six squares of crisp, well-buttered
la maître   toast. Put a pat of *maître d'hôtel* butter upon the top of each egg the
d'hôtel.   size of a shilling, and send them up with the butter melting over them.
                For the butter, *see* No. 7.

MENU VI.

Fried smelts.
Grilled partridge, with potato chips.
Eggs à l'Indienne.
Oat-cakes.

A dozen smelts of moderate size will yield a nice dish for six. Egg and crumb them with finely sifted stale crumbs, and fry them one by one in very hot fat, drain on blotting-paper, and send them dry and crisp upon a fish-paper, with slices of lemon for garnish. If fried without colouring overnight they will be all the crisper when fried again in the morning.

16. *Fried smelts.*

Make sure when you order a grill that it is *grilled*—i.e., done on the gridiron. Grills are too often cooked in the frying-pan, and are unsatisfactory in consequence (*see* No. 29). Besides this, mark the difference between a grill and a "devil"; the former need not necessarily be highly seasoned or strongly peppered. The remains of four partridges of which part of the breasts alone have been used will give a nice dish of grill; let them be neatly cut up, then butter the pieces, sprinkle them with salt and black or white pepper, and cook them on the gridiron, which should be warmed and buttered to receive them. Dish them, piled up, in a hot *entrée* dish, and send a plate of potato chips with them. For chips, remember you use raw potato sliced thinly and evenly, dried carefully, and then boiled, as it were, in very hot fat.

17. *Grilled partridge, with potato chips.*

The pan should be deep and not wide, so as to ensure a *bath* of fat; not too many chips should be done at a time; do them in relays, drain, dry on a hot cloth in front of the fire and serve. For cutting chips an even thickness, Woolf and Co.'s "vegetable slicer" is a most handy instrument.

Œufs à l'Indienne are *poached* eggs smothered with a thickish curry sauce, and are not to be confounded with curried eggs. Prepare six squares of fried bread as in No. 9, lay a nicely poached egg upon each of them, and send them up at once with the

18. *Eggs à l'Indienne.*

following sauce poured evenly over them: Shred one shallot very finely, fry the slices in one ounce of butter, or clarified dripping, over a low fire till turning a pale brown; then mix with them a dessertspoonful of curry *paste* and a dessertspoonful of curry *powder*; mix, fry at least for five minutes, and stir in a teaspoonful of rice flour; dilute the jam-like paste now formed with broth or milk by degrees, stirring over a moderate fire till you have about a pint of liquid, add to this a dessertspoonful of desiccated cocoanut, a teaspoonful of sweetish chutney, with a small teaspoonful of salt. Let the sauce boil; skim off the scum, simmer for ten minutes, and then pass through the pointed strainer over the eggs. The English practice of spoiling all preparations of curries with sliced apples, green gooseberries, and other acids, should be carefully avoided: there is ample sub-acid in all good curry *paste*—viz., tamarind. In India it is not the custom to use acid adjuncts beyond this, or a little lime juice. This sauce can of course be made on the previous day.

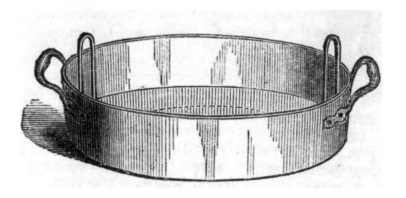

MENU VII.

ABSTINENCE.
Broiled mackerel.
Mushroom curry—rice.
Eggs in the dish.
Sally Lunus.

The mackerel must of course be split, laid open, and broiled. I recommend this sauce—a good one for all fatty fishes: Proceed as usual to make a breakfastcupful of melted butter sauce; when nice and smooth, stir in a tablespoonful of C. F. Buckle's "horse-radish zest," a pungent and well-flavoured composition very little known. The yolk of a raw egg—stirred in off the fire—is an improvement.

19. Broiled mackerel.

Having peeled, trimmed, and cleaned a dozen fairly large mushrooms, put them (overnight) to simmer gently in the curry sauce described for the eggs in No. 18 for half an hour. Keep in a china dish during the night, warm up, without actual boiling, in the morning, and serve in a hot *entrée* dish.

20. Mushroom curry—rice.

For the rice there is only *one* method, easily learnt. Having cleaned and sifted the rice—say six ounces—prepare a large vessel of boiling water, a gallon not too much, put into the water a dessertspoonful of salt, and the juice of half a lemon to preserve the whiteness of the grains. When the water is at a gallop—*fully boiling*—throw in the rice, and stir it round with a wooden spoon; watch the clock for ten minutes, stirring every now and then; after ten minutes, test a few grains by pinching them between the finger and thumb; as soon as soft, probably in twelve or thirteen minutes according to the size of the grains, stop the boiling instantly by a dash of cold water, immediately remove the vessel, and drain off every drop of the water from the rice, returning the latter to the now dry, hot pot in which it was boiled. Shake well, replace this upon the hot plate, or put it in front of the fire (a moderate heat required), and cover the rice with a folded cloth—do not use the lid—shake the vessel now and then, and after ten minutes' rest the rice will be fit to serve. The last process is necessary to dry and disintegrate the grains.

N.B.—Never *soak* rice before boiling, or put it into *cold* water, as some advise.

21. *Eggs in the dish.* Spread an ounce of butter on a fire-proof dish sufficiently presentable to send to table; sprinkle a thin dusting of salt and pepper over the surface, break six eggs carefully into the dish, dust a fine layer of salt over them, and set the dish on the hot plate with brisk heat beneath; pass the salamander over the surface of the eggs, so as to give heat above as well as below the dish, and in about four minutes, when the whites are set, the eggs will be ready. A dusting of finely grated cheese may be given over the eggs before serving if approved; send up in the dish in which they were cooked.

To obtain the appearance called *au miroir* the salt should only be sprinkled over the whites, and a teaspoonful of butter melted should be poured over the yolks. This can be set in the oven.

MENU VIII.

Fish cutlets.
Veal kidneys à l'Italienne.
Omelette with mushrooms.
Devilled biscuits.

To about a pound of any cold fish left at dinner cut up into a coarse mince, add four ounces of crumbs soaked in fish-boilings or stock, blend together, moistening with a breakfastcupful of warm sauce (that remaining after dinner should thus be used), with the yolk of an egg mixed into it. Stir the mixture over a low fire to thicken, then spread it upon a dish to get cold and set during the night. The mixture should be about half an inch thick when thus set. In the morning **22. *Fish cutlets.*** cut out of it as many cutlets as you can with a cutter; egg and bread-crumb them, and fry in boiling fat as explained for smelts in No. 16. Serve with a breakfastcupful of ordinary white sauce with this flavouring, a tablespoonful of Harvey sauce, a dessertspoonful of mushroom ketchup, and a teaspoonful of anchovy sauce.

Either broil the kidneys *à la brochette (see* No. 2) or crumb them, broiling four minutes on each side. For the sauce: thicken half a pint of gravy or stock with a quarter of an ounce of butter and a quarter of an ounce of flour, stirring in a tablespoonful of mushroom ketchup and a teaspoonful of anchovy **23. *Veal kidneys à l'Italienne.*** vinegar *(see* No. 10). Next slice up two tomatoes, boil up in the sauce, simmer for ten minutes, seasoning with a saltspoonful of salt and one of roughly ground fresh black pepper, then pass through the pointed tin strainer into a hot sauce boat. To this sauce *may* be added a mince composed of ham, mushroom, and parsley—a dessertspoonful each of the two former, and a teaspoonful of the latter, both of course previously cooked.

Make the *omelettes* as described in No. 6, omitting the herbs; having cut up four fairly sized mushrooms, or a quarter of a pound of any size, and fried the mince in butter immediately beforehand. Keep the mince hot in the pan in which it was

24. Omelette with mushrooms. cooked, and as soon as one *omelette* is ready to turn into the hot dish, rapidly pour half of the former over the surface of the latter, which will envelop it as it rolls over from the pan to the dish. Repeat the process with the second *omelette*.

MENU IX.

Fish Pudding.
Cold meat cutlets, with grilled bacon.
Eggs with anchovies.
Wholemeal cakes.

Pick about a pound of cold cooked fish free from bones, skin, &c. Make with the latter and any of the fish-boilings saved (flavoured with one onion sliced, pepper, salt, and a pinch of powdered mace), about a pint of nice broth; strain this. Next take of cold cooked potato the same bulk as you have of fish, and boil three *25. Fish* eggs hard. Measure two ounces of butter and a tablespoonful of minced *pudding.* parsley. Have the sauce left at dinner preserved for this. Empty the fish and potato into a roomy bowl and mash them together, adding the cold sauce, and moistening with the broth to get the mixture to work easily. Crush the hard-boiled eggs with a fork and add them to the fish and potato; mix a teaspoonful of salt with one of white pepper, and a saltspoonful of mace, and dust the seasoning into the mixture; stir in the parsley and butter, and lastly a tablespoonful of milk. All being blended, put the pudding into a buttered mould, put this into a pan with boiling water round it half the depth of the mould, heat it thoroughly in the oven, and then turn it out carefully; shake some fine crust raspings over it, and send to table. If liked, ordinary melted butter and anchovy sauce may accompany in a boat.

These are to be made with any cold cooked meats—overnight—in the *26. Cold* same manner as the fish cutlets described in No. 22. Serve them with *meat cutlets,* fried parsley and tiny rolls of crisply fried bacon. Any brown sauce left *with grilled* at the previous evening's dinner may be warmed up to accompany. *bacon.*

27. *Eggs with anchovies.* Prepare six squares of crisply fried bread, as in No. 9, butter them with anchovy butter (*see* No. 10). Put a nicely poached egg on each square thus buttered, and lay two little strips of anchovies, cut from the filleted fish, crosswise, on the top of each egg.

MENU X.

Fried soles—capers butter.
Devilled turkey.
Eggs with vegetable marrow.
Tea-cake, not sweetened.

For breakfast it is desirable to cut the soles into pieces, across— say two inches wide; to egg and bread-crumb these, and fry them as explained for smelts (No. 16). Serve after draining and drying in the same manner.

28. Fried soles —capers butter.

For capers butter *see* No. 7, and proceed in the way therein given, mixing into the butter a dessertspoonful of well-pounded capers instead of the parsley and lemon.

On Grills and Devils.—For breakfast few dishes are more popular than these, while the excellence of devilled bones for a *very* late supper need hardly be mentioned. The utensil necessary for their preparation is the *gridiron*. Many cooks spoil their grills by using the frying-pan, for though the bones may be served in a wet as well as in a dry form, they must be themselves broiled over a clear fire. The meat attached to the bone, whether a turkey leg, or the bones of a saddle of mutton, must be scotched with a sharp knife criss-crosswise, and bountifully peppered with this seasoning:— one teaspoonful of Nepaul pepper, one teaspoonful black pepper coarsely ground, two teaspoonfuls of salt, mixed well together. Following these proportions a bottle of "grill-seasoning" can be made, and labelled for use when required. Mix your mustard for your grill with Worcester sauce instead of water or vinegar, and if you want "the very devil" of a grill, add to it six drops of *Tabasco*. Smear this over the seasoned bones, rub the bars of the gridiron

29. Devilled turkey.

with butter, lay the bones thereon, and grill them. If here and there they scorch a little, so much the better. Serve without delay "from the grid to the plate," so to speak. This is a dry grill. For a wet grill proceed exactly as directed for the dry, but roll the bones, after broiling them, in a *sauté pan* for a few minutes in this sauce:—

Devil Sauce.—Take a breakfastcupful of gravy, or a broth made from scraps, and half an ounce of glaze or a teaspoonful of Brand's essence; put this into a saucepan and add to it a tablespoonful of hot yet sweetish bottled chutney, a tablespoonful of mustard mixed with Worcester sauce, a tablespoonful of mushroom ketchup, a tablespoonful of Marsala, half a teaspoonful of red-currant jelly, and a teaspoonful of chilli vinegar; heat all together to melt the jelly and blend the ingredients, then strain, and thicken with half an ounce of butter, and half an ounce of flour, heat this up to boiling point in a frying-pan, and roll the grilled bones in it off the fire, serving them quickly with the rest of the sauce in the pan poured over them.

A moderately sized young vegetable marrow, cold boiled, and six hard-boiled eggs will be wanted for this dish. Cut the marrow into fillets freed from seeds, one and a half inch long, three-quarters of an inch wide, and the depth of the marrow; slice each egg in half longitudinally; take the water in which the marrow was boiled (an onion

30. *Eggs with vegetable marrow.*
boiled with it would have been an improvement), and using an ounce of butter and one of flour proceed to thicken it; season with a saltspoonful of black pepper, half one of powdered mace, and a teaspoonful of salt: add a tablespoonful of chopped parsley and a teaspoonful of chopped chervil. Now arrange the eggs and fillets of marrow neatly in a hot *entrée* dish, add a tablespoonful of milk, with which one raw yolk has been well mixed, to the sauce off the fire, and pour it over the fillets and eggs, steaming hot.

MENU XI.

Fish fritters.
Kidneys stewed with mushrooms.
Eggs "mollets" with "ravigote."
Muffins.

For these fritters, which will be found very tasty, about half a pound of any cold fish, such as whiting, fresh haddock, gurnard, or plaice, that will pound easily, will be enough. A batter must be made as follows: Beat up the yolks of four eggs with two tablespoonfuls of beer, one tablespoonful of salad oil, and five *31. Fish* tablespoonfuls of water. Having pounded the fish well, mix it with the *fritters.* beaten eggs, &c., and add a saltspoonful of salt, and enough flour to bring the mixture to the consistency of a thick batter. Put the frying fat into a small but deep pan, and while it is heating, beat up the whites of the eggs to a stiff froth, add this to the batter the last thing, and then, when the fat is *very* hot, proceed to put about a tablespoonful of the mixture into it at a time. The batter will frizzle up at the moment of contact, and assume an irregular shape. Each fritter having been cooked a rich golden brown, should be drained with a perforated slice and laid on a hot cloth to dry before dishing. Pile the fritters on a hot dish, and serve with slices of lemon.

About three-quarters of a pint of good broth or gravy, six kidneys, and six medium-sized mushrooms are wanted, and the preparation should take place on the previous day. Take a stewpan and commence by thickening the gravy in the usual manner, then add the kidneys cut into slices; stew them very *32. Kidneys* slowly; if allowed to boil they will be as tough as leather. After they *stewed with* have simmered for about half an hour put in the mushrooms, with *mushrooms.*

a teaspoonful of salt and one of black pepper, and half a sherry-glass of mushroom ketchup; continue the stewing now till the kidneys are done, then put the stew into a china dish to keep till the next day. In the morning put it into a stewpan, and if any additional liquid is necessary add a little milk; warm up in the *bain-marie*. When ready to serve, stir in a dessertspoonful of Marsala.

Boil six eggs for exactly four minutes; put them at once into cold water; when cold carefully remove the shells; the eggs will be soft to the touch, the yolks inside them not having hardened. Have ready a pint of nice white sauce seasoned with pepper and spiced salt; flavour this with a tablespoonful (mixed) of finely *33. Eggs* chopped tarragon, parsley, chives, and chervil, and sharpen it with *"mollets" with* a dessertspoonful of anchovy vinegar; put the eggs on a hot dish, *"ravigote."* and pour the sauce boiling hot over them. Serve.

MENU XII.

Fish custard puddings.
Purée of grouse in scallops.
Eggs with mushrooms.
Scones.

These are tasty little fish puddings very easily made. Any cold fish will **34. *Fish*** do. Choose six *dariole* moulds, fluted or plain; butter them, and sprinkle ***custard*** a layer of finely minced, dry parsley over this lining. Make enough ***puddings.*** ordinary thick custard to fill the moulds about half full each, seasoning it with salt and pepper instead of sugar. Pick the cold fish free from bones and skin, and cut it up into a coarse mince; dust into this a saltspoonful of spiced pepper; fill the moulds loosely with this, and then pour the custard over each, allowing time for it to settle well, and adding more custard till the moulds are filled; put a round of buttered paper over each of them, and place them in a *sauté* pan with enough boiling water round them to poach them nicely. When set, pick off the papers, and turn the moulded custards out. A saltspoonful of anchovy sauce may be stirred into the custard before filling the moulds if liked. Excellent with cold salmon.

Pick and mince the meat from the birds overnight, and make as much well-flavoured broth from the bones as you can. This having been prepared, the work the next morning will be quickly done. Simply thicken the broth, flavour it with half a teaspoonful of red-currant jelly and a dessertspoonful of Marsala, season it with salt, and a teaspoonful of spiced pepper. Then stir in the mince, keep **35. *Purée*** it hot in the *bain-marie* while you butter six scallop shells, into which, ***of grouse in*** when ready, pour the mince, shake a layer of pounded crumbs over ***scallops.***

the surface of each, and heat well in the oven or Dutch oven; brown the crumbs with a salamander, and send up.

36. *Eggs with mushrooms.* On six squares of fried bread place six nicely poached eggs, pouring over each about a tablespoonful of this sauce. Stew four medium mushrooms, or a quarter of a pound of small ones, in milk, having first cleaned them carefully and cut them up into a coarse mince; season with pepper and salt; when ready stir in a tablespoonful of milk with which a raw yolk has been mixed, off the fire, and use as directed.

MENU XIII.

Fried flounders, tomato butter
Curry cutlets, chutney sauce
Eggs with green peas.
Bannocks.

Procure enough flounders for the party, and fry them as explained for **37. *Fried*** smelts (No. 16); serve drained dry on a hot dish lined with a fish-paper, ***flounders,*** and this butter on a plate: To two ounces of Brittany butter add a good ***tomato*** tablespoonful of French tomato *conserve* (it is much thicker than sauce), ***butter.*** season if necessary, and work them together with the butter-bat. A little of this should be taken as an adjunct with the fish, and allowed to melt over it.

Prepare overnight enough minced veal, mutton, lamb, or even mixed meats—partly of fowl and mutton, for instance—as will suffice for half a dozen good cutlets. Dilute this with the sauce given for No. 18, using gravy or broth instead of milk, and stirring into it the yolks of two raw eggs; thicken gently over a low fire, carefully **38. *Curry*** avoiding boiling, then turn the mixture out upon a dish, patting it into ***cutlets,*** a rectangular shape, a quarter of an inch thick, with a wooden spoon; ***chutney*** set this aside in a cool place for the night. In the morning it will be quite ***sauce.*** firm; cut out of it six or eight neat cutlets with your cutter, bread-crumb and fry them a golden brown, and serve with them the sauce given for No. 8.

If fresh peas are not available—those left from the previous evening's **39. *Eggs*** dinner, for instance—a very nice dish for a change can be made with a ***with green*** small tin of French *petits pois* in this way: Open the tin, and placing a ***peas.*** block-tin strainer over a bowl, empty the contents of the tin into it, drain thoroughly, catching all the liquid: next, with half an ounce of butter and half an ounce of flour make a thickening at the bottom of a small stewpan over a low fire; when smooth add the liquid from the tin, stir well, increasing the heat and adding a coffeecupful of milk; bring to the boil, and when nice and thick put in the peas with a saltspoonful of salt, one of sugar, and half one of white pepper. Now set the stewpan in the *bain-marie*. When required turn the peas with their sauce into a hot *entrée* dish, and lay on the surface six nicely poached eggs, garnishing with sippets of fried bread. A spoonful of cream may of course be added just before dishing the peas.

MENU XIV.

ABSTINENCE.
Khitchri (Indian).
Macaroni à la Livornaise.
Eggs in white sauce.
Sally Lunns.

This dish, from which the so-called "kedgeree" of English cookery books was doubtless taken, was originally a dish of rice cooked with butter and an Indian pea called *dál*, but now it may either be composed of cold cooked fresh fish, or of salt fish that has been soaked and either boiled or fried. Choose which you prefer—about one pound will be enough—and with a fork divide it into small pieces. Boil six ounces of rice, as explained for No. 20. These preparations can be made overnight. Boil three eggs hard, and with a 40. *Khit chri (Indian).*

fork crush them, whites and yolks together, to a coarse mince. Melt over a low fire three ounces of butter, and fry a very finely minced shallot therein till it is a yellow colour; now stir in the rice, using a wooden spoon, and the pieces of fish, season with pepper and salt and sufficient *turmeric* (about a teaspoonful) *to tint the rice a nice light yellow colour;* lastly, shake into the mixture the crushed hard-boiled eggs, and empty the whole into a very hot dish.

N.B.—Both onions and turmeric may be omitted, if it be desired, without prejudice to the mixture generally.

Boil six ounces of macaroni; stew six medium-sized mushrooms in milk, and season them with pepper and salt. Make a breakfastcupful of tomato *purée*. Put a layer of macaroni in a well-buttered, fire-proof baking dish, moisten it with some of

41. *Macaroni*   the *purée,* put a little of the stewed mushroom over that, and then
à la   another layer of macaroni, finally dusting the surface over with a
Livornaise.   layer of grated cheese. Bake, and send up very hot.

Six hard-boiled eggs sliced in halves longitudinally, a pint of white sauce, seasoning
of pepper, salt, and powdered dried herbs. A tablespoonful of milk with the yolk of
an egg beaten up with it. Season the pieces of egg, and arrange them on
42. *Eggs in*   a hot *entrée* dish; heat the sauce very hot, stir into it, off the fire, the
white sauce. tablespoonful of milk, &c., and pour it over the eggs. Serve.

MENU XV.

Smoked brill.
Mutton kidneys bread-crumbed.
Eggs in cases.
Oatmeal cakes.

This method of serving fish for breakfast is a *spécialité* at the Bombay and Madras clubs. I recommend its trial with brill because that fish is more like the Indian "pomfret" than any other English fish; at the same time the system is applicable to any kind of flat fish or slices of fish, from salmon downwards. Choose a fish of about a pound and a half or two pounds. **43. *Smoked brill.***
Take the flesh from the bones as you do the fillets of a sole, trim them neatly, and dry them with a cloth. Now prepare a fire of cocoanut fibre (procurable at Treloar and Sons, 70, Ludgate Hill); when damped it makes a great volume of smoke; place the gridiron over the fire, but well in the smoke, butter the fish fillets on both sides, lay them side by side on the gridiron, covering them, as they are cooking in the vapour, with the lid of a tin fish-kettle to concentrate the smoke. In about ten minutes the fish will turn a rich warm brown on the side nearer the fire; then turn it and smoke the other side, which will take about five minutes. The fillets can now be served with any plain sharp sauce. The process can be conducted in an ordinary fire-grate if the kitchen range be a closed one, and in smoke produced from damp clean straw, or shavings laid on a wood fire.

44. *Mutton kidneys bread-crumbed.*

Breaded kidneys. Six kidneys will do for the party. Proceed as laid down for kidney *à la brochette* (No. 2). Skewer them, omitting the bacon; egg and bread-crumb them, boil over a bright, clear fire, and serve on the skewers, garnished with crisply fried curls of bacon. The sauce given for No. 23 will do.

Choose six little scallop shells, or mince-pie patty-pans; put into each a piece of butter the size of a cobnut, and a teaspoonful of minced *"fines herbes"*—*i.e.,* chopped

45. Eggs in cases. mushroom, chopped parsley, and finely chopped stem of fresh green onion, or chives, the proportion of the mixture being equal measure of the first two ingredients to one-third of the measure of the last. Warm the shells over the hot plate, and when the butter has melted break an egg into each of them; shake a layer of finely sifted bread-crumb over the surface, and keep over moderate heat till the eggs set, then brown them with the salamander, and serve.

MENU XVI.

Fricassee of cod and oysters.
Rissoles of ham and chicken.
Omelettes with tomatoes.
Buttered toast.

Presuming that the fish for dinner has been cod and oysters, a fricassee of what remains of them will be nice for breakfast the next day. Pick the meat in firm, flaky pieces from the bones; put the former aside, while with the latter and the fish-boilings you make a strong broth, using an onion and seasoning to assist the operation; strain and turn this into a moderately thick white sauce, and flavour it with a teaspoonful of essence of anchovy. Now arrange the cod in a stewpan, moisten it with the sauce, and heat it gently up in the *bain-marie* to steaming point; lastly, add the remaining oyster sauce, and empty the fricassee into a hot *entrée* dish. Or the mixture may be put into a fire-proof dish, dusted over with raspings, and baked.

46. Fricassee of cod and oysters.

These can be made the previous day, and can be easily heated for breakfast. Having prepared your *salpicon,* or coarse mince of ham and chicken (a quarter of a pound of the former to half a pound of the latter), with a good thick sauce, in which the yolks of two raw eggs have been mixed, roll out rather thinly half a pound of nice puff paste, and out of it cut six or eight circular pieces four inches in diameter. Put a tablespoonful of the *salpicon* upon each of these, turn over the paste, and wet and pinch the edges all round. The *rissoles*—now of a semi-circular or cocked-hat shape—should be plunged

47. Rissoles of ham and chicken.

into very hot fat and fried fast. The next day let them be heated on a hot napkin in the Dutch oven. Fried parsley is the usual garnish, and a boat of tomato sauce a good accompaniment. Please note that bread-crumbed mixtures of meats *(croquettes)* are not *rissoles,* though often called by that name.

I will now give you the variation in *omelette*-making promised in No. 6. Select a roomy *omelette* pan; see that it is clean and dry; break, one after another, five eggs,

48. Omelettes with tomatoes. carefully separating the yolks from the whites; put these into separate basins, whisk the whites to a stiffish froth, and mix the yolks well with a fork. Place the pan on the fire with half an ounce of butter; let this get hot as for the *omelette* in No. 6, and when it is ready quickly amalgamate the contents of the two bowls and pour the mixture into the pan; let it alone for three minutes, shake, and turn the *omelette* over upon a bed of tomatoes, as explained for No. 12. The minced herbs mentioned in No. 6 can be stirred in with the yolks if liked, and a teaspoonful of salt should be mixed with them also.

If you possess a glazing-iron, heat it, and pass it closely above the surface of the *omelette* while the bottom is setting. In any case the upper side remains frothy, and is buried as the *omelette* laps over in dishing. It is as light as a *soufflé,* and sweet *omelettes* thus cooked are excellent.

N.B.—Owing to the frothiness of the mixture a large pan is necessary. If this be not available it will be safer to divide the mixture, putting it into two bowls separately, and to cook each independently. The fire should not be too fierce.

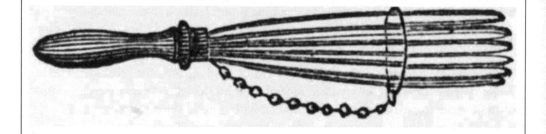

MENU XVII.

Sardines au gratin.
Crêpinettes or mixed game.
Eggs with prawn butter.
Devilled biscuits.

Accidents may sometimes occur when it may be found very convenient to fall back on the tin of sardines. On such an occasion this will be found a useful recipe:— Carefully lift out a dozen sardines one by one, lay them on a medium-sized joint dish, separately; tip the dish up, and pour gently over the little fish a stream of very hot water, to carry off the fishy oil; pour this *49. Sardines au gratin.* off once or twice, drain, and the sardines will be clean. Now choose a flat *gratin* dish, or fire-proof baking dish, butter it liberally, and strew over the butter a goodly sprinkling of the *"fines herbes"* given in No. 45. Lay the sardines on this bed, putting a saltspoonful of the *herbes* on each of them, dredge lightly over all a dusting of fine salt and white pepper mixed together, pour a few drops of melted butter over them, and a thin layer of crust raspings; heat thoroughly in the Dutch oven, and serve.

Although the term is usually applied to preparations of minced meats, wrapped in pig's caul, crumbed, and fried, a *crêpinette* is literally a thing frizzled, or made crisp, and pancakes are very useful as envelopes for *salpicon* of any kind. Make two or three ordinary thin pancakes plainly seasoned with salt and pepper instead of sugar, and a sprinkling of finely chopped parsley. Let them get cold, then cut out of them a dozen pieces five inches long and four *50. Crêpinettes* wide; lay these on a floured pastry board, brush a coating of white *of mixed* of egg over the upper surface, upon this put a good tablespoonful of *game.*

hare, grouse, partridge, or mixed game *purée,* moistened with a thick brown sauce, as given for No. 35, and roll the pancake up as you would a sausage-roll. A very thin slice of cold cooked bacon may be laid over each of the *crêpinettes* first, and the mince over it. This much can be done the evening before. To prepare the *crêpinettes* for the table: Egg and bread-crumb them, and either fry them in boiling fat, or bake them. Curls of fried bacon can accompany them.

Poach the eggs, lay them on squares of fried bread, and send them up with a pat of this butter melting over them: Choose six nice boiled prawns; pick them; pour a jug of cold water over the shells and meat also; when quite clean pound meat and shells *51. Eggs with* together in a stone mortar, using an ounce of butter to assist the *prawn butter.* pounding. When thoroughly pounded pass the paste through a hair-sieve into a bowl of cold water, skim it off the water, drain it, and add it to another ounce of butter with the butter-bat, seasoning it with a saltspoonful of salt, white pepper, and mace blended. Shrimps may be substituted for prawns.

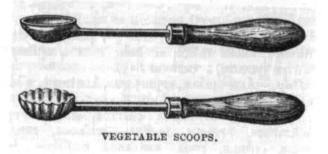

VEGETABLE SCOOPS.

MENU XVIII.

Fried plaice, shrimp butter.
Fowl (or turkey) marinaded.
Eggs in bread sauce.
Tea-cake—not sweetened.

Skin and trim a plaice, dividing it into fillets two inches and a half long, and one and a half wide: marinade them all night, as recommended in No. 73. In the morning wipe them dry, egg, bread-crumb, and fry these as explained for smelts (No. 16). Serve on a neat fish-paper garnished with slices of lemon, and send in with them a little plate of shrimp butter made as explained for prawn butter (No. 51).

52. Fried plaice, shrimp butter.

Cut up a chicken or half a large fowl into neat pieces as for fricassee. Put these overnight into a soup-plate in a *marinade* composed of two tablespoonfuls of salad oil, two of vinegar, one finely sliced shallot, one inch length of celery shredded, a dozen peppercorns, a sprig of parsley chopped, and a saltspoonful of salt. In the morning drain the pieces, dry them, prepare a bath of boiling fat, dip the pieces in frying batter (No. 116), fry a golden brown; drain, dry, and pile upon a napkin.

53. Fowl (or turkey) marinaded.

Flavour a pint of milk as you would for bread sauce—*i.e.*, cut in quarters and blanch a three-ounce onion in boiling water for five minutes, drain the pieces and simmer them in the milk with six cloves and a saltspoonful of salt. When nicely flavoured turn the milk into a white sauce, with half an ounce of butter and the same of flour. Choose a large fire-proof baking dish, butter it, pour over the bottom of it a layer of the sauce at least a quarter of an inch

54.· Eggs in bread sauce.

deep; over this strew a layer of pounded bread crumbs seasoned with salt, pepper, and mace blended. Put the dish in the oven for a few minutes to heat without boiling, take it out and slip into it carefully, without breaking one of them, six eggs; dust a layer of very fine raspings over the surface, and return the dish to the oven just long enough for the eggs to set. Grated cheese may be mingled both with the crumbs and the raspings if liked.

MENU XIX.

Dried haddock, with egg sauce.
Devilled kidneys.
Curried eggs.
Vienna rolls.

Soak and boil the haddocks (two required, if small) till the meat can be   *55. Dried*
picked easily from the bones and skin; make a good pint of egg sauce   *haddock,*
slightly flavoured with anchovy, arrange the picked haddock on a very   *with egg*
hot dish, season it with a little salt and black pepper, pour the egg sauce,   *sauce.*
steaming hot, over it, and serve.

Impale the kidneys as described in No. 2, give them a broil for two minutes, then
roll them on a dish, upon which you have spread a thin layer of   *56. Devilled*
made mustard; now dust over the mustard-coated kidneys a good   *kidneys.*
seasoning of salt and black pepper, and continue the broiling till they
are done. Serve with the sauce given in No. 8.

Curried eggs differ from eggs *à l'Indienne* (No. 18), inasmuch as they are hard-boiled,
while the latter are poached, and are simmered *in* the curry sauce, not merely covered
with it as the poached eggs are. Boil overnight six eggs hard, slice   *57. Curried*
them when cold in halves longitudinally, cut twelve nice fillets of cold   *eggs.*
cooked vegetable marrow or stewed cucumber, each piece to be about

the size of one of the half eggs. Prepare a curry sauce as given for No. 18, put into it the eggs and pieces of marrow, and slowly heat them up to steaming point; let them rest all night thus prepared, and simply re-heat the dish in the morning. The curry will be far better if allowed thus to *marinade* for twelve hours in its own sauce. Fried ham or bacon may accompany.

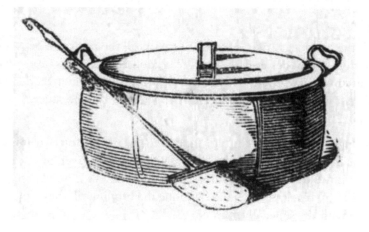

MENU XX.

Lobster cutlets à la Turque.
Irish stew à la Wyvern.
Poached eggs with Italian sauce.
Barley meal scones.

Either fresh or tinned lobster may be used. Take enough lobster to form, with an addition of one-third of its bulk of panada, about six or eight nice cutlets; season the mixture, after pounding an mixing it well, with salt, white pepper, and *58. Lobster* mace blended; moisten it over a low fire with white sauce (in which *cutlets à la* the raw yolk of egg has been mixed) for a few minutes to thicken, *Turque.* and let it set firmly in a dish. Thus much having been done overnight, procced the next morning to form the mixture into cutlets or balls and cook in the manner described for No. 22. Rice *à la Turque* should accompany—*i.e.*, "yellow rice" thus prepared: Boil six ounces of rice according to the directions for it in No. 20, then drain, shake over it a teaspoonful of turmeric powder, mixing it well into the rice; a dust of nutmeg may be also given. Pile the rice on the hot dish prepared for it, and arrange the cutlets or balls round it. If liked the sauce mentioned for No. 8 may accompany.

I adopt a slightly different way of making Irish stew, which I think may be liked. Take the best end of the neck of mutton, cut from a small-sized sheep and not too fat. Divide this into eight or ten equally sized cutlets, and put them into a large stewpan with eight ounces of onions, four of carrots, four ounces of turnip, and *59. Irish* an ounce of celery, with a seasoning of salt and black peppercorns. Bring *stew à la* once to the boil and then simmer slowly for an hour. When nicely done, *Wyvern.* and the meat quite tender, strain off the broth, and set it to get cold and throw up the fat; put the cutlets on a dish, and the onions on another separately. Now peel and boil two and a half pounds of potatoes, which, when ready, drain and mash in their own hot saucepan, mashing the onions from the stew with them, and moistening the whole with enough of the now skimmed broth to bring the vegetables to the consistency of a good *purée*. If required, a little more salt and freshly ground black pepper seasoning can now be added. Next put the cutlets into a stewpan, add a spoonful or two of the broth to the *purée* of potato and onions, pour this over the meat, and slowly heat up the stew to steaming point. Dish in this way: arrange the cutlets in a row in a hot silver dish, and mask them with the *purée*. Some add milk or cream to Irish stew, but I do not think it necessary. In my way you have all the flavour of the mutton broth and *no grease,* while the potato is creamy and free from lumps, with the onion *there,* but not *en evidence.*

60. *Poached eggs,*   Put six poached eggs on six squares of fried bread, and pour
with Italian sauce.   enough of the sauce given in No. 23 to cover each nicely.

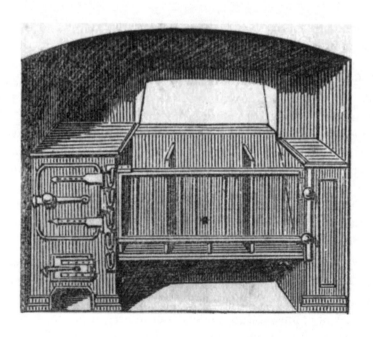

MENU XXI.

ABSTINENCE.
Fillets of sole, with shrimps.
Spaghetti à la Milanaise.
Omelette with artichokes.
Muffins.

Have a good-sized sole neatly filleted. Order the bones and trimmings to be sent in with the fish, and with them make a good fish broth. Also order half a pint of picked shrimps, mince them not too finely, and season the mince with salt, white pepper, and a pinch of mace. Lay the fillets on a board, brush the upper sides of them with white of egg, and spread over each a coating of the mince after having moistened it with a quarter of a pint of white sauce made with the fish broth and thickened with a raw egg. Roll up the fillets and poach them in the remaining broth to set the farce. Let them get cold. If thus prepared overnight they can be lightly floured or bread-crumbed and fried for breakfast, anchovy or shrimp butter accompanying.

61. Fillets of sole, with shrimps.

Spaghetti seems more delicate than macaroni. Weigh six ounces of it and boil the spaghetti till tender,[1] then drain; while hot, and in the same saucepan, quickly melt a couple of ounces of butter into it, stir it well about with a wooden spoon, flavour it with a teaspoonful of spiced pepper, and finish with three ounces of grated cheese; stir all together vigorously, and then serve piled up on a hot dish, steaming.

62. Spaghetti à la Milanaise.

Cut six artichoke bottoms into six pieces each, toss them in chopped parsley and butter, seasoning with white pepper and salt; make an *omelette* in either of the ways

63. *Omelette with artichokes.* already explained. Dish as follows: Melt a pat of butter at the bottom of the hot *entrée* dish, put in the artichokes, upon them lay the *omelette,* and serve.

[1]Boil macaroni or spaghetti exactly as you do rice (No. 20) for all ordinary purposes. It should be firm not pulpy.

MENU XXII.

Whitings au gratin.
Little moulds of ham and chicken.
Buttered eggs with grated beef.
Wholemeal cakes.

Choose two large or three medium whitings, untouched by the fishmonger. Have them simply trimmed and *scored*—*i.e.,* cuts about a quarter of an inch deep, made at two-inch intervals along both sides. Thus prepared they will lie *flat* on the *gratin* dish, not curled round in the manner invariably adopted by the fishmonger. Butter the baking dish well, sprinkle over its surface **64. *Whitings au gratin.***
a saltspoonful of salt and one of white pepper, and dredge about two tablespoonfuls of fine raspings over all. Brush the whitings on one side with egg, and sprinkle over them some finely minced mushroom, put them in the dish with this side upwards, melt half an ounce of butter and moisten the surface of the mushrooms, sprinkle a layer of chopped parsley over that, and two more tablespoonfuls of raspings, moisten with a coffeecupful of broth, and set the dish in the oven for ten or twelve minutes; serve in the same dish laid on a napkin.

N.B.—The mushroom is, of course, optional.

Pound well on the day previously seven ounces of cold cooked chicken and five ounces of cold lean ham, after first passing the meat through the mincing machine; incorporate with this six ounces of panada, one ounce of butter, a saltspoonful of white pepper, half one of mace, and a pinch of salt; mix all together with two well-beaten eggs, and about **65. *Little moulds of ham and chicken.***

two tablespoonfuls of thick white sauce made with broth extracted from the bones and trimmings of the chicken. Now butter six or eight *dariole* moulds, shake a thin lining of rasped crumbs over this, then proceed to fill the little moulds with the mixture; shake them down well so that the latter may settle closely into them, then with the back of a saltspoon scoop out a hollow in each; into these little cavities put a teaspoonful of the sauce, and close them with a cap of the mixture you took out, smoothing over the surface with the blade of a dessert-knife dipped in water. Now poach the little moulds till set firmly, and put them in a cold place till morning, when they can be gently warmed *en bain-marie* and turned out.

66. Buttered eggs with grated beef.   Prepare six squares of hot buttered toast, cover each with a canopy of buttered eggs, and sprinkle a layer of finely rasped Hamburg or cold salt beef (red) over the top of each; serve as hot as possible.

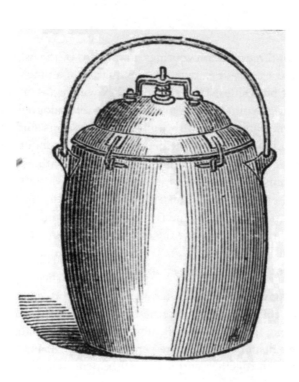

MENU XXIII.

Salt cod with egg sauce and potatoes.
Calf's liver à l'Italienne.
Eggs with shrimp cream.
Oatmeal scones.

Steep a pound and a half of salt cod for six or eight hours in lukewarm water, changing it three times, finally leaving it in cold water for three hours longer. Put it on to boil in *cold* water; as soon as boiling ease off the fire, and let it simmer for five minutes, drain it, set it on a hot dish on a bed of nicely mashed potato, and pour a pint of well-made hard-boiled egg sauce over it. The potato should be worked more as a *purée* in the French way—that is, diluted with stock or milk until it can be *poured* out of the saucepan about the consistency of porridge.

67. Salt cod with egg sauce and potatoes.

Slice up about a pound or so of calf's liver lengthwise, about half an inch thick, season with a seasoning composed of salt, white pepper, and powdered dried herbs in equal portions, and a saltspoonful of mace blended with it. Melt four ounces of clarified dripping or veal suet in a frying-pan; when this is hot put in the liver, fry for three minutes on one side, then turn the slices and fry three minutes on the other side; take the slices out and lay them on a hot *entrée* dish closely covered. Now put into the frying fat one ounce of flour, work it well, add one shallot chopped small, a couple of mushrooms also chopped, and enough broth to bring the sauce to a nice consistency; finally add a tablespoonful of chopped parsley; skim well, pour through a pointed strainer over the liver, and serve.

68. Calf's liver à l'Italienne.

69. Eggs Poach six eggs, and lay them on squares of fried bread, and cover
with shrimp them with this sauce: Half an ounce of butter, half an ounce of
cream. flour, and enough milk to make a rather thin sauce. Season with a
saltspoonful of salt and black pepper blended, and stir in enough
potted shrimps to thicken the sauce well.

MENU XXIV.

Stewed fish.
Epigrams of mutton.
Eggs with Soubise sauce.
Sally Lunns.

For this choose any cheap yet *clean* fish—*i.e.,* not *"fatty,"* as herrings, mackerel, &c.; about one and a half pounds enough, have the fish filleted if you wish, but ask that all the "cuttings" may be sent with it. With the latter, assisted 70. *Stewed* by two or three onions, a bit of celery, six peppercorns, a seasoning *fish.* of salt, a bunch of parsley and herbs, and a tablespoonful of grated *horseradish,* make a good fish broth; strain when quite done, and thicken, then put the fillets into it, and simmer them till they are cooked; lastly, stir in the yolk of an egg, off the fire; dish on a hot dish, and serve.

Select about a pound and a half of breast of mutton, cover it with cold water, and stew it, with ordinary broth, vegetables, and seasoning, till it is tender, then strain off the broth, take out the mutton, remove the bones (they will come 71. *Epigrams* out easily), sprinkle some salt and pepper over the meat, and put it *of mutton.* on a dish under a weight for the night, setting the broth in a bowl. In the morning cut the meat into convenient pieces; egg, bread-crumb them, and fry them a nice colour in very hot fat; dish on a hot dish, and send this sauce with them: Take the fat off the bowl of broth, put about half a pint of it into a saucepan, colour it a nice brown with browning, and mix into it a teaspoonful of red-currant jelly, a tablespoonful of Harvey, one of mushroom ketchup, a teaspoonful of anchovy vinegar, and a dessertspoonful of Marsala. If the fire be clear the pieces of mutton may be broiled instead of being fried.

Prepare six "*œufs mollets*" (No. 33), put them in a hot *entrée* dish, and pour over them a pint of sauce Soubise—*i.e.*, three two-ounce onions boiled till tender in milk or broth, then passed through the sieve—heated up in the same liquid slightly thickened with arrowroot, seasoned with pepper and salt, and finished with a yolk of a raw egg if liked. Prepare the sauce overnight.

72. Eggs *with* Soubise *sauce*.

MENU XXV.

Fried brill.
Salmis of game.
Devilled eggs.
Muffins.

About one pound and a half of filleted brill. Parboil them overnight, and lay them, when cold, in a *marinade* composed as follows: Four tablespoonfuls of salad oil, one of vinegar, an onion sliced in rings, a tablespoonful of chopped parsley, one of mixed green herbs, the peel of half a lemon, and a teaspoonful of black pepper and salt blended. In the morning take the fillets out of the *marinade,* wipe them, egg, bread-crumb, and fry them as explained for smelts (No. 16). *73. Fried brill.*

N.B.—*Maître d'hôtel* butter may accompany.

Although a true *salmis* should be made with game which has been only partly cooked beforehand, a very eatable dish can be concocted out of the remains of birds, provided that they have not been over-roasted. Presuming, then, that you have some remains of game—hare, grouse, black game, or partridges—you can proceed in this way on the evening before: Cut off all the available *74. Salmis of game.* meat, and, giving it a dust of salt and white pepper, put it by. With all the bones, skin, and any gravy that may be over, make the best game broth possible. For this pound all the *enamelled* bones before putting them into the pot, add any trimmings of bacon or ham, a bunch of sweet herbs, and an ounce of glaze; cover with warm water, boil, and simmer. When satisfied that you have got all that the ingredients can yield, strain the liquid off, and leave it in a bowl all night. The next morning thicken this, add a tablespoonful of Marsala, a teaspoonful of red-currant jelly, one of anchovy vinegar, and such seasoning as you may consider necessary. When fully flavoured put in the meat, and let the *salmis* warm slowly to steaming point without boiling, keep in the *bain-marie* till required, and serve. If the *whole* process were carried out overnight, the dish would be all the better, gentle re-heating being alone necessary the next day.

75. Devilled Eggs. These may be either poached eggs on toast, capped with "devil sauce" (No. 29, slightly thickened), or hard-boiled eggs cut in halves lengthwise, placed in a hot *entrée* dish, and moistened with "chutney sauce" (No. 8) as steaming hot as possible.

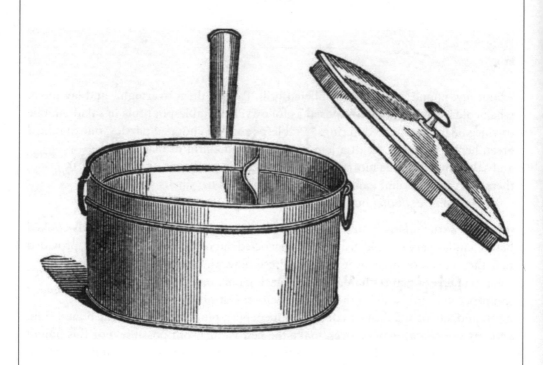

MENU XXVI.

Fried fish à l'Indienne.
Kubàb of liver and oysters.
Buttered eggs with shrimps.
Crumpets.

This depends upon a peculiar batter in which the fish is dipped **76. *Fried fish***
before frying. Fillets of whiting may be chosen. Having prepared ***à l'Indienne.***
a bath of boiling fat, fry them, after having dipped them in this
mixture:—

    Beat up two raw eggs in half a pint of milk, thicken this to the consistency of a
batter that coats the spoon when lifted from it with *pea*-flour, add a saltspoonful
of turmeric, a saltspoonful of ground ginger, and the same of salt and white pepper
blended.

This is only a *kubàb* in so far that the viands are strung upon skewers in the Oriental
manner. Choose about a pound of lamb's or calf's liver, and cut it into slices one-
third of an inch thick, an inch wide, and an inch and a half long, egg **77. *Kubàb***
and crumb them with finely pounded stale crumbs; take one dozen ***of liver and***
cooking oysters, and wrap each of them in a very thin slice of streaky ***oysters.***
bacon; egg and bread these also with fine crumbs. Now pass these on
to your skewers in alternate order—first a piece of liver, then an oyster, then a piece
of liver, and so on; melt a couple of ounces of clarified dripping in a frying-pan, and
fry for three minutes on one side, then turn the skewers, and fry for three more on
the other side; drain, dry, and serve on a very hot dish.

78. *Buttered eggs with shrimps.*   A pint of picked shrimps, six eggs, and six toasts. Make buttered eggs of the eggs, butter the toasts, and toss the shrimps in a frying-pan in a couple of ounces of butter; let them absorb the butter, then turn them on to the toasts, and pour the hot buttered eggs over them.

MENU XXVII.

Fried shell-fish.
Chicken purée with mushrooms.
Egg molé.
Oatcakes.

A dish of fried shell-fish, as is often presented at the Italian breakfast, is a nice variation from the ordinary routine. Take a dozen fair-sized shelled prawns, and a dozen shelled scallops; make two pieces of each prawn by slicing it lengthwise, and slice the scallops in the same way; spread a layer of flour on a clean cloth, and roll the pieces of shell-fish in it; let this dry, and then turn them, a ladleful at a time, into a bath of boiling fat. Fry a golden yellow, drain, and pile the crisp fritters (like whitebait) on a napkin; dust salt over them, and serve with slices of lemon, brown bread-and-butter. *79. Fried shell-fish.*

N.B. Scallops alone are quite acceptable when thus presented.

Enough minced chicken for the party should be made in the usual manner, and six mushrooms, each the size of a five-shilling-piece, should be broiled or fried in butter. Butter six squares of fried bread, cover them with the steaming mince, and lay a fried mushroom on the top of each square. *80. Chicken purée with mushrooms.*

Lay six poached or hard-boiled eggs in a hot silver *entrée* dish, and pour over them a sauce made like that given in No. 13, only use milk instead of fish broth for the moistening. *81. Egg molé.*

MENU XXVIII.

ABSTINENCE.
Semolina fritters of fish.
Vegetable curry (Malay).
Eggs à la voyageuse.
Indian crumpets.

Boil twelve ounces of semolina in sufficient milk to form a paste. Let it get cold, then roll it out a quarter of an inch thick, and line a dozen oval tartlet moulds with it. Fill these with a stiffly reduced shrimp sauce, in which the shrimps, cut into dice, are plentiful. Close over each little patty thus formed with a covering of semolina paste, wet the edges, pinch the tops securely to the lining, and then take them out of the moulds, egg, bread-crumb, and fry in very hot fat, like *rissoles*. Drain, dry, and send in on a napkin with fried parsley. These can be prepared, all but the frying, overnight. Remains of lobster, oysters, scallops, or prawns, may be similarly cooked.

82. Semolina fritters of fish.

Choose the following vegetables: Six cooked artichoke bottoms, the same weight of cooked vegetable marrow or cucumber, six sprigs of the flower of not over-cooked cauliflower, three cooked potatoes of moderate size. Cut the artichoke bottoms into four pieces each, cut the vegetable marrow also into pieces about the same size, and slice the potatoes into similarly small discs. Then proceed as explained for curried mushrooms (No. 20), serving rice with the curry as therein described.

83. Vegetabe curry (Malay).

ABSTINENCE   59

Lay six poached eggs on six fried toasts, and pour over each a little of this sauce: half a pint of milk thickened with a quarter of an ounce of butter, and the same of flour, flavoured with a tablespoonful of Harvey sauce, a dessertspoonful of tomato ketchup, a teaspoonful of anchovy vinegar, and salt to taste. A tablespoonful of milk with one raw yolk beaten up in it may be stirred in as a finishing touch, off the fire, just before using the sauce.

84. *Eggs à la voyageuse.*

MENU XXIX.

Orlys of fillets of hake.
Twice-laid of salt beef.
Eggs à la Bordelaise.
Bannocks.

---

85. *Orlys of fillets of hake.* Trim the hake into convenient pieces for frying, and *marinade* them as explained for the brill fillets (No. 73). Before cooking them, wipe the pieces carefully, make a good frying batter (No. 116) and prepare a bath of boiling fat. Dip the pieces into the batter, and fry them a rich golden brown. Serve piled upon a hot napkin.

86. *Twice-laid of salt beef.* This simple dish can be made very tasty with a little trouble. Pass half a pound of lean Hamburg spiced or salt beef through the mincing machine; cut the fat into dice, fry them till well melted, then empty the contents of the pan into a hot saucepan containing about a pint and a half of well-mashed potato: stir well together with a wooden spoon, adding by degrees the minced beef, and moistening the mixture with a few spoonfuls of broth or milk. Turn the whole into a well-buttered mould, and bake until thoroughly hot, then turn out, and shake some fine raspings over it. Garnish with curls of bacon.

87. *Eggs à la Bordelaise.* Bake overnight three good-sized onions on a buttered dish until they are quite soft. Boil six eggs hard. The next morning take off the browned outer skin of the onions, and mince them, and take four sardines from the tin, free them from oil, and cut them up rather small. Put an ounce of butter into a frying-pan, throw into it the minced onion, set the pan on a low fire, add the sardines, fry very gently; meanwhile warm the hard-boiled eggs by putting them into hot water. All being hot, empty the mince into a hot *entrée* dish, slice the hard eggs, across, into pieces, strew them over the mince, and serve very hot.

MENU XXX.

Kippered salmon.
Croquettes of mixed meat.
Omelettes with asparagus.
Muffins.

Cut six nice pieces from a kippered salmon, and, if necessary, soak them awhile to remove some of the saltness, then dry them, butter them, and dust some pepper over

88. Kippered Salmon. them, then wrap in well-oiled papers, and broil over the clearest fire on a gridiron.

These can be made of mixed cold meats overnight, and will be much improved by the remains of a *pâté de foie gras,* sweetbread, a spoonful of ham or tongue if it can be spared, and the same of minced cooked mushroom. But none of these expensive things is essential. Having minced the meat, seasoned, and flavoured it, stir it in a bowl in which you have poured a quarter of a pint of thick white or brown, sauce,

89. Croquettes of mixed meat. with the yolks of two raw eggs blended with it; warm all in a saucepan together, but without boiling, then put aside the mixture to set firmly. Next morning strew a pastry board with finely powdered and sifted crumbs, divide the mince into equally sized parts, roll them into drumlike shapes, egg, crumb, and fry them in boiling fat till of a nice yellow-brown colour; drain, dry, and serve piled up upon a hot napkin. Any nice brown sauce can accompany.

Cooked asparagus, either fresh or tinned, may be employed in this dish. Cut all the tender part into quarter-inch dice, boil the stalks in milk, strain, thicken the milk,

90. Omelette with asparagus. season it with salt and pepper, and put the dice into it. Make two omelettes as recommended in No. 6, and add the asparagus as described in No. 24. Serve as hot as possible.

MENU XXXI.

Whitebait.
Vienna steaks.
Omelettes with shrimps.
Knotted rolls.

Few dishes of fish are nicer for breakfast than whitebait. They are none the worse for having been fried overnight; on the contrary; for a plunge into very hot fat for two, or three minutes at most, and careful draining and drying, they are all the crisper. Serve them with slices of lemon and thin brown bread-and-butter in the usual way.
91. *Whitebait.*

Vienna steaks are made in this way: Take half a pound of lean veal uncooked, and half a pound of lean beef also uncooked; mince the two meats finely, season with spiced pepper and salt, and add a dessertspoonful of chopped parsley and a teaspoonful of finely minced shallot; mix into this two well-beaten eggs, and turn the whole out upon a flat dish. The mixture should be about three-eighths of an inch thick. This having been done the previous day, in the
92. *Vienna steaks.*
morning all that has to be done is to cut the now firm mass into rounds with a three and a half inch cutter; flour and fry them *(sauté)* in butter three minutes on one side, turn, and three minutes on the other, serving them on a hot dish in a circle, with a small mound of mashed potato in the centre. Plain brown gravy may accompany in a sauce boat.

The *omelettes* should be cooked in either of the ways already described *(see* No. 6, or 48), and the shrimps should be added in the manner explained for the mushrooms in No. 24. They should be
93. *Omelettes with shrimps.*

prepared as follows: Having picked enough boiled shrimps to fill a half pint measure generously, pound the shells of the tails in a mortar with one ounce of butter, pass all through a hair-sieve, and put it into a small saucepan over a low fire, add the picked shrimps and a dust of mace, stir well to heat thoroughly, and spread half of the contents of the saucepan over the surface of each *omelette* just before turning the latter into the dish.

MENU XXXII.

Slices of Salmon, grilled.
Ham steaks.
Eggs in cases with mushrooms.
Irish scones.

Cut a piece of salmon into six slices half an inch thick. If the piece be a deep cut from the middle of a fine fish three slices will be sufficient each being divided into two pieces down the naturally marked division of the fish. Remove the skin, and let the prepared slices lie all night in a *marinade* composed of four tablespoonfuls **94. *Slices of salmon, grilled.*** of salad oil, two of red wine vinegar, a dessertspoonful of chopped chives or finely shredded shallot, a tablespoonful of chopped parsley, and a sprinkling of spiced salt. In the morning lift the slices from the *marinade*, wipe them, and wrap them in well-buttered papers, twisting the ends of the papers to secure them firmly. Butter the bars of a well-cleaned gridiron, lay the cutlets one by one thereon, and boil them over a clear fire, turning them frequently. They will take about twelve minutes. If cut thicker, say three-quarters of an inch, and not wrapped in paper, they will be done in a quarter of an hour. In this case the slices must be buttered before being laid on the gridiron.

These are cut out of a raw ham in quarter-inch thick slices and broiled over a clear fire. The secret of success lies in having the ham, or a portion set aside for steaks, soaked as if for boiling, and to send the steaks in absolutely straight from **95. *Ham steaks.*** the grill. Excellent steaks can thus be cut from a gammon of prime bacon, but the soaking and speedy service must be carried out with the same care.

Stew a quarter of a pound of trimmed mushrooms in milk; when done, drain them, chop them up small with a silver dessert-knife. Thicken the milk custard-wise with

96. Eggs in cases with mushrooms.

the yolks of two raw eggs, stir in the minced mushroom and enough finely sifted white crumbs to bring the mixture to the consistency of a farce, seasoning with salt and a saltspoonful of spiced pepper. With this line half a dozen well-buttered china cases, leaving a hollow in the centre of each, into which break a fresh egg. Set the cases in a shallow pan with hot water an inch deep round them, and poach them in the oven for eight or ten minutes. Pour enough of the sauce mentioned below to mask the top of each, dust over with fine raspings, and serve.

Sauce: only six dessertspoonfuls wanted. Take the trimmings of the mushrooms, wash, dry, and simmer them in just enough milk to cover them, for twenty minutes, season with a pinch each of salt and pepper; afterwards strain, thicken the broth thus obtained, and use as directed.

N.B.—The mushrooms should be prepared the day before.

MENU XXXIII.

Fish pudding with rice.
Grilled breast of mutton.
Eggs in coquilles.
Indian crumpets.

Any cold fish carefully picked from the bones will do, or a combination of fish such as salmon and whiting, for a little salmon improves the pudding greatly. Take eight ounces of this, and four ounces of boiled rice, one hard-boiled egg crushed with a fork; mix together in a bowl, seasoning with a saltspoonful of spiced pepper, and one of salt, and moistening with any fish sauce that may have been left, or milk, with one well-beaten egg. When worked to the consistency of a pudding, put the mixture into a buttered mould, place a round of paper over the exposed end, and set the mould in a large stewpan in boiling water one third of its depth; cover the vessel, and let it steam for forty minutes (see p. 99). The mould can then be taken from the stewpan and the pudding turned out. If any fish broth be available, a white sauce, flavoured with a few drops of anchovy sauce, may be poured over the mould.

97. Fish pudding with rice.

Trim and stew a breast of mutton or lamb with six ounces of onions, four ounces of carrot, an ounce of celery, a bouquet of herbs, and seasoning, with sufficient water to cover all well, till tender. Take the breast out of the broth, remove the bones at once, and place it between two dishes with a weight upon the upper one. This must be done while the meat is hot on the afternoon of the previous day. Save the broth. In the morning release the piece of meat from the weight, and cut it into neat pieces three inches long by one and a half wide. Score, and season these highly, grill, and serve with crisply fried parsley,

98. Grilled breast of mutton.

and the "devil" sauce given for No. 29, using some of the broth that was saved in its making.

Boil six eggs hard. Fry a couple of fairly large mushrooms. Take the yolks out of the boiled eggs, chopping the whites into little squares, and treating the mushrooms in a similar manner. Mix the chopped whites and mushrooms, season with spiced pepper

99. Eggs in coquilles. and salt, and moisten them with a spoonful or two of good brown sauce; add the crushed yolks with a little more sauce—just enough of the latter in all to form a nice moist mince. Butter six china scallop shells, put an allowance of the mince in each, smoothing the surface in dome shape; shake a layer of finely sifted white crumbs over them, pour a few drops of butter melted upon each, and set in the oven till nicely browned. Serve very hot.

MENU XXXIV.

Cod's-roe cutlets.
Croustades of mixed meats.
Eggs on the dish à la Monaco.
French rolls.

Put a whole cod's roe, with the skin intact, into boiling water for five minutes. Take it out, put it on a sieve, and pour a jug of cold water over it. Then return it to the stewpan, to the water in which add a tablespoonful of vinegar and one of salt. Simmer slowly for twenty minutes, or thirty if a large roe. Then drain, and set it in the larder to get cold. When required in the morning, cut the roe into half-inch slices, trim these into cutlets with a cutter, egg, bread-crumb, and fry them a nice colour, then drain and dry, serving with brown bread-and-butter and sliced lemon.

100. Cod's-roe cutlets.

These can be made out of any combination of cold meat, and if the following proportions be maintained—approximately—will be found very nice for breakfast: To two-thirds finely minced cold roast beef, mutton, veal, or fowl, allow one-third minced ham, tongue, mild lean bacon, or lean pressed beef. Blend a mince thus apportioned, season it with spiced pepper, and prepare half a pint of nicely flavoured brown gravy, slightly thickened. A good flavour will be got by adding to the gravy one tablespoonful mushroom ketchup, one dessertspoonful of Harvey sauce, a teaspoonful of vinegar from the walnut pickle, and a teaspoonful of Marsala. For seasoning a saltspoonful of sugar and one of salt. For the *croustades* choose six small stale dinner rolls; slice off the rounded top of each as you take the top off a boiled egg; then, using a fork,

101. Croustades of mixed meats.

pick out the crumb without injuring the outer crust. Six bread-cases having thus been prepared, fry them in very hot beef dripping till pale golden in colour; drain, dry, and keep till wanted. In the morning butter the inside of the cases, sprinkle over this a layer of finely minced parsley. Next, taking enough mince to fill each case, put it into a bowl, dilute with the sauce till nice and moist, fill the cases, strew a layer of fine crumbs over the tops, set them on a buttered baking tin, and put this into the oven for a few minutes, just till thoroughly hot . Meanwhile fry six curls of bacon, crisply, and when serving the *croustades* put a curl on the top of each one.

102. *Eggs on the dish à la Monaco.* In a small saucepan put a claret-glassful of tomato sauce, with a tablespoonful of melted glaze; season with a saltspoonful of spiced pepper, dilute with broth or milk to bring the liquid to the consistency of thin cream, then pass it through a strainer into a fire-proof china dish; break six eggs into this carefully without breaking, and put a few drops of melted butter on each egg; then set the dish in the oven, and as soon as the whites are set take it out, and serve on a napkin laid upon a larger dish.

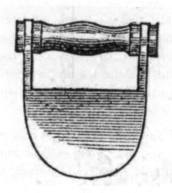

MENU XXXV.

Haddock in a mould.
Chicken cutlets, Indian way.
Eggs on the dish with bacon.
Crumb-muffins.

Take the flesh from both sides of a medium-sized haddock. Put the head, skin, bones and tail, with an onion sliced, six peppercorns, and a bouquet of herbs, into a stewpan with sufficient water to cover all; season with a saltspoonful of salt, boil, and simmer for half an hour, then strain off the broth, which should be thickened with butter and flour (one ounce of each to half a pint), and finally enriched—off the fire—with the yolk of a raw egg. *103. Haddock in a mould.*
This being ready, proceed to pound the flesh of the haddock in a mortar, moistening it during the operation with a spoonful or two of the sauce. When well pounded pass the fish through the sieve, and to it add half its bulk of white bread-crumb that has been soaked in milk; pound all together, moisten slightly with the sauce and two well-beaten eggs, seasoning with spiced pepper. When well mixed, butter a plain pudding mould, fill it with the mixture, and poach it *"au-bain marie"*—i.e., place it one-third deep in boiling water, watch it come again to the boil, then lower the fire and steam as you would a pudding, closely covered, for three-quarters of an hour. In the morning set the mould again in hot water, and keep it so until thoroughly heated through, when it should be turned out upon a hot dish. Any unexpended sauce there may be should be warmed and poured over the mould.

The legs and thighs of fowls, the breasts of which have been used for an *entrée,* will do well. The meat may be cooked or not. The remains of a turkey may be thus utilised. To three-quarters of a pound of cold cooked meat allow six ounces of cold cooked pork sausage. *104. Chicken cutlets, Indian way.*

Mince the meat, not too finely, and chop up the sausages, removing the skin; add a teaspoonful of minced shallot, a dessertspoonful of parsley, and a sprinkling of salt; mix all together with two raw eggs, spread the mixture on a dish three-eighths of an inch thick, and let it stiffen during the night. In the morning cut it into cutlets with a cutter, flour them, and lay them in a *sauté* pan with an ounce of butter. Fry six minutes (three on each side), and dish in a circle with fried parsley as garnish.

Cut into thin slices enough cold cooked bacon to cover the bottom of a large fire-proof dish. Slightly butter the dish, cut the slices into inch squares, and lay them over the bottom of the dish. Put it into the oven, let the bacon cook for five minutes on one

105. *Eggs on the dish with bacon.*
side, then turn the pieces and cook five minutes longer. Now take the dish out of the oven and break six eggs into it, return it to the oven till the whites are set, then dish in the manner described for No. 102.

MENU XXXVI.

ABSTINENCE.
Sole as whitebait.
Mushroom fritters.
Omelette à la Soubise.
Barley-meal scones.

This is a fanciful way of serving fried sole, which, as a change, may be acceptable. Skin a medium-sized fish, and detach the long fillets on either side of the spine. Cut these into strips about the size of a largish whitebait, toss them in a floured cloth, and plunge them in relays into a bath of boiling lard or clarified suet, in which a frying-basket has been set; in six or seven minutes they should just turn colour, when lift the basket out of the bath, drain for a moment over the pan, then turn out upon a sheet of blotting-paper placed in front of the fire so as to dry. When all have thus been fried, drained, and dried, sprinkle them with salt, dish on a very hot dish, serving with brown bread-and-butter and lemon cut into quarters.

106. Sole as whitebait.

Half a pound of good fresh mushrooms should be chosen. It is never advisable to buy these very nice fungi after they have turned black. Commence by boiling two eggs hard; while this is proceeding, trim, peel, and prepare the mushrooms, putting all the stalks and peelings into a saucepan, with a pinch of mignonette pepper and two of salt; cover with milk, milk and water, or water, according to your resources, and bring once to the boil, simmering afterwards for twenty minutes; then strain through muslin—for there may be grit in the mushroom trimmings—and save the broth in a bowl. Thicken this

107. Mushroom fritters.

with a quarter of an ounce of butter and a quarter of an ounce of flour, reducing it somewhat, and lastly add (off the fire) the yolk of a raw egg. Next cut the mushrooms up into a coarse mince, and, putting this into a *sauté* pan with an ounce of butter, fry it for five minutes over a moderate fire. Remove the pan from the fire. Chop up the hard-boiled eggs, whites and yolks together, and add this to the fried minced mushroom, seasoning with a teaspoonful of spiced pepper and salt. Dilute this with a few spoonfuls of the sauce, and again, over a moderate fire, proceed to cook the mixture, adding a little more sauce if it seems necessary. When the mixture thickens well, stop, turn the contents of the pan out upon a dish, pat it into shape with a wooden spoon, making it about a quarter of an inch thick, and leave it to get firm during the night. In the morning cut this into cutlets; egg, bread-crumb, and fry a golden brown, and serve with fried parsley.

In this case an onion *purée à la Soubise* is added to an *omelette* just as the latter is on the point of being passed into the dish. Cook the *omelettes* (for there had better be two, as already advised) in either of the methods (No. 6 or 48) that have been given, adding, at the period indicated, this *purée*, which would of course be made overnight.

108. Omelette à la Soubise.

Mince six ounces of onion, plunge this into boiling water to blanch for seven or eight minutes; strain carefully, turn the mince into a stewpan, and over a low fire; stir it about to dry thoroughly, then add a tablespoonful of milk, simmer, and continue adding by degrees till the onion is covered with milk; now simmer till the onion is cooked, then strain, pass the mince through the sieve, thicken the milk in which it was boiled with a quarter of an ounce of butter and the same of flour, pass in the *purée*, amalgamate thoroughly, adding the yolk of an egg beaten up in a tablespoonful of milk to finish with.

MENU XXXVII.

Sea-bream on the dish.
Chicken à la chevalier.
Buttered eggs with mushrooms.
Brown rolls.

Fillet a sea-bream neatly. With all the trimmings make a broth as described in No. 103; when this is ready strain it into a shallow pan just large enough to hold the fillets; a copper *sauté* pan with an upright rim will do; place this on the fire, bring to the boil, put in the fillets, and in three minutes reduce the heat to simmering; in eight or ten minutes the fillets will **109. Sea-bream on the dish.** be sufficiently done for our purpose. Put them aside for the night, carefully saving the broth. In the morning thicken the broth, giving it a teaspoonful of anchovy sauce, and having arranged the fillets on a buttered flat dish that will stand the oven pour the sauce over them in sufficient quantity to mask them neatly; dust over the surface a layer of finely grated cheese, and set the dish in the oven just long enough to heat thoroughly; remove it when this has taken place, pass a heated glazing iron over the surface to make it a yellowish brown, and serve. Any cold cooked fish may be similarly dressed. Serve of course on the dish in which it was cooked.

An easy way of presenting a *réchauffé* of chicken, fowl, or turkey. Remove the legs and thighs from a pair of cold roast or boiled birds, put them aside while you pick off all the remaining meat on the car-cases. Pick all the burnt skin out **110. Chicken à la chevalier.** of this, and chop up the bones that remain, with which proceed to make a broth. Pass the meat through the mincing machine or chop it upon a board. Season this with spiced pepper and salt. Thicken the broth slightly, and moisten the mince with it, heating the mixture in the *bain-marie*. Score, season, and grill the joints that were cut off in the first instance, dishing as follows: On the bottom of a hot silver dish place a piece of crisply fried bread for each piece of grilled fowl, spread a layer of the mince on each of these, and place the leg or thigh over that, garnishing the whole with crisply fried curls of bacon. In the case of a turkey the joints must be cut crosswise into convenient pieces.

Buttered eggs with mushrooms can either be served upon toasts—first the mushrooms and then a covering of the egg mixture—or a layer of mushrooms can be laid on the

111. *Buttered eggs with mushrooms.* bottom of a hot silver dish with the buttered eggs over them. A third way is to incorporate the mushrooms with the buttered eggs the last thing before dishing the latter. Prepare the eggs as shown in No. 3, and the mushrooms as in No. 36.

FRYING-PANS.

MENU XXXVIII.

Cutlets of moulded fish.
Ox-tongue fillets devilled.
Eggs in cases with ham.
Crumpets.

Prepare on the day before the cutlets are wanted a mould of fish as explained in the case of "haddock mould" (No. 103). This can be made of mixed fish, and if any salmon, remains of lobster, or shrimps can be worked in with it, so much the better. Put the mould away at night, and in the morning cut it into neat pieces—cutlet shapes if liked—which egg, bread-crumb, fry in boiling fat a golden brown, and serve crisp and dry with fried parsley.

112. Cutlets of moulded fish.

Cut from a cold boiled tongue eight or ten neat slices a quarter of an inch thick; prepare as many rounds of fried bread; get ready half a pint of the "devil sauce" already explained in No. 29. Trim the tongue slices free from skin, and season them with grill seasoning (No. 29). Give them a few turns on the gridiron, lay them on the toasts, and pour the sauce over them.

113. Ox-tongue fillets devilled.

Butter six china cases or scallop shells; take enough finely grated ham to fill an afternoon teacup; moisten this with twice the quantity of good brown sauce and stir in the yolk of a raw egg off the fire when the mixture is ready. With this line your cases or shells, leaving a hollow space in the middle of each to hold an egg. Put the cases in hot water to poach and set the lining, then take them out. In the morning warm the cases, slip a poached egg into the hollow of each of them, pour a dessertspoonful of hot brown sauce over every egg, and serve.

114. Eggs in cases with ham.

MENU XXXIX.

Baked smelts.
Kromeskis of chicken.
Eggs with oysters.
Devilled biscuits.

Large smelts are the best for this dish. Butter an oval fire-proof dish, sprinkle finely minced parsley over it, on this bed lay one dozen smelts; moisten them with half a pint of white sauce, strew them over with fine raspings pretty thickly, put into a moderate oven for ten minutes, and serve in their dish placed on a napkin.

115. *Baked smelts.*

Make a mixture of chicken—or veal with ham, lean bacon, or any tasty adjunct—as if for *croquettes* (No. 89). In the morning mix a frying batter: Put four and a half ounces of flour into a bowl, make a hollow in the centre and put into it a quarter of a pint of water, half a saltspoonful of salt, the yolks of two eggs, and two tablespoonfuls of salad oil. Mix thoroughly till the batter coats the spoon with a coating the eighth of an inch thick, adding water, if necessary, to attain that consistency. Twenty minutes before using stir in the whites of the two eggs well whipped. For the kromeskis cut out of thinly sliced cooked bacon eight or a dozen pieces about three inches long and two inches wide; lay a tablespoonful of the minced meat in the centre of each of these, roll them up, dip them into the batter, and fry in a bath of boiling fat till they turn a light brown colour; drain, dry, and serve on a napkin.

116. *Kromeskis of chicken.*

The oysters should be prepared the previous evening. The operation is very simple, yet it requires care. Order a dozen sauce oysters to be sent up *with their liquor.* Strain the latter, for it is often gritty with little atoms of shell, into a small saucepan, putting in with it the beards taken from the oysters; add fish broth, milk or water to moisten well, and boil, simmering afterwards for half an hour. Strain off this liquid, let it get cold, put the bearded oysters into it, empty it all into a saucepan and set it on the fire—the heat moderate—watch now, and the moment *signs* of boiling can be detected, stop; reduce the heat to the *lowest* simmering temperature, and in two minutes the oysters will be ready. If allowed to boil the oysters will be leathery. Now take out the oysters, thicken the broth, put them *117. Eggs* in again, and keep this in a china or earthenware bowl during the *with oysters.* night.

In the morning boil six eggs hard; cool them in cold water; slice them crosswise, butter a fire-proof baking dish, put a layer of the eggs at the bottom of it, arrange the oysters, now taken out of the sauce, over this, and cover with another layer of egg slices, seasoning each layer with pepper and salt, moisten the whole with the oyster sauce, cover the surface with raspings somewhat thickly strewn, and put the dish in the oven until steaming, when serve. This is obviously an easy way of disposing of any oyster sauce left from dinner the previous evening.

VEGETABLE KNIFE.

MENU XL.

Scalded whitings.
Potato cutlets.
Poached eggs à la Colbert.
Barleymeal scones.

Get the whiting untouched by the fishmonger except cleaning. Put the fish (three or four, according to size) upon a dish overnight, squeeze a lemon over them, and sprinkle with salt. In the morning put a fish-kettle with drainer on the fire with

118. *Scalded whitings.* as much water as you think will cover the fish nicely, add to it a dessertspoonful of vinegar and a teaspoonful of salt, wipe each fish, and when the water boils put them into the kettle; this will stop the

boiling; let it come up to the boil again, then draw back the vessel; from five to eight minutes must now be allowed, according to size; drain as soon as tender, getting rid of all the water from the fish, and serve with slices of lemon and brown bread-and-butter. This is perhaps the most easily digested dish of fish that can be presented either at breakfast or any other meal. It is equally practicable with small-sized fresh haddock.

Take two pounds of potatoes (weighed after paring), steam or boil, pass through the sieve, moisten in a bowl with two well-beaten eggs, work to the consistency of smooth

119. *Potato cutlets.* dough, adding a spoonful of milk if necessary. Spread a slight layer of flour on a board, turn the potato dough upon it, flour and roll it out as you would ordinary dough for pastry. Sift a thin layer of

finely grated cheese over the surface, and dust over with salt and spiced pepper; fold over, roll out again, fold, and put it away. Prepare eight or ten tablespoonfuls of any nice minced meat, moistening it as explained for *croquettes* (No. 89). Set this aside also. In the morning roll out the potato paste a quarter of an inch thick with a three-inch cutter, cut this into rounds, put a tablespoonful of the *croquette* mixture on each round, fold over, and pinch the edges securely. Brush over with egg, roll in finely sifted crumbs, and either heat them up on a buttered baking tin in the oven, or plunge till well coloured in boiling fat.

Choose six scallop shells; put into them a lining of roughly minced kidney prepared in this way:— Take a pair of fine mutton kidneys, or half a veal kidney, previously cooked—those taken out of a cold roast joint will do; cut them up into small squares, moisten the mince with a quarter of a pint of any brown sauce there may be left, or thickened gravy from a joint, flavoured with a tablespoonful of mushroom ketchup. Heat up this 120. *Poached eggs à la Colbert.* in the morning and use as follows: — Having lined each shell with the mince, slip a poached egg into the hollow, put a teaspoonful of the sauce on each egg, and serve.

TURBOT KETTLE.

MENU XLI.

Herring fillets fried.
Rabbit au gratin.
Eggs with artichokes.
Tea-cake—not sweetened.

Take the flesh from four fresh herrings, one long fillet from each side. Save the roes. Put the fillets overnight on a flat dish, sprinkle them with salt, and squeeze a few drops of lemon juice over each of them. Give the roes a fry and put them away—they will come in for "a savoury" at dinner the next day. In the morning **121. *Herring*** wipe, egg, bread-crumb, and fry the fillets as crisply as possible in ***fillets fried.*** boiling fat, serving them nicely dried after draining on a napkin, slices of lemon accompanying.

Pick all the meat remaining from a couple of boiled rabbits, the back fillets of which may have been used at a previous meal; save all the onion sauce that may have been left, and as much of the boilings as may not have been used. Butter a fire-proof baking dish, strew this over with finely minced parsley, arrange the pieces of meat over this, dusting them with spiced pepper and salt, an moistening **122. *Rabbit*** with the onion sauce supplemented with a spoonful or two of the ***au gratin.*** boilings thickened. Having finished the packing, dredge a good layer of raspings over the surface of the rabbit, and put the dish into a moderate oven to heat thoroughly. If well moistened, this will be found a nice dish for a change.

This should be made with artichoke bottoms *(fonds d'artichauts)*, but a decidedly nice combination can be made with Jerusalem artichokes. Arrange six cooked artichoke bottoms on a buttered fire-proof dish, pour a few drops of melted butter on each, warm in the oven, take out the dish, put a nicely trimmed poached egg upon each, sprinkle a dust of spiced pepper over each, or a drop or two of tarragon vinegar, and serve. When made with Jerusalem artichokes, the *purée* is the simplest method to choose for the vegetable; line a well-buttered fire-proof dish with this, dust a fine layer of grated cheese over the surface, dress the poached eggs neatly in hollows scooped out of this bed, and serve.

123. *Eggs with artichokes.*

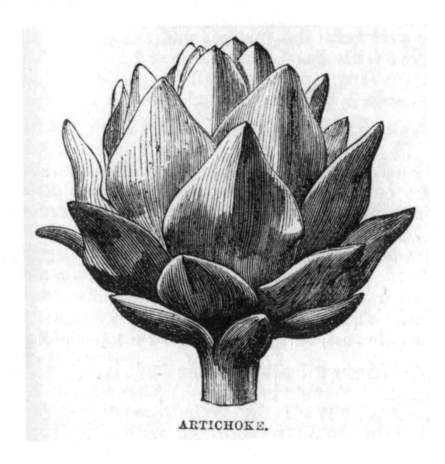

ARTICHOKE.

MENU XLII.

ABSTINENCE.
Trout fried and marinaded.
Croquettes of vermicelli.
Eggs with green herb sauce.
Crumpets.

Practicable with small trout. Clean six quarter.-pounders, trim, sprinkle them with salt, and fry them in butter in the *sauté* pan. Put them, when thus cooked, in a deep dish, and let them get cold, pouring over them a marinade composed of four tablespoonfuls of salad oil and three of anchovy vinegar, seasoned with a teaspoonful

124. *Trout fried and marinaded.* of finely grated horseradish, a tablespoonful of chopped parsley, a teaspoonful of chopped thyme or marjoram, and one of chives if not objected to. Let this stand all night, and serve as it is. An excellent summer dish.

Prepare the vermicelli exactly as explained for spaghetti (No. 62), cutting it up small and adding a coffeecupful of tomato conserve to it, a quarter of a pint of white sauce, and two raw eggs. Stir altogether over a low fire, then spread the mixture upon a dish during the night for it to stiffen. In the morning shape this into little ovals as

125. *Croquettes of vermicelli.* described for meat *croquettes* (No. 89), and cook in the same manner. If liked, the ovals may be rolled in crushed uncooked vermicelli instead of bread crumbs.

Pound in a mortar two ounces of carefully picked and scalded leaves of chervil,

126. *Eggs with green herb sauce.* parsley, chives, tarragon, and watercress with six capers and the fillet of a boned anchovy; pass the whole through the sieve, and stir it into half a pint of white sauce. Arrange six poached eggs on fried squares of bread and pour a portion of the sauce over each.

MENU XLIII.

Oyster cutlets.
Sausages with potatoes.
Eggs à la Portugaise.
Brown flour scones.

For these turn to No. 117, and follow the directions therein given both in regard to the making of the oyster broth, and the cooking of the oysters, but using eighteen sauce oysters instead of twelve. After the latter have been cooked drain them from the broth, and put them on a plate. Next, presuming there is about half a pint of broth, proceed with half an ounce of butter and half an ounce of flour to thicken it; while cooling somewhat, cut the **127. *Oyster cutlets.*** oysters up into small pieces and put them with two ounces of bread-crumb soaked in milk and the yolks of two raw eggs into the broth, stir together over a low fire to thicken, but do not boil on any account, and then turn the mixture out on a dish, and leave it in a cool larder for the night. In the morning shape the mixture in flat oval shapes with two wooden spoons, or cut them with a cutlet cutter, egg, bread-crumb, and fry in boiling fat; drain, dry, and serve with slices of lemon and brown bread-and-butter.

This homely dish can be made worthy of service at any table if a little trouble be taken with the potato, the dishing up, and the frying of the sausages. Taking the last first, to preserve the sausages in shape without bursting, *time* must be taken—that is to say, the sausages, having been pricked, must be put in melted beef dripping over a *low* fire and cooked slowly and thoroughly. People who think that sausages are too rich will find them much plainer if they be partly **128. *Sausages with potatoes.*** boiled before frying. Prick them well, put them into hot water, bring slowly to the boil for fear of bursting, then simmer for five minutes; after this they can be drained and fried till brown. For the potato: Boil or steam half a dozen fairly sized potatoes, drain, mash, pass through the sieve, moisten with an ounce of butter and a coffeecupful of milk, season with a teaspoonful of spiced pepper and a dessertspoonful of grated cheese, add the yolk of a raw egg, mix thoroughly, pat into six neat, elongated ovals, set these on a buttered baking tin, which put in the oven till thoroughly hot; take the tin from the oven, with a slice lift the potato ovals, lay them on a hot dish, put a well-drained sausage, free from all fat, upon each, and serve.

Cut up six tomatoes weighing in all, say, three-quarters of a pound; cut up very finely one small shallot, say, half an ounce. Put half an ounce of butter at the bottom of a small stewpan, melt it and put in the minced shallot, season with spiced pepper and salt, fry over a low fire till turning pale golden brown, then add the tomatoes, increase the fire, now stirring the tomatoes well, the object being to reduce their wateriness somewhat. When nicely pulped, pass the mixture through the sieve and put it aside. In the morning butter a fire-proof china dish, arrange the *purée* on the bottom of it, warm this in the oven, take it out, hollow out with a spoon six little cavities in the tomato bed and slip a raw fresh egg into each of them. Place the dish in the oven again till the eggs have set nicely, and serve.

129. *Eggs à la Portugaise.*

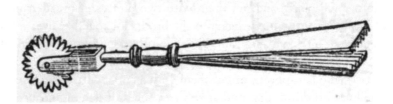

MENU XLIV.

Fillets of brill à la meunière.
Devilled sheep's tongues.
Fried eggs and bacon.
oatmeal scones.

Having procured eight or ten nice fillets of brill, lay them on a flat dish, lightly sprinkle them with salt, and squeeze a few drops of lemon juice over them. In the morning wipe them, flour them, and having melted a couple of ounces of butter in a *sauté* pan over a low fire, put them therein, turning them frequently till done; then drain and arrange them on a hot dish; add another ounce of butter (melted) to the butter in the *sauté* pan, let this **130. *Fillets of brill à la meunière.*** turn a pale brown; then take the pan from the fire, add a teaspoonful of anchovy sauce to the butter, let it froth, and stir in little by little a couple of tablespoonfuls of vinegar that has been warmed separately, and a teaspoonful of finely-minced parsley. Empty this over the fried fillets, and serve. The point of this method of cooking fish will be entirely lost unless the dish containing the fillets be as hot as possible, and the sauce that is added equally so. It must be served without any delay whatever.

The six sheep's tongues must be cooked until tender, and skinned on the previous day. In the morning trim off the unsightly roots of the tongues, dip them in melted butter, lay them on a buttered gridiron, and let them just catch the fire nicely. Arrange them upon a hot dish on *croûtons* of fried bread **131. *Devilled sheep's tongues.*** with a crisp curl of bacon between each, and a masking over them of the sauce given for No. 29, the basis of which can be the broth in which the tongues were cooked.

One of the very commonest of breakfast dishes in the British Isles is fried eggs and bacon. In the majority of cases it may be described as an arrangement of eggs in a condition of boot-leather, surrounded by greasy slices of bacon, and resting upon a layer of discoloured melted fat. Now it is by no means easy to fry an egg properly. The usual way in vogue is to put the eggs, three or four at once, into the far too scanty quantity of melted fat in which the bacon was cooked. This method is altogether wrong. In the first place, the eggs and the bacon must be prepared separately, the former being fried one by one as follows: Empty four ounces of fresh lard into a small but deep frying-pan, just large enough to hold the fat when melted and accommodate one egg. Heat the lard as for whitebait, and when ready, slope the frying-pan so that you can slide gently upon its surface a fresh egg, previously broken from the shell into a large spoon. It will set very quickly, lift with a perforated slice, drain thoroughly, and proceed with the next. Six eggs having thus been fried, dried, and trimmed as to their edges, lay them on squares of fried bread upon a hot dish, garnishing with curls of crisply-fried bacon, or with bacon cut into small squares and similarly *dry*-fried.

132. Fried eggs and bacon.

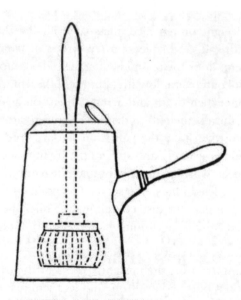

CHOCOLATE MILL.

MENU XLV.

Fried sprats.
Broiled fowl with mushrooms.
Eggs with liver.
Irish scones.

When sprats are in season they make a nice breakfast dish. Treat them as much as possible as you would whitebait: flour, fry at a gallop in a boiling fat, *133. Fried* drain, dry well, sprinkle with salt, and serve with brown bread-and- *sprats.* butter and lemon. They may be egged, crumbed, and served as smelts, but this is more troublesome than flouring.

Choose the drumsticks and thighs of a couple of cold roast fowls; *134. Broiled* score, rub with butter, season with salt and spiced pepper, and grill *fowl with* on a well-buttered gridiron. Treat six or eight nice-sized mushrooms *mushrooms.* in like manner. Dish the latter on *croûtons* of fried bread with the broiled fowl arranged round them.

If there happen to be any fowl, turkey, or rabbit livers available, or three ounces of lamb's or veal liver, cooked, cut it up into small squares, which keep ready on a plate, dusting them over with salt and spiced pepper. Put into a small saucepan *135. Eggs* half an ounce of butter with half an ounce of finely-minced shallot, fry *with liver.* till turning colour over a low fire, then add half an ounce of flour, mix and continue the frying for five minutes, then stir in half a pint of broth, meat gravy, or soup that may have been left, let the sauce come to the boil, then simmer, adding one tablespoonful of mushroom ketchup, a teaspoonful of walnut-pickle vinegar, and half one of red-currant jelly. Mix well and pass through a strainer into a clean bowl, empty the mince into this, and set it aside for the night. In the morning warm the liver sauce in the *bain-marie,* adding a dessertspoonful of marsala. Keep this hot while you prepare a fire-proof china dish, then put in the liver, making little hollows for the reception of six fresh eggs. These having been put in, set the dish in the oven till the eggs are set, and serve.

MENU XLVI.

Salmon fritters.
Veal and ham scallops.
Buttered eggs with fines herbes.
Indian-meal rolls.

These can be made out of the remains of cold salmon in this manner: Cut up the salmon in small pieces, take an equal quantity of breadcrumb—say six ounces of each—empty both into a bowl, season plainly with pepper and salt, moisten with any sauce that has been left, or with a quarter of a pint of white sauce made with the salmon boilings. Add two raw yolks, mix thoroughly, and spread the mixture upon a flat dish, a quarter of an inch thick, cover, and leave for the night. In the morning cut with a two and a half inch cutter a series of rounds out of the flattened mixture, flour them, or dip them in frying batter (No. 116), plunge them into boiling fat till golden-brown; drain, dry, and serve with sliced lemon.

136. Salmon fritters.

Having prepared a mince of cold veal and ham—two-thirds of the former to one of the latter—season it with salt and spiced pepper, and moisten it with a white sauce made out of veal broth. Butter six or eight fire-proof china scallop-shells, or a large baking-dish, sprinkle over the butter a coating of finely-minced cooked mushroom, put in the minced meat, dust over the surface of the scallops with fine raspings, pour a few drops of butter, melted, over them, and warm in the oven, serving with a curl of fried bacon on each.

137. Veal and ham scallops.

This is a variation of buttered eggs. *Fines herbes* is to be described as a mixture of mushrooms, parsley and shallot, or chives if procurable, in these proportions—equal measure of the two former to one-third of last. For this dish a tablespoonful of chopped mushroom (well cleaned fresh trimmings will do) and one of chopped parsley to a dessertspoonful or rather less of chopped shallot. Begin by frying the shallot in a quarter of an ounce of butter, a pinch of pepper and one of salt, over a low fire for five minutes, then stir in the parsley and mushroom, fry for five minutes more. Empty the contents of the pan into a bowl and set aside. In the morning put a quarter of an ounce of butter into a small saucepan, add a quarter of an ounce of flour, cook over a low fire for four or five minutes, then stir in a quarter of a pint of milk, bring to the boil to thicken, simmer, adding the *fines herbes* and a dessertspoonful of milk, with which a raw yolk has been beaten, keeping it hot afterwards in the *bain-marie*. Now make the buttered eggs (No. 3), adding the *fines herbes* mixture as a finishing touch. Serve as hot as possible.

138. Buttered eggs with fines herbes.

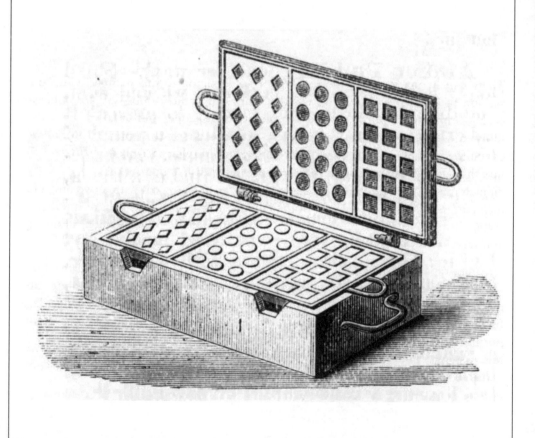

MENU XLVII.

Cod in custard sauce.
Dry curry on toast.
Matelote of eggs.
Vienna rolls.

Take a pound and a quarter of cold boiled cod-fish and break it up into nice flaky pieces. Put these into a stewpan, season with pepper, salt, and a grate of nutmeg, and moisten with enough of the boiling, saved the previous evening, to cover; set this in the *bain-marie* to heat up slowly, while with the yolks of a couple of eggs you proceed to turn half a pint of the boilings to a savoury custard, when ready drain the now hot pieces of fish from the liquid in which they were warmed, arrange them on a hot dish, and smother with the custard. Serve as hot as possible.

139. Cod in custard sauce.

This is a very nice breakfast "savoury." Make on the day previous a good curry of one pound of mutton, veal, or lamb cut into neat squares, and put it away for the night in a china dish. In the morning prepare eight or ten two and a half inch squares of fried bread, and lay these in close order in a hot silver dish. Pick the pieces of meat out of the curry gravy, and melt half an ounce of butter in a stewpan or earthenware casserole, set this over a very low fire, put in the curried meat, stirring it about so as to heat up and dry at the same time. The process must be patiently carried out, and care must be taken to prevent burning. When quite hot the dry curry should be arranged on the fried bread, and served with curls of crisply fried bacon or fried ham. If preferred the curry may be simply warmed, without drying, in the *bain-marie,* and poured over the toasts. This,

140. Dry curry on toast.

it need scarcely be said, is a handy way of serving the remains of a curry left at a previous meal.

Put an ounce of butter at the bottom of a stewpan over a low fire, melt it, add an ounce of flour, slowly cook these together for seven minutes till browning lightly, **141. Matelote** then add a pint of broth, gravy, or clear soup that may have been left, **of eggs.** flavour with a tablespoonful of mushroom ketchup, a saltspoonful of spiced pepper, salt if necessary, and a sherry-glass of light claret; boil, skim, and pass this sauce into a fire-proof dish, then slip six eggs into it, put the dish in the oven and poach them till set, when serve.

N.B.—When red wine is used in cookery the vessel should either be enamelled or glazed earthenware: tinned utensils have a prejudicial effect on the colour of the sauce in these circumstances.

MENU XLVIII.

Water-zootje.
Fritot of pigeons.
Eggs with tarragon.
Devilled biscuits.

If this dish has been presented on the previous evening it can be easily heated for breakfast, for which meal, owing to its plainness, it is very well suited. A zootje can be made of any fish, or any mixture of fish, including the fresh   142. *Water-* water varieties. The flounder is a favourite subject for treatment in   *zootje.* this fashion, but whiting, small haddock, slips, &c., are very nice in a zootje. The first thing to do is to fillet the fish and make a good broth with the heads, bones, and trimmings, using the adjuncts mentioned in No. 103, and when nicely flavoured to strain it off and employ it as the "water" in which the fillets are to be cooked. Bring the "water" to the boil, put in the fillets, let it return to the boil for a minute, then simmer the fillets till done; bunches of green parsley should be boiled with a zootje, the scraped root of parsley also, and a tablespoonful of grated horseradish is an improvement if there be as much as three pints of water or broth. Serve the fillets in a deep dish with the parsley and the broth as well, brown bread-and-butter accompanying. In hot weather a nice breakfast dish is *cold* zootje, for if the decoction of the heads and bones be strong, and the dish be set in a very cold larder or upon a bed of crushed ice, it will solidify in a firm jelly. A little gelatine may be added.

Three pigeons will be enough if of a good size. Slightly roast and   143. *Fritot of* split them in halves. Marinade these during the night with three   *pigeons.*

tablespoonfuls salad oil, the juice of a lemon, a bunch of parsley shredded, a half ounce shallot also sliced finely, a dozen pepper corns, and a dust of salt. In the morning take out of the marinade and wipe the pieces of pigeon, **144. Eggs with** dip them in milk, flour them well, plunge them in very hot fat (as **tarragon.** for *croquettes*) when they turn a pale brown, drain, dry, dish on a napkin or paper, garnish with fried parsley, and serve. Should there be any bread sauce available it would be an appropriate adjunct. By saving the livers of the birds you can dish them effectively in this manner. Fry the livers in butter, empty them and the butter into a mortar, pound them, add for six livers a teaspoonful of anchovy essence, season with a saltspoonful of spiced pepper, and spread the mixture on six nicely fried toasts, heat in the mouth of the oven, and lay a half pigeon on each, serving immediately.

This may be done with either poached or hard-boiled eggs. If the former, put an ounce of butter in a small saucepan, take it off the fire when half melted, so that it may camplete the melting in the hot saucepan, add a teaspoonful of lemon juice and the same of chopped tarragon, or, if tarragon be out of season, a teaspoonful of tarragon vinegar instead of lemon juice ; a teaspoonful of this should be poured over each of the six poached eggs after the latter have been arranged on squares of buttered toast. For hard-boiled eggs: Slice them in halves, longitudinally, and lay them in a hot silver dish, masking them with white sauce flavoured with chopped tarragon.

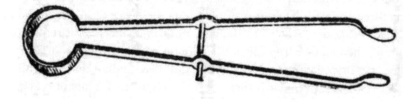

MENU XLIX.

ABSTINENCE.
Soles in the oven.
Egg croquettes.
Omelette with oysters.
Bannocks.

Prepare one large or two medium-sized soles as if for frying, No. 28, but in this instance the fish can be left whole. Butter a flat *gratin* dish, sprinkle this over with finely chopped parsley, lay the sole upon it and moisten the upper side of the fish with butter, melted. Put this in the oven; after eight minutes' cooking carefully turn the sole, baste again with butter, **145. *Soles in the oven.*** and six minutes afterwards it will be done. Lift the fish with a slice and put it upon the hot dish prepared for it; to the butter in the *gratin* dish add a tablespoonful of minced parsley and the juice of a lemon: pour this over the dished sole and serve immediately. As in all cases where butter melted forms the sauce of a dish of fish great care must be taken to have things as hot as possible, to prevent greasiness.

For these follow the directions given for No. 107, but with this difference as to proportions: Four hard-boiled eggs instead of two, and a quarter of a pound of mushrooms instead of double that quantity. Mix the two minces as therein explained, adding one filleted anchovy, minced small, or a teaspoonful of the es- **146. *Egg croquettes.*** sence. When thickened pat the mixture into shape in the same way, but making it about two-thirds of an inch thick. In the morning divide the mass into pieces, which when rolled in fine crumbs will be about the size of a guinea-fowl's egg. Brush over with beaten egg and crumb these, plunging them one by one into very hot fat; as soon as they turn a nice golden colour take them out, drain, dry, dust over with salt, and serve piled up on a napkin or paper.

See No. 117. In this instance, before being finally added to the thickened broth, each oyster should be cut into two pieces. Divide the mixture in halves—one for each *omelette* (which can be made in either of the ways given—No.6 or 48, as may be preferred), and having heated it in the *bain-marie* pass one portion into each *omelette* as done in the case of No. 93.

147. *Omlettes with oysters*.

MENU L.

Fillets of brill with tomatoes.
Jambalaia of fowl.
Omelettes with salmon.
Sally lunns.

For this please turn to No. 109, and treat a nice-sized brill exactly in the manner described for the sea bream. Proceed in all respects similarly until the thickening of the broth stage, when the teaspoonful of anchovy sauce should be 148. *Fillets* omitted, and two tablespoonfuls of tomato conserve added instead. *of brill with* This, when nice and smooth, should be poured over the fish fillets *tomatoes.* as explained in the before-mentioned recipe; the glazing is, however, unnecessary.

A *"jambalaia"* is a species of European khitchri; that is to say, it consists of minced chicken and ham tossed in rice, the process being thus conducted: Boil six ounces of rice as for curry (No. 20); chop up five ounces of uncooked lean 149. *Jambalaia* ham, and eight or ten ounces of cold cooked chicken. Put the ham *of fowl.* into a small frying-pan with an ounce of butter and give it a fry till fit to serve, then stir in the cooked chicken, season with spiced pepper, and turn the contents of the pan into the vessel containing the hot rice, which by this time should be drained and dry. Serve well mixed on a very hot dish.[1]

Here the method is as nearly as possible the same as that adopted 150. *Omelettes* for the oyster *omelette,* and by its means half a pound of cold *with salmon.*

cooked salmon can be turned to capital account. Break up the salmon, but not too finely, and moisten it in a stewpan over a low fire, or in the *bain-marie,* either with the sauce left the previous evening or a quarter of a pint of melted butter sauce made with the salmon boilings. Add half of this, quite hot, but not boiling, to each of the *omelettes* in the same way as the oysters in No. 147.

[1]This dish is improved by stirring into the rice a coffee-cupful of tomato ketchup and giving the whole a dusting of grated Parmesan.

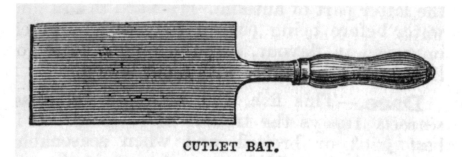

CUTLET BAT.

APPENDIX.

HINTS ON BAKING AT HOME.

Fancy bread has become an almost essential portion of the English breakfast. It is susceptible of considerable variety, and in view of this fact I have suggested various kinds of rolls, scones, bannocks, &c., in the *menus*. These have now to be explained. While many of them must, of course, be old familiar friends, some, I think, will be found uncommon; at any rate, there are twenty different sorts to choose from, and as I propound the simplest possible system of baking—with baking powder—little or no difficulty should be experienced in working out the whole category. Still, it must be admitted that as in all branches of cookery, so in this, experience in regard to details is necessary. Flours vary in quality. With some less moistening fluid is necessary than with others, in consequence of which exact proportions may sometimes not be hit off without an experiment or two. With perseverance, however, success is certain. A very important factor in the operation is the oven. This demands close observance on the part of the cook, for ovens seem to be as variable in their dispositions as human beings. A great advance has, however, been made in the construction of ranges, and happy is the home baker who possesses one with regulating power in regard to the heating of the baking apparatus. In some (I might say *all*) ordinary old-fashioned kitchen stoves the ovens are deficient in bottom heat, quite an essential feature in the baking of bread, cakes, *soufflés,* &c., and many a cook is, I fear, unfairly blamed for failures that might be traced to this defect in her appliances.

If fancy bread baking be carried out nearly every day, it is desirable that the cook should keep a set of utensils separately for this branch of her work—a shallow white enamelled milk pan, two wooden spoons of a largish size, a dozen round patty pans for ordinary rolls two and a half inches in diameter, half a dozen muffin rings, a wire drainer as used by confectioners, a baking sheet, and six special tins for French rolls.

The milk pan is recommended for the kneading of the dough, for which process the wooden spoons should be used. Thus, work with the hands is unnecessary, and greater lightness is obtained. If little round rolls be set in buttered patty pans they preserve their shape and bake nicely, and French roll tins are useful in a similar manner.

Touching materials, I recommend Yeatman's baking powder, because I have had sixteen years' experience of it, and have proved its reliability. In regard to flours, there are many varieties to choose from. For white fancy bread such as rolls, Hungarian or Vienna is considered the best, while for the different digestive cakes, scones, &c., brown flour, wholemeal or wheatmeal, oatmeal, barley-meal, Indian-meal and so on, are called into play. It is, I presume, scarcely necessary to add that all flour used in baking should be as dry as possible.

In the directions given for home baking on a small scale, it often happens that certain rule-of-thumb dry measures are given which cannot be considered definite, such as "cups" of flour, and "teaspoonfuls"—"heaped up" or not, as the case may be—of baking powder. Many find it difficult to decide what cup to choose, and all teaspoons are not made exactly the same size. I have accordingly adopted a system of weights for everything, excepting a saltspoonful of salt, which have been carefully verified and can be trusted.

Touching "a saltspoonful of salt." It will be found on careful examination that a heaped up ordinary kitchen saltspoonful weighs two drachms, and a mere bowlful *not* heaped up half that quantity. For the sake of clearness, then, I would explain that when I say "a saltspoonful" I mean the former, and when I say "a small saltspoonful" I mean the latter.

With liquids there is less risk of ambiguity than with dry measure, for you cannot "heap" them up—a full tablespoonful may be accepted as a fixed quantity, *i.e.,* four tablespoonfuls equal half a gill or a common *sherry* glass, for the term *wine*glass is not explicit.

1. HOT ROLLS.—For eight rolls one and a half ounce each, take eight ounces of flour, a quarter of an ounce of Yeatman's powder, a saltspoonful of salt, and half an ounce of butter. Spread the flour in the enamelled pan, sprinkle the baking powder and salt over its surface, mix well, then rub the butter into it. This having been done, begin to moisten with milk or buttermilk by degrees, working the dough with the wooden spoons. Nine tablespoonfuls, provided that the flour be of fine quality, should suffice if the operator work skilfully. When ready, turn this out upon a floured pastry board, divide the dough into eight equal portions, pat them into a round shape with the spoons, and place them in eight buttered patty pans. Arrange these upon a baking sheet, wet the surfaces of the rolls with a brush that has been dipped

into milk, and slip the sheet into the oven, which should be rather brisk. When the rolls have risen and taken a pale brown colour, they may be taken out of the oven, turned out of the patty pans, and served in a hot napkin. Time, from twelve to fifteen minutes.

2. FRENCH ROLLS.—For six French rolls exactly double the quantities given in the preceding recipe should be taken, with the addition of one fresh egg. Work in the same way, adding the egg well beaten at the commencement of the moistening, then enough milk to form a firm dough. When smooth, turn this out on a floured pastry board, divide it into six portions, and pat these into elongated oval shapes; lay these in well-buttered French roll tins, brush them over with milk, and set them upon a baking sheet, finishing as in the previous case.

3. VIENNA ROLLS.—The difference here consists in the shape alone. Having worked the dough as for French rolls, turn it out on a floured board, divide it into six portions, roll these out into sausage shapes an inch and a half thick in the centre, tapering somewhat towards the ends, curve them in the form of crescents, lay them on a buttered baking tin, brush them over with milk, and bake about fifteen minutes.

4. KNOTTED ROLLS.—Here again variety is obtained by shaping the dough in a different manner: a crisp crusty roll is thus produced. Roll the portions of dough out into long tubular shapes the thickness of your little finger, tie them in knots, and finish as in the case of Vienna rolls.

5. INDIAN-MEAL ROLLS.—For these the proportions of flour only are altered, viz., twelve ounces of fine flour to four ounces Indian-meal (maize flour). For the rest the ingredients are the same as for French rolls, and the method of work also. They may be shaped as "Hot Rolls" (No. 1), and baked in patty pans.

6. BROWN ROLLS.—In this case substitute the best wholemeal, well dried, for flour; in other respects proceed as detailed for "Hot Rolls" (No. 1). Another wholesome variation can be obtained by a mixture in these proportions: Five ounces of wholemeal to three of fine well-dried oatmeal, while a milder digestive roll is got by substituting flour for wholemeal, and mixing three ounces of fine oatmeal with it.

7. SIR HENRY THOMPSON'S WHOLEMEAL CAKES.—"Take two pounds of coarsely-ground whole wheatmeal, and add half a pound of fine flour, or, better still, the same weight of *fine* Scotch oatmeal. Mix thoroughly with a sufficient quantity of baking powder and a little salt; then rub in two ounces of butter and make into dough—using a wooden spoon—with cold skimmed milk or milk and water, soft in consistence, so that it can almost be poured into the tin ring, which gives it form when baked. In this manner it is to be quickly made into flat cakes (like tea cakes), and baked on a tin, the rings used being about an inch high and seven or eight inches in diameter, each enclosing a cake. Put them without delay into a quick oven at the outset, letting them be finished thoroughly, at a lower temperature."

"The object of making this bread in flat cakes or in scones is to ensure a light and well-cooked product. It is difficult to ensure these two qualities in the form of loaves except of the smallest size. A larger proportion of oatmeal, if preferred, can be adopted by either method."

N.B.—Half an ounce of Yeatman's baking powder and a saltspoonful of salt per pound of meal will be found correct.

8. MUFFINS.—Sift together a pound of fine flour, an ounce of Yeatman's powder, and two saltspoonfuls of salt, stir in enough milk by degrees to form a smooth, but rather stiff, batter. Butter four muffin rings, lay them on a buttered baking sheet well heated, half fill them with the batter, and put them in the oven. When the batter has risen level with the top of the rings, turn them gently and bake till a good straw colour, when take out the tin, turn the muffins out of the rings, open them, toast slightly on the inside, butter them, fold the two pieces together again, and serve at once. About a pint of milk or a little more will be probably required to form the batter. Time, about twenty-five minutes.

9. CRUMB MUFFINS.—Weigh half a pound of stale white breadcrumb, eight ounces of flour, and half an ounce of baking powder. Beat up two eggs. Soak the crumbs till soft in warm milk. Mix the flour and baking powder well, adding a saltspoonful of salt. Combine the two, diluting first with the beaten eggs, and then with enough milk, if necessary, to form a stiff batter. Put this into buttered muffin rings upon a hot buttered baking tin, and bake in a quick oven fifteen minutes.

10. SALLY LUNNS, NOT SWEETENED.—Rub two ounces of butter into a pound of flour, with which half an ounce of baking powder has been thoroughly sifted and a saltspoonful of salt. Convert this into dough by first mixing with it two well-beaten eggs, and then milk enough by degrees to bring it to the consistency of thick batter. For the rest, treat this as explained for "Crumb Muffins."

11. TEA CAKES, UNSWEETENED.—Beat up a couple of eggs in a bowl, warm a quarter of a pint of milk, and melt in it two ounces of butter. Mix these together well, and then stir in by degrees three-quarters of a pound of flour, with which half an ounce of baking powder and a saltspoonful of salt have been well incorporated. If necessary, add a little more milk or flour, as the case may be, to obtain the consistency of a firm batter. Put into rings, and proceed as in No. 8.

12. SCONES.—Under this denomination there are several varieties. The ordinary English sort may be described in the following manner: With one pound of flour mix well a saltspoonful of salt and half an ounce of Yeatman's powder; then rub into this two ounces of butter, and when that has been thoroughly done, commence moistening with a well-beaten egg and enough milk (something rather less than half a pint) to form a light dough. Lay this on a floured board, roll it out half an inch thick, divide this into a dozen neat oblongs. Bake on a buttered baking tin in a hot oven eight or ten minutes, and when nicely browned, serve piled up in a hot napkin.

13. BARLEY-MEAL SCONES.—Follow the previous recipe, substituting barley-meal for flour. Properly speaking, according to old Scottish custom, these scones should be cooked on a "girdle," *i.e.*, a thick circular piece of iron about a foot and a half in diameter, which should be suspended or held over a clear fire and heated till a few grains of salt laid upon its surface crackle; this having been brushed off, the cakes or scones should be laid upon the girdle, occasionally turned, and taken off with a slice (the "spurtle") when they are nicely browned. But this process is in these days of closed ranges unnecessary, ingenious as it may have been when the cook had to do her best with only a primitive open fire to work with. Scones can now be cooked "girdle" wise in a thick iron plate or frying-pan on the hot plate of the range, or on a baking sheet in the oven. A good bottom heat is obviously the thing that is needed. You can see scones beautifully cooked by electricity at Messrs. Verity's, in Regent Street, on this principle. But to return to the case in hand. Having mixed the dough as in No. 11, turn it out upon a board, dredge it over with flour, and roll it out a third of an inch thick, cut this into three-inch squares, double the opposite corners over, forming three-cornered shapes, and bake on a buttered tin in the oven eight or ten minutes; or lay them upon a heated iron frying-pan upon the hot plate, and treat them in the manner just described for the girdle scones.

14. BROWN FLOUR SCONES.—Mix with a pound of wheatmeal half an ounce of baking powder and a saltspoonful of salt; rub two ounces of butter into this, and when that has been done, commence moistening with a well-beaten fresh egg, adding just enough milk or buttermilk to bring it to the consistence of a light dough. Finish as described for No. 11.

15. BANNOCKS.—A pound of fine oatmeal, a saltspoonful of salt, and half an ounce of baking powder having been sifted and mixed, rub into it an ounce of butter, and then moisten with water in sufficient quantity to make a thick dough. Roll this out as thin as possible, divide it into quarters, and halve each of them; lay these one by one on a heated iron frying-pan upon the hot plate, bake, turning them on each side. Toast afterwards in front of the fire till crisp.

16. IRISH BANNOCKS.—Warm half a pint of milk and dissolve in it three ounces of butter; mix into this a pound of wheatmeal, half an ounce of baking powder, and a saltspoonful of salt. Mix to a stiff dough. Turn this upon the board, roll it out three-quarters of an inch thick, and cut into six cakes. Bake in the manner just described, and serve dusted over with flour on a hot napkin.

17. OAT CAKES.—As a rule, the directions given for these wholesome cakes counsel the cook to roll them out as thin as possible. This, of course, is simply a matter of taste, and with cheese perhaps the thin cake is very nice, but for breakfast I think a thicker cake is better. For these take one pound of oatmeal—coarse or fine, as may be preferred—rub into this two ounces of butter with a small teaspoonful of salt, and then moisten with sufficient water to make a smooth dough. Pat this into a round

mass and lay it upon a floured board, roll it out not less than *a quarter of an inch* thick, cut this into three and a half inch squares, halve these by cutting them across from corner to corner, forming triangular shapes, and bake in the pan till firm and thoroughly done. Dust over with sifted meal and serve in a hot napkin.

18. DEVILLED BISCUIT.—Take a dozen plain water biscuits, or six "Bath Olivers." If the former be only two inches in diameter, six can be done at a time in a large, or three in a medium, pan as follows: Put an ounce of butter into a large, or half an ounce into a small, frying-pan over a low fire: as soon as it begins to melt, lay the biscuits upon it, turning them over the fire till the butter browns, pepper well with grill seasoning (page 37). Put them on a very hot dish, and pour the browned butter over them, and serve. Or if liked very dry, lay them, after having been thus cooked, on a wire drainer, and set them in the oven for a minute or two, serving *as hot as possible,* closely covered in a hot silver dish.

Biscuit à l'Indienne is prepared as the foregoing, but curry powder is dusted over it instead of the plain seasoning of pepper and salt. Some even like an addition of a couple of drops of tabasco on each biscuit.

Bath Olivers or three-inch water biscuits ought to be done separately one after another.

19. CRUMPETS.—In London and most towns crumpets can be so easily procured from "the manufacturer," that very few people take the trouble to make them at home. In the country this is different; besides, there may be some who, among other experiments, would like to try this:—Thoroughly mix together twelve ounces of Vienna flour, a small saltspoonful of salt, and three-quarters of an ounce of Yeatman's baking powder; then stir in an ounce of butter, melted, one egg well beaten, and enough milk to form a smooth batter. With this half till six or eight well-buttered muffin rings, which should be laid beforehand on a heated iron pan. Watch, and when the batter rises somewhat, turn each crumpet carefully, and finish the baking without further turning. Toast lightly, butter, and serve in the usual manner, Coming straight from the pan in this way, they will be found nicer than those bought cold and toasted afterwards.

20. SOUTHERN INDIAN CRUMPETS, OR "APUMS."—Put one pound and a half of rice flour into a pan, dilute it to a stiff paste with lukewarm water, in which half an ounce of fresh German yeast has been dissolved. Let this remain all night; next day moisten this with the juice of a cocoanut to the consistency of firmish batter, and put a gill of this at a time into a heated and buttered pan over the hot plate, covering the pan closely. When nicely risen and browned round the edges the "apum" is ready. Repeat the process with similar quantities of the mixture till all of it is expended: serve very hot on a napkin, dusted over with salt.

Cocoanut juice is made as follows: Scrape the nutty part of a cocoanut into fine shreds, put these in a bowl, pour scalding water over them, moistening them well. After half an hour's infusion, strain the liquid into a bowl, and putting the nut scrapings into a piece of muslin, squeeze all the moisture out of them into the strained juice. This extract of cocoanut is what the Southern Indian cook uses in curry making under the name of "cocoanut milk," a fluid that it resembles in appearance. The water inside the nut is not "cocoanut milk" from this standpoint.

21. OATMEAL PORRIDGE.—This is a deservedly popular thing for breakfast. To prepare it, weigh a couple of ounces of oatmeal, put three-quarters of a pint of water in a saucepan, set it on the fire and bring it to the boil; cast into it a *pinch* (the eighth of an ounce) of salt, and then dredge in the oatmeal, stirring with a wooden spoon while the operation is being carried out. Simmer for forty minutes, by which time the oatmeal should have absorbed the water and be swollen and soft. It can now be served accompanied by a jug of hot milk, sugar or salt being added according to taste, the latter obviously for choice. Cream is, of course, a favourite adjunct with many, but does it not detract from the well-known wholesomeness of the porridge? I think so.

Those who like their porridge at its best will find the following process a good one:—Let the prepared oatmeal be sent in its saucepan, set this on a spirit lamp in the breakfast-room, stirring in cold milk in sufficient quantity to bring the porridge to the desired consistency; wait till air bubbles begin to rise to the surface, and turn it into a very hot soup plate. *Hot* milk can be used if liked, but remember that there is a difference in the flavour of boiled and unboiled milk. By this plan a properly hot porridge is certain in a couple of minutes.

The proportions given will yield two large or three small portions. If the oatmeal absorbs the water too quickly in the cooking, additional hot water should be stirred in. Some oatmeals are more floury than others, and as much as a pint of water may be needed for two ounces.

22. DRY TOAST.—A very simple thing to be sure, yet how often is it maltreated—scorched outside, spongy within, and flabby? The bread should not be new; it should be cut in quarter inch slices, and toasted at *some little distance* from the clear smokeless embers, patiently, till each side has turned a nice pale golden brown. Sir Henry Thompson's dry toast is made in this way:—The slices are cut somewhat thicker—three-eighths of an inch—and slightly coloured on both sides. A sharp knife is then passed horizontally through the softish centre part, making two pieces of each slice. The inner sides are now toasted, and nice crisp dry toast is the result.

23. ANTI-FAT TOAST, for those who have to think twice about eating bread, is easily made as follows:—Cut a stale tin-baked loaf into thin slices (one-eighth of an inch thick at the outside), lay these on a wire drainer in the oven till they crispen and turn yellowish brown. If a good quantity of it be prepared, this toast can be kept in a biscuit tin, and will be quite nice for two or three days. Excellent whether for breakfast, luncheon, or dinner.

Index.

DISHES OF FISH.

DISHES OF MEAT.

DISHES OF EGGS.

FANCY BREAD, ROLLS, &C.

MISCELLANEOUS.

Epilogue

Since this biography was first written, reports of the death of the English Breakfast have been much exaggerated, as the writer Mark Twain said of his own passing after discovering that his obituary had been published in error. So here is what has happened to the meal, beginning with the breakfasts of the second half of the twentieth century, which were very different to those of the first half—and some not English at all.

The 'Oslo Breakfast' almost became the English Breakfast as a matter of national policy. It was a children's meal developed in the late 1920s to improve the health of Norwegian children. Highly nutritious, the Oslo Breakfast consisted of:

The Oslo Breakfast

Wholemeal bread, 2 oz; butter, 1.2 oz; yeast (as extract), 1/8–3/8 oz; cheese, 1 oz; tomato, ½ oz; herring or sardine, 1 oz, fresh or tinned; milk, 1 pint; 1 apple or half orange.

Children given this simple cold meal daily, it was reported, showed a marked improvement in growth, vitality and alertness and freedom from infectious illness (Henning 1942). In the 1930s, as nutrition emerged as a science, there was widespread concern about the nation's health, as a result of the privations of World War I followed by an economic depression. Advocating a national policy of nutrition, the Fabian Society of Britain argued for communal feeding, envisioning 'schools as centres of health', where mass-catered nourishing breakfasts could be served to every child (Drake 1936:27), ensuring that they would have one good meal a day, and the most important one at that. World War II intervened but in 1942, well before the war was over, plans to use the Oslo Breakfast to improve the health of British children were considered at the highest levels of government. Even if communal feeding proved impractical, it was hoped that the Oslo Breakfast could easily be served at home, and to adults, in larger portions, as well as to children. The main advantage of the Oslo Breakfast was that it required no cooking, a boon to poorer families who suffered from 'the lack of proper cooking conveniences in small flats and tenements, and the excessive cost of fuel which is bought and used in small quantities' (Drake 1933:17). It also supplied more nutrition than the cereals, flour, oatmeal, rice and potatoes that featured large in working class diets. Whether or not the Oslo Breakfast would have appealed to the British palate, most of its ingredients were rationed until 1954 and the scheme was abandoned, leaving people to find other breakfasts in a sparse foodscape and a rapidly changing world.

The wealthy could take the first meal of the day in hotels, which had been a bastion of the English Breakfast through the war. Restaurants and hotels were not subject to rationing, and those who could afford it had their meals there, with some choosing to live in hotels for the duration of the conflict and the post-war food restrictions. In hotels, breakfast was often eaten in the privacy of the bedroom, rather than in the dining room. With room service, the challenge was always to deliver the food before it cooled, and to transport it from kitchens to bedroom without mishap. Here, the 'art of the tray' was all. The Council for the Hotel and Catering Trade issued detailed instructions on how the tray was to be laid and breakfast presented, in a style that has not altered to this day. For a full breakfast, the heaviest dish—say, eggs and bacon, or kippers—would be in the centre, under a cloche or food cover. The lighter items, such as toast in a toast rack, half a grapefruit, dishes of butter and of jam, mustard, salt and pepper, sugar cubes and tea or coffee pots along with cutlery and cups were placed along the outside, arranged to spread the weight evenly. The tray was to be balanced on poised fingers, not flat on the palm of the hand nor resting on the shoulder. 'The clever waiter', the instructions continued, 'will balance a tray in his outspread palm on a level with his shoulder, so that his right hand is free to open the door handle of the room he is about to enter' (National Council for Hotel and Catering Education 1947:42–4).

Outside the hotels, things were very different. *'Starvation in the Midst of Plenty'* had been one of the rallying calls of the pre-war Fabian food reform movement and, ironically, this worsened after the war, not just among the poor, but in the population generally. At the war's end, trying to keep the breakfast flag flying, the food writer Ambrose Heath opened his book *Good Breakfasts* (1945:9) in this way: 'the lack of bacon has disturbed our native breakfast-dish and brought doubt and distress into many an early morning kitchen. The purpose of this little book is to help to dispel these two concomitants of war time, and still to promote what Izaak Walton called "a good, honest, wholesome, hungry breakfast"'. With rations for

adults comprising 1 fresh egg and 4 ounces of bacon or ham per person weekly, Heath's recipes consisted of subterfuges to make bacon go as far as possible and ingenious versions of traditional English breakfast dishes using non-rationed foods like cod's tongues and rabbit; however, they required lengthy preparation, and time was something people no longer had. The voice of the New Woman was increasingly heard in the land, and in a new breed of cookery books devoted to making everything quick and easy. As one of these modern cookery writers put it, 'We cannot devote so much time to cooking. And frankly, we don't want to, except perhaps on especially cold and dreary days' (Terry 1947:6). This writer urged the use of 'carry-overs'— not to be confused with 'sad-looking leftovers'—which, if well chosen, could do for dinner, and the next morning's breakfast.

Reflecting this new mood, Good Housekeeping Institute, the authority on the domestic arts, published a booklet called A Good Housekeeping Book of Meals in a Hurry (1948:1), which began, 'In most households these days many meals have to be prepared in a hurry, it may be breakfast in the morning when there are trains to catch', and continued, 'For a great many people today, breakfast is prepared and eaten with one eye on the clock' (1948:3). A well stocked and carefully arranged store cupboard, it went on to say, was the first essential for hurried meals—tinned goods, dry stores and especially packaged cereals. Breakfast cereals were increasingly eaten by adults and children at any time of day, because they were a quick and convenient 'meal in a minute', one that even a man could easily make. In the early 1950s, Selfridges Department Store in London offered forty-eight different kinds of breakfast cereal, including Fig Vita-Bran and 'Aviator' Wheat Flakes.

Out in the working world, women were encountering their own catering challenges. For post-war career girls pursuing independence, the longed-for 'room of one's own' in a large house recently converted into bedsitting rooms often had no separate cooking facilities. While this had long been a problem among the poor, it came as a shock to young middle-class women. In the 1950s, gas was replacing coal for domestic heating and the Gas Council, seeing an opportunity, published booklets with titles like One Room Cookery (1950:3), which began: 'A room of your own . . . perhaps you are one of the many thousands of women . . . who live in one-room flatlets. Probably the room was not originally designed as a bed-sitting room . . . How about your cooking arrangements?' Now the midday meal was taken outside the home, often in the works canteen, but that still left breakfast and supper to prepare in a pre-fast food era. To solve the problem, an array of gas-powered cooking appliances, specifically designed for use in a bedsit, appeared. There were table-top portable grills and small ovens, and for boiling and frying, gas rings with or without attached hotplate. Under these conditions, cooking had to be simple, and cookbooks began to have sections entitled 'Breakfast and Supper Dishes' because now these were often the same: eggs prepared in many different ways—'something eggy on a tray', as Noël Coward reportedly put it—and, especially, toast which became something

ONE-ROOM COOKERY

of a national obsession. *One Room Cookery* (1950:26) devoted a chapter to 'Toast Dishes', urging, 'if you have not much time to spare, "something on toast" is a good idea. Make your toast underneath the gas grill, or with the aid of a toasting fork, in front of the gas fire', and following with recipes for mushroom toast, cheese and walnut on toast, fish toast, tomatoes on toast and many more. Flour producers

and millers' associations also promoted toast enthusiastically as an ideal start to the day. Seeking to expand this repertoire, Good Housekeeping published *100 Ideas for Breakfast and High Tea*, with recipes that could serve for both meals, and which had been devised to make the most of un-rationed meats.

In bedsits, breakfast may have been truncated to 'something on toast', but as food finally came off rationing in 1954, people could indulge themselves in the most basic form of the English Breakfast—the old favourite of bacon and eggs—in a new setting. With women going to work outside the home in large numbers, and with the democratisation of society in the post-war years, what came to be described as the 'working class café' emerged. Now commonly, though inaccurately, described as the 'Full English' breakfast, this version of the meal was assumed to be rooted in the distant past, but this was not the case, and nor were 'working class cafés' as old as they are assumed to be today. The Victorian urban poor ate street food such as puddings and penny pies purchased from hawkers (Mayhew 1969). Establishments, however humble, in which they could sit and eat food cooked to order at leisure were beyond their means and, even when their lot improved, visits to cafés and eating houses were a rarity. In the pre-war years, for those of restricted means, freshly cooked eggs and bacon were not cheap, and as for tinned baked beans—regarded today as the quintessential working class food—they began as a highly expensive luxury food. Imported from America, they were sold only at the exclusive Fortnum and Mason in London until the end of the 1920s, when they began to be produced by Heinz in the UK (Alberts 1974). Cafés now became the redoubt of the cooked breakfast for the general population. The cafés also cooked proper lunches, but as sandwich bars began to develop, cutting into the luncheon market, the cafés focused increasingly on breakfast, which they began to serve all through the day. Café décor, regarded as iconic today, was very much of the 1950s that saw their emergence: shiny Formica counters and tables, plastic bottles of tomato ketchup and brown sauce, cruets of vinegar, shakers of pepper and salt, and a large shaker of sugar to sweeten mugs of tea and coffee served in Pyrex cups and saucers. The menu was usually chalked up on blackboards—egg and bacon; egg, bacon and sausage; egg, bacon and tomatoes; sausages, chips and beans; sausage, egg and chips (Davies 2005). If bedsits were a woman's world with a menu of toast, cafés were a man's world where lorry drivers, shopkeepers, labourers, office workers and businessmen could enjoy the greasy delights of a 'fry-up' in steamy, smoky fraternity.

The English Breakfast may have been flourishing in cafés and hotels but, with rationing over, producers of breakfast foods now faced the challenge of re-establishing the home-cooked breakfast—indeed, proper home cooking in general—with the result that food 'marketing boards' proliferated. Their objective was to sell the foods they promoted by re-educating the cooking and eating public, often through the issuing of free recipe booklets and leaflets. Now classed as 'ephemera' and hard to find, they were more influential than cookbooks in their day, both reflecting popular opinion and forming it, and their use in this history takes advantage of a highly valuable but often overlooked resource.

The challenge faced by the post-war marketing boards was substantial. As the Butter Information Council (1959:2) put it, 'With fifteen years of rationing it is not surprising that many of us have forgotten—and many never even knew—all the things that butter does to make good food better and still more delicious'. Breakfast was of particular interest to the Butter Information Council, who appealed to both toast-eaters and devotees of the fry-up:

> We need to eat a good breakfast. We need nourishment to help us face up to the day's work ahead of us. But it isn't everyone who feels like a cooked meal at breakfast time . . . Then of course there are the late risers or early starters who simply 'haven't got time' for big breakfasts. From the time they get up, life is a continuous fight against the clock until they arrive, slightly exhausted, at work . . . For these people butter is essential at breakfast. Tea or coffee and toast liberally spread with butter may comprise their first meal of the day . . . A good cup of coffee, crisp toast with cool, delicious butter—that is breakfast for many people. It's a good breakfast too. But what about those who want a *real* breakfast—even if they have time for it only on Sunday? As a change from eggs and bacon, kidneys, and kippers (served with a knob of butter of course) a popular alternative is buttered eggs . . . It is scarcely necessary to add that buttered eggs must be made with *butter* and served on *buttered* toast. (Butter Information Council 1959:5, original italics)

The Egg Marketing Board went for a more direct approach, with what became one of the most famous advertising slogans of the twentieth century: 'Go to work on an egg'.

Breakfast was also a target for the British Grower's Publicity Council, whose booklet *101 Recipes for English Tomatoes*—'English tomatoes are by far the best and they have one supreme virtue—they are fresher'—offered breakfast recipes for tomato omelette, haddock and tomato in casserole, kidneys and tomatoes, scrambled eggs and tomatoes, egg and tomato rings, baked tomato and egg, fried tomato and bacon, and tomato kedgeree:

Tomato Kedgeree

½ lb English tomatoes. ¼ lb cooked fish. 1 hard boiled egg. 4 oz cooked rice. 1 oz butter. Dip the tomatoes in boiling water. Remove the skin. Slice them finely and cook them gently in the butter until quite soft. Remove any skin and bone from the fish. Flake it finely. Add this to the tomatoes along with the rice. Remove the yolk from the egg. Chop the white and add this to the kedgeree. Season very thoroughly and heat through, stirring all the time. Arrange in a pyramid on a hot dish. Press the yolk of egg through a strainer and use as a garnish. (British Grower's Publicity Council 1950s:6)

By 1959, *Good Housekeeping* declared that there were now two kinds of breakfasts: 'Traditional English Breakfasts' and 'Breakfasts for Moderns'. The

former were the bountiful meals of the Victorian and Edwardian era, described in the opening chapters of this book—a time when 'the many types of breakfast cereals so popular today were unknown, and fruit was rarely included in the breakfast'. Altogether, *Good Housekeeping* (1959:5–6) concluded, 'the breakfast enjoyed by our grandparents was a meal to be reckoned with, the symbol of a leisurely era when domestic labour was cheap. Times have changed—but we can still have some of these savoury dishes on our breakfast tables, even if we provide only one each day instead of a lavish array', going on to provide recipes for old favourites such as potted ham, bloater paste, breakfast bannocks and fried herring, North-Country style, the latter two being regional specialities—a subject that will be returned to later. As for 'Breakfast for Moderns', while acknowledging that breakfasts had to be simple to prepare and quickly and easily eaten, *Good Housekeeping* urged:

> Nevertheless, most dieticians agree that a good breakfast is best for health, and obviates any need for mid-morning snacks . . . The oft-quoted Continentals who breakfast on coffee and a roll, it must be remembered, devote most of the time between noon and two o'clock in the afternoon to a really good leisurely meal. But in this country many people have only a hurried snack lunch—sometimes not even sitting down to eat it— and an extra fifteen minutes in the morning spent in preparing and eating a nourishing breakfast would help to prevent many digestive troubles. (*Good Housekeeping* 1959:14)

A breakfast in the modern style, *Good Housekeeping* suggested, should take advantage of the many ready-to-eat breakfast cereals—'many of them from across the Atlantic'—and canned fruits, adding a simple cooked dish using quick-frozen foods now widely available. Among the recipes given was 'fish sticks and tomatoes' using packets of frozen fish fingers, grilled herrings using frozen herrings, and pineapple and bacon toast using tinned pineapple juice and slices.

Meanwhile, the marketing boards continued their efforts, with those responsible for promoting eggs and bacon facing a different challenge to that of the others. Their aim was to escape from their strong associations with breakfast, and to promote their foods to a wider market. In their booklet *Thank Goodness for Eggs*, the Egg Information Bureau presented a collection of 'Anytime, any day, egg recipes', setting the stage for what happened to breakfast next. 'Brunch'—a combination of 'breakfast' and 'lunch'—is an English invention, being neither more nor less than the elaborate late breakfasts of the Victorian era, described earlier in this book. Having fallen out of fashion in Britain, it survived in America where it was first developed into a lavish meal offered at the weekend by hotels, private social clubs and society hostesses, then imitated more widely. For Americans, the great appeal of brunch was conviviality in a more informal setting, with guests able to serve themselves from a wide variety of foods. In the 1970s—with great irony—brunch was imported back to Britain as an American invention.

A great populariser of brunch was the Anglophile American food writer and television chef Robert Carrier, who espoused a lighter and more cosmopolitan menu and declared war on the cooked English breakfast. 'Half the nation', he wrote, 'starts the day inadequately fed, or so overstuffed with morning "stodge"—fried bread, egg, tomato and greasy bangers—that they are more fit for a return to bed than for the morning's activities . . . why not take up the American habit of the breakfast party—late breakfast, of course—and invite friends around for an imaginative feast where sausages, bacon or kippers served on their own are absolutely banned. No traditional British "stodge" allowed here—but only the lightest, most sophisticated of fare' (Carrier 1971:8–9). At the centre of Carrier's brunch were croissants and brioche, stalwarts of the French 'Continental breakfast' which, decried by *Good Housekeeping* a decade earlier, had been making steady inroads on the cooked English breakfast as people took up the habit on the foreign holidays that were becoming ever more affordable. Since there were few Continental bakeries in Britain outside the major cities, Carrier included recipes for croissants and brioche along with American popovers and baking powder biscuits. Other offerings included corned beef hash and grilled grapefruit with cinnamon but, true to his word, no traditional 'stodge'. A very different version of brunch was offered by Fanny Cradock, the television chef and food writer noted for her theatrical cooking style and elaborately presented dishes. Her cold Sunday brunch, which stretched over three separate programmes broadcast by the BBC in 1970, consisted of a collation which in spirit might have come straight out of Georgiana Hill's *Breakfast Book* in this volume. Fanny Cradock's brunch menu consisted of: hot or cold beetroot soup, prawn or shrimp border mould, raw mushroom salad; Roman-style cold duck with cherries, crudités with mayonnaise and vinaigrette; Fanny's chocolate refrigerator cake and Fanny's special iced coffee with home-made vanilla ice cream. As noted in Chapter Three, brunch is a meal that slips in and out of fashion. After enjoying a period of popularity in the early 1970s, it was gradually eclipsed by a very different kind of eating and had largely disappeared as a form of private entertaining by the end of the decade, leaving behind the baked goods of the Continental breakfast which ended the reign of toast.

The new style of eating that displaced the relaxed sophistication of brunch arose from the earnest and arduous whole food health movement. Although commonly thought to be an American invention, there had long been a British interest in health foods, natural cures and diet reform, often mixed with radical politics and practices like fruitarianism and vegetarianism. The British interest in natural health and vitality continued through the 1950s and early 1960s, sustained by herbal remedies and homeopathy, beliefs about the benefits of products like molasses, cider vinegar and honey, and the practice of calisthenics and yoga. In the late 1960s and 1970s this native health faction, previously marginal, melded with the American whole food movement and went mainstream.

On both sides of the Atlantic, the whole food movement was a direct outgrowth of the sweeping social changes of the period, in which the cultural values practices of the 1950s and early 1960s were roundly rejected. 'Quick-and-easy' cuisine, sugary processed cereals, anything tinned, and all the instant foods promoted as 'modern' became anathema as what became known as the 'diet revolution' took hold. This was not a monolithic movement but many, sometimes contradictory, influences that came together to challenge conventional practice. New nutritional, economic, gender,

spiritual and ecological values found expression in changed patterns of living and eating. In the 1950s, the new had been preferred to the old, and the mass-produced to the handmade. The key word had been convenience, and the aim had been to make life easier and save time. Now all that was reversed. In the 1960s, the old came to be valued over the new, and the hand-made preferred as 'authentic'. Time spent was no longer seen as time lost, but as meaning gained. Instead of convenience food and 'making easy', there was a new discourse of real, natural food and 'making hard'— planting, weeding, chopping, stirring, kneading, peeling, cooking for hours—because nothing of true worth was now believed to come easily or quickly. These breakfasts took a long time to make and to eat. Instead of white bread and cornflakes there were wholemeal loaves and granola; instead of dairy butter and coffee there were nut and seed spreads and herbal tea, and everywhere there was lots of plain, natural yoghurt —which Evelyn Waugh once said 'tasted so foul it simply had to be good for one' (in Gill 2008:97). No longer a simple act of nourishment or a companionable activity, eating was seen as nothing more or less than restoring kinship with the Whole Earth (Lee 1976), and ideally every breakfast was a peace-and-love experience. 'Just being together in a peaceful, warm atmosphere will make all the difference in how they get through their day. Food eaten in this relaxed and leisurely manner will be digested much more easily than when one eye is on the plate and the other on the kitchen clock', urged the authors of *Laurel's Kitchen*, a key cookbook of the movement (Robertson, Flinders and Godfrey 1976:112).

Ironically, the heyday of the whole food diet revolution saw the advent of a diametrically different way of eating. McDonalds, originator of breakfast fast food in America, opened in Britain in 1974, and the old-style fry-up cafés began to melt away. Trying to keep up with both new trends, the Eggs Information Bureau (1970s:1) brought out a recipe leaflet, *Get 6 More British Eggstra*, with instructions for preparing an 'egg and gammon bap'—effectively an Egg McMuffin—at home, and on the same page ran a recipe for a 'yoghurt breakfast' consisting of a mixture of bran, brown sugar, natural yoghurt, a sliced apple and a raw egg, mixed together.

Egg and Gammon Bap

1 thin gammon steak or rasher
1 egg
fat for frying
1 large white or brown bap, buttered.

Grill gammon steak. Meanwhile heat a little fat in a frying pan over a moderate heat. Break egg into pan, allow to start setting, then baste egg with fat until cooked to your liking. Place cooked gammon steak on bottom half of map, top with fried egg and other half of bap.

Taking the opposite tack, the Bacon Marketing Board fought valiantly against the new fast food and whole food breakfasts, declaring, 'bacon is part of our national heritage!' Mindful of the need for quick nourishment in children, it recommended, 'If the children are not used to a cooked breakfast, give them bacon sandwiches, either fried or toasted. Give them bacon and baked beans for a meal that is full of protein which they won't refuse' (British Bacon 1979:26), and among the breakfast suggestions for adults was an old-fashioned recipe:

Bacon Fraize

4 rashers streaky bacon, 2 oz plain flour, 1 egg, ½ pint (125 ml) milk, pinch of salt. Derind the bacon and cut the rashers into small strips. Mix together the flour, egg, milk and salt to make a smooth, creamy batter. Take a 7 ins/17.5 cm frying pan and fry a quarter of the bacon strips gently without extra fat until they are crisp. Add a quarter of the batter and cook until just set. Fold and serve on a warm plate. Repeat process for each serving. (British Bacon 1979:30)

'Fraize' or 'Froise', according to the food historian and folklorist Florence White (1932:32–3), was a very old English dish, a country speciality which could also be made with sausage meat, flaked fish or fruit. Its appearance in a collection of mainstream recipes bespoke a coming trend: the rediscovery of traditional English regional cooking.

Unaccustomed to cooking breakfast at home, city dwellers were discovering that the one place the full English Breakfast could still be found was in the countryside. Bed and breakfast accommodation had burgeoned after World War II, and there were still many independent country inns and small hotels. Waking up to their appeal, the English Tourist Board brought out a special guidebook called *The Taste of England*, highlighting 750 country restaurants that offered 'real English food', especially breakfasts. The guide urged:

> Two world wars and the lingering blight of rationing cast a dark shadow over the English kitchen. Fortunately today's generation is rediscovering the gourmet splendours of yesteryear. Good, fresh English food, cooked in the traditional way, is now firmly back on the map . . . Our Victorian ancestors knew better. It is impossible to build an Empire on a cup of coffee and a slice of toast. (English Tourist Board 1977:4)

It is easy to imagine hopeful breakfasters, in flight from McMuffins and granola, motoring through the English countryside accompanied by the guide, in keen pursuit of oak smoked kippers, Oxford sausages, frumenty, black pudding and devilled drumsticks.

Meanwhile, back in town, breakfast was undergoing another transformation. Now, in the 1980s greed-is-good world of high capitalism, Reaganomics and yuppies, lunch was for wimps and breakfast became the meal where the business got done. 'Power' was the buzz word—the 'power look', 'power dressing', 'empowerment' and, inevitably, the 'power breakfast'. The Regency Hotel in Manhattan claimed to be the birthplace of the power breakfast, but soon early morning meetings of movers and shakers were taking place in centres of influence across the country. Apart from getting business under the belts when dawn had scarcely broken, the aim was to see and be seen to be important enough to have to make the most of every minute. Here the people that mattered could eat the fat of the land together, although since this was also the heyday of high performance fitness, aerobics, spas and no-cholesterol culture, many power breakfasters made a show of eschewing the Eggs Benedict and high stacks of pancakes drenched with maple syrup and butter for joyless but virtuous egg white omelettes and power shakes. Crossing the Atlantic with the American bankers, brokers and firms who were an increasing presence on the City of London scene, the power breakfast went through its British incarnation, finding a home in the hotels where the English Breakfast had always flourished. At the time, Sir Mervyn King, then a professor of economics at the London School of Economics and later the Governor of the Bank of England, described the power breakfast as one of 'America's three great contributions to civilisation', along with central heating and showers (*New York Times* March 1987, in Hunter 2009).

On both sides of the Atlantic, the power breakfast faded with the 1980s economic boom, but deep in the British countryside the culinary movement that had started with the rediscovery of English regional foods now went political.

There had always been a superficial similarity in the ordinary breakfast dishes common to England, Ireland, Scotland and Wales—tea being the traditional hot drink in all cases—but now the local produce and regional specialities that had given the meal character took on a new importance. By the 1990s, devolution – the new term for what had been known as 'home rule'—became a volatile issue, with Wales and Scotland both demanding independence from Britain and central government, seeking the right to manage their affairs through their own national assemblies. Now, the 'Scottish' and 'Welsh Breakfasts' referred to in Chapter Three, which had always been part of the British foodscape, came to the fore as emblems of the emerging nationalist identities, repeating the process that had led to the emergence of the English Breakfast as symbol and sacrament in the nineteenth century.

Terroir—the distinctive and almost spiritual quality of local foods—became highly significant, and although they had previously been seen as variants of the English Breakfast, the Scots and Welsh now insisted that their breakfasts be seen as national meals in their own rights. The Scots were the more militant in their approach. Going back in history, the relationship between England and Scotland has always been uneasy, and writing about the two has habitually taken the form of a discourse of difference—a perpetual rehearsal of the ways they are profoundly unlike each other. The cultural history of Scottish cookery is as much comparative as it is descriptive. As F. Marianne McNeil, the doyenne of Scots food history, wrote, 'The Scots are

a fish-eating, and the English a flesh-eating people', and 'instead of the wheat of the south, the cereals of Scotland were oats and barley', concluding, 'Why even to describe Scottish porridge as English porridge is an injustice to Scotland!' (McNeil 1971:8). She goes on to cite the English writer Samuel Johnson (1971:56):

> In the breakfast, the Scot, whether of the Lowlands or mountains, must be confessed to excel us . . . If an epicure could move by a wish in quest of sensual gratification, wherever he had supped, he would breakfast in Scotland.

Fish is to the Scottish breakfast what bacon is to breakfasts in Britain generally, the best known being the smoked Findon or Finnan and Moray Firth smoked haddock, Arbroath smokies, Loch Fyne herrings and salmon, smoked and in many other forms. The Scots claim to have made two contributions to the English Breakfast. The first —porridge—is not unique to Scotland, although they have their own ways of milling and cooking it, in the old days preceding the porridge with a dram of whiskey. The second contribution—marmalade—was not invented in Scotland either, although the Scots can be credited with establishing the use of marmalade, previously a dessert sweetmeat, as a breakfast food (Wilson 2002).

There is a third contribution that the Scots themselves often overlook—the 'Breakfast Tea' blend popularised by Queen Victoria. The royal tradition of tea drinking began in 1664 when the Court of Directors of the East India Company presented King Charles II with the princely gift of two pounds of tea, and their full bodied Royal Breakfast blend is still offered. Over time, different blends developed, and one invented in Scotland which had a high proportion of black tea gained favour with Queen Victoria, becoming known as Breakfast Tea. It is now the most popular type of tea blend sold in Britain. As for the food, in Scotland, there are many regional and season variations, but this may be regarded as a representative traditional 'Scottish Breakfast' (after McNeil 1932:24):

Scottish Breakfast

Porridge, with Milk or Cream
Fresh Herring Fried in Oatmeal
or
Wind-blown Whitings, Broiled
Boiled Eggs
Wheaten scones   Barley Bannocks   Oatcakes
Butter   Toast   Marmalade
Tea

Instead of militant difference and looking outwards, the Welsh approach to their national cuisine looks inward, emphasising identity and the need to consolidate and express 'Welsh-ness'. As S. Minwel Tibbot, the doyenne of Welsh culinary historians, put it, 'Food and drink form an important part of a nation's heritage, and (there is a) need to retain information about the dishes that were once synonymous with the Welsh way of life' (Tibbot 1976:11); cuisine is an instrument of nationalism. Oats were the main cereal crop of Wales, and bacon—rather than lamb—the everyday meat of its people, but although oatmeal and bacon figure in the Welsh breakfast, they are not at its heart. Instead, that place was given over to seaweed and shellfish. Wales has some 1,200 miles of coastline, and most of the population lives on or very near to the sea, the source of the small clams called cockles and edible porphyra seaweed called laver, or *lawr* in Welsh. The consumption of these foods is assumed to be rooted in antiquity, but they gained importance as a cheap food for the miners and factory workers who made Wales a thriving centre of industry in the nineteenth and early twentieth centuries. Cockles and laver grow in proximity to each other, and were traditionally gathered by women and children who went 'out on the sands' while the men were at work. Cleaned of sand, the seaweed—the same type as is used in sushi—is boiled for about seven hours, until it forms a dark green marine porridge which is eaten as-is, or mixed with oatmeal to make laverbread or *baralawr*. The cockles were also boiled and, along with the seaweed, sold ready-cooked by the cockle women, from door to door or in the markets. The emblematic breakfast is prepared as follows: Welsh bacon is fried and set to one side, then the cockles and laver are fried in the bacon fat, and all are served together. Sometimes eggs or sausages are added, but this is the core breakfast that is regarded as 'the taste of Wales'.

Welsh Breakfast

Laver or Laverbread

Cockles   Bacon

Fried Bread

Tea

At the turn of the millennium, the English Breakfast was beleaguered. Smart sandwich shops and coffee bars were now offering breakfasts that were short and sweet in all senses—muffins, croissants, bagels, brownies, cake and cupcakes partnered by a bewildering array of designer coffee. In these places, the English Breakfast was telescoped into breakfast baguettes, breakfast wraps and 'all-day-breakfast' sandwiches consisting of egg, bacon, sausage and tomato trapped between some form of bread. Then came a series of financial crises—the housing boom collapse, credit crunches, stock market instability and global recession. If ever comfort, reassurance and the certainties of tradition were needed, it was now—and the English Breakfast once again came into its own. The meal that had become a solitary, snatched, on-the-run affair was now a Breakfast Club that everyone wanted to join, and the grand hotels opened their doors to a new clientele.

This was a new style of power breakfast—quieter, more discreet, assured rather than brash—and the food fit the mood. In establishments like the Dorchester, the Savoy and the Ritz, the culinary history of the previous decades can be seen on the menu. The current mode consists of several set breakfasts, variations of 'British Organic', 'Continental' and 'Light and Healthy' options with pride of place going to an 'English Breakfast' consisting of a combination of eggs, bacon, ham, sausage, black or white pudding, mushrooms and tomato. Swimming alongside are the traditional fishy favourites—haddock, kippers, smoked salmon—along with naturalised imports like baked beans, American pancakes, Belgian waffles, Danish pastries, French patisserie and Viennoiserie, frittatas and that defining dish of sumptuous breakfasting, Eggs Benedict. Outside the hotels, the English Breakfast also enjoyed a revival. In London, the reigning temple of breakfast—the award-winning Wolseley brasserie in Piccadilly—has a menu that is a social document of the democracy *de luxe* that characterises upscale breakfasting in Britain today. Alongside their version of the English breakfast, the Wolseley offers everything from caviar omelettes and Scottish haggis with duck eggs to sausage sandwiches and crispy bacon rolls, along with that quintessentially English nostalgic nursery favourite, boiled eggs with the strips of toast called 'soldiers'. Less formally, breakfasters sought out the new independent establishments that opened in opposition to the fast food chain breakfasts, and also made for the few surviving fry-up cafés, now regarded as national treasures. Even the chains are offering seductive new breakfast choices like Eggs Benedict sandwiches. For others, staying in has become the new going out. Home-cooked breakfasts are once again objects of desire, promoted enthusiastically by producers of butter, bacon and eggs, as the marketing boards did decades ago. Brunch is back in fashion, and people can make their own grand breakfasts and host brunches using the recipes in this book.

* * *

Two world wars, several economic booms and depressions, sweeping social changes, new nationalisms, imported foods, fluctuating fashions in eating; the English Breakfast has accommodated them all, and remains the best meal of the day. As the popular patriotic World War II song put it, 'There'll Always Be An England'—and, it seems, there will always be an English Breakfast.

EPILOGUE ILLUSTRATIONS

A Good Housekeeping Book of Meals in a Hurry and *Good Housekeeping's 100 Ideas for Breakfast and High Tea*, courtesy of the Hearst Corporation. *One-Room Cookery*, The Gas Council; *Butter For You*, Butter Information Council; *101 Recipes for English Tomatoes*, The British Growers' Publicity Council; *Get 6 More British Eggstra*, Eggs Information Bureau—all from author's collection. Royal Breakfast tea, courtesy of the East India Company. Breakfast Tea, courtesy of Fortnum & Mason.

References and Bibliography

Abels, Richard. 1998. *Alfred the Great: War Kingship and Culture in Anglo-Saxon England*. Addison Wesley Longman, London and New York.

Adburgham, Alison (Ed). 1969. *Yesterday's Shopping: The Army and Navy Stores Catalogue 1907*. David and Charles, Newton Abbot.

Alberts, R.C. 1974. *The Good Provider: H.J. Heinz and His 57 Varieties*. Arthur Barker, London.

Allen, Miss M. L. 1884. *Breakfast Dishes for Every Morning of Three Months*. J.S. Virtue & Co, London.

Anderson, Benedict. 1991. *Imagined Communities: Reflections on the Origin and Spread of Nationalism*. Revised Edition. Verso, London.

Anon. 1872. *Modern Etiquette in Public and Private*. Frederick Warne and Co, London and New York.

Appadurai, Arjun. 1988. How to Make a National Cuisine: Cookbooks in Contemporary India. *Comparative Studies in Society and History*. Vol 30, No. 1:3–24.

Arnold, Bettina. 2001. Power Drinking in Iron Age Europe. *British Archaeology*. Vol. 57:12–19.

Aylmer, Ursula with Caroline McCrum. 1995. *Oxford Food: An Anthology*. Chosen and edited by Ursula Aylmer, with recipes from the colleges edited by Caroline McCrum. Bodleian Library, Ashmolean Library, University of Oxford.

Ayrton, Elizabeth. 1975. *The Cookery of England*. Andre Deutsch, London.

Bakels, Corrie and Stefanie Jacomet. 2003. Access to Luxury Foods in Central Europe During the Roman Period: the Archaeobotanical Evidence. *World Archaeology*. Vol. 34, No. 3/3:542–557.

Beetham, Margaret and Kay Boardman (Eds). 2001. *Victorian Women's Magazines: An Anthology*. Manchester University Press, Manchester and New York.

Beeton, Isabella (Ed). 1888. *Mrs Beeton's Book of Household Management*. Ward Lock, London.

Bergier, Jean-Louis. 1998. Food and Material Culture. In Scharer, Martin R. and Fenton, Alexander (Eds) *Food and Material Culture*. Tuckwell Press in association with Alimentarium, Vevey, Switzerland and The European Ethnological Research Centre, Edinburgh.

Bishop, Frederick. 1864. *The Wife's Own Book of Cookery*. Houlston and Wright, London.

Boisard, Pierre. 2003. *Camembert: A National Myth*. University of California Press, Berkeley, Los Angeles and London.

Boxer, Arabella. 1991. *Arabella Boxer's Book of English Food*. Hodder & Stoughton, London and Toronto.

Brillat-Savarin, Jean-Anthelme. 1970. *The Philosopher in the Kitchen*. Translated by Anne Drayton. Penguin Books, London.

British Growers' Publicity Council. *One Hundred and One Recipes for English Tomatoes*. London, British Growers' Publicity Council.

Brown, Marjorie A. 1998. The Feast Hall in Anglo-Saxon Society. In Carlin, Martha and Rosenthal, Joel T. (Eds) *Food and Eating in Medieval Europe*. The Hambledon Press, London and Rio Grande.

Brown, Rose. 1898. *The Breakfast Book*. Simpkin, Marshall & Co, London.

Browne, Phillis. 1882. *The Girl's Own Cookery Book*. The Religious Tract Society, London.

Browne, Phyllis (Hamer, Sarah Sharp). 1898. *Dictionary of Dainty Breakfasts*. Cassell and Co, London.

Butter Information Council. 1959. *Butter*. London, Butter Information Council.

Carrier, Robert. 1971. *Breakfast and Brunch Party Menus*. London, Pan Books.

Clark, Priscilla P. 1975. Thought for Food I: French Cuisine and French Culture. *The French Review*. Vol 49, No. 1: 32–41.

Cole, Rose Owen. 1885. *Breakfast and Savoury Dishes* by R.O.C. Chapman and Hall, London.

Coleridge, Lady Georgina (Ed). 1972. *The Lady's Realm: A Selection from the Monthly Issues November 1904 to April 1905*. Arrow Books, London.

Conrad, Joseph. 1925. Preface. In Conrad, Jessie. *Handbook of Cookery*. William Heinemann, London.

Cosh, Stephen R. 2001. Seasonal Dining Rooms in Romano-British Houses. *Britannia*. Vol. 32: 219–242.

Counihan, Carole and Penny Van Esterik. 1997. Introduction. In Counihan, Carole and Van Esterik, Penny (Eds) *Food and Culture: A Reader*. Routledge, London and New York.

Cradock, Fanny and Johnnie Cradock. 1970. *Fanny Cradock Invites...*BBC Publications, London.

Crook, J. Mordaunt. 1999. *The Rise of the Nouveaux Riches: Style and Status in Victorian and Edwardian Architecture*. John Murray, London.

Crossley-Holland, Kevin. 1982. *The Anglo-Saxon World*. Oxford University Press, Oxford.

Dalby, Andrew. 2000. *Empire of Pleasure: Luxury and Indulgence in the Roman World*. Routledge, London and New York.

Davidoff, Leonore and Catherine Hall. 1994. *Family Fortunes: Men and Women of the English Middle Class 1780–1850*. Routledge, London and New York.

Davies, Hester. 1921. *A Handbook of Plain and Household Cookery, with a Preface by Lady Aberdare*. Tudor Print Works, Cardiff.

Davies, Russell M. 2005. *Egg, Bacon, Chips and Beans: Fifty Great Cafes and the Stuff that Makes Them Great*. Harper Collins, London and New York.

Donahue, John F. 2003. Toward a Typology of Roman Public Feasting. *American Journal of Philology*. Vol. 124: 423–441.

Douglas, Mary. 1970 (1996). *Natural Symbols: Explorations in Cosmology*. Routledge, London and New York.

Douglas, Mary. 1975 (2003). *Deciphering a Meal* In *Implicit Meanings: Selected Essays in Anthropology*. Routledge, London and New York.

Douglas, Mary. 1997. Introduction. In Kuper, Jessica (Ed) *The Anthropologists' Cookbook*. Kegan Paul, London, New York and Bahrain.

Douglas, Mary and Baron Isherwood. 1979. *The World of Goods: Towards an Anthropology of Consumption*. Routledge, London and New York.

Douglas, Robin. 1933. *Well, Let's Eat*. Cassell and Company, London, Toronto, Melbourne and Sydney.

Drake, Barbara. 1936. *Nutrition: A Policy of National Health*. New Fabian Research Bureau and Victor Gollancz, London.

Driver, Christopher. 1983. *The British At Table: 1940–1980*. Chatto and Windus—The Hogarth Press, London.

Egg Information Bureau. 1960s. *Thank Goodness for Eggs*. Egg Information Bureau, London.

Egg Information Bureau. 1970s. *Get 6 More British Eggstra*. Egg Information Bureau, London.

Elias, Norbert. 1994. *The Civilising Process*. Blackwell, Oxford.

Emina, Seb and Malcolm Eggs. 2013. *The Breakfast Bible*. Bloomsbury, London.

English Tourist Board. 1977. *A Taste of England: 750 Restaurants offering English Food Prepared in the Traditional Way*. Quarto Publishing, London.

Esmonde Cleary, Simon. 1993. Approaches to the Differences Between Late Romano-British and Early Anglo-Saxon Archaeology. *Anglo-Saxon Studies in Archaeology and History*. Vol 6: 57–63.

Finke, Laurie A. and Martin B. Shichtman. 2004. *King Arthur and the Myth of History*. University of Florida Press, Gainsville.

Fischer, David Hackett. 1989. *Albion's Seed: Four British Folkways in America*. Oxford University Press, Oxford.

Flandrin, Jean-Louis. 1996. Mealtimes in France Before the Nineteenth Century. *Food and Foodways*. Vol 3, No. 4: 261–282.

Flandrin, Jean-Louis and Massimo Montanari. 1999. Introduction. In Flandrin, Jean-Louis and Montanari, Massimo (Eds) *A Culinary History of Food*. Columbia University Press, New York and London.

Franklin, Jill. 1981. *The English Country Gentleman's House*. Routledge and Kegan Paul, London and Boston.

Galsworthy, John. 1906. *The Man of Property* (First book of *The Forsyte Saga*). Heinemann, London.

Gas Council. 1950. *One-Room Cookery*. The Gas Council, London.

Gill, A.A. 2008. *Breakfast at the Wolseley*. Quadrille, London.

Gilmour, Robin. 1981. *The Idea of the Gentleman in the Victorian Novel*. George Allen and Unwin, Boston, London and Sydney.

Girouard, Mark. 1971. *The Victorian Country House*. Clarendon Press, Oxford.

Girouard, Mark. 1978. *Life in the English Country House*. Yale University Press, New Haven and London.

Good Housekeeping Institute. 1947. *A Good Housekeeping Book of Meals in a Hurry*. Gramol Publications Ltd, London and Chesham.

Good Housekeeping Institute. 1948. *100 Ideas for Breakfast and High Tea*. Gramol Publications Ltd, London and Chesham.

Good Housekeeping. 1959. *English Recipes Old and New*. National Magazine Company, London.

Goody, Jack. 1982. *Cooking, Cuisine and Class: A Study in Comparative Sociology*. Cambridge University Press, Cambridge and New York.

Goody, Jack. 1998. *Food and Love: A Cultural History of East and West*. Verso, New York and London.

Grigson, Jane. 1992. *English Food*. Penguin Books, London.

Grossmith, George and Weedon Grossmith. 1892 (1968). *The Diary of a Nobody*. Penguin Books, London and New York.

Hagen, Ann. 1992. *A Handbook of Anglo-Saxon Food: Processing and Consumption*. Anglo-Saxon Books, Pinner, England.

Hammond, P. W. 1993. *Food and Feast in Medieval England*. Alan Sutton, Stroud and Dover, New Hampshire.

Hass, Hans (Translated by James Cleugh). 1954. *Under the Red Sea*. Arrow Books-Jarrolds, London.

Heath, Ambrose. 1940. *Good Breakfasts*. Faber and Faber, London.

Heath, Ambrose. 1945. *Good Breakfasts*. Faber and Faber, London.

Helstosky, Carol. 2003. Recipe for the Nation: Reading Italian History Through *La Scienza in Cucina* and *La Cucina Futurista*. *Food and Foodways*. Vol. 11: 113–140.

Henning, S. Belfrage. 1942. *Design for Britain: The People's Food*. J. M. Dent, London.

Hieatt, Constance B. and Robin F. Jones. 1986. Two Anglo-Norman Culinary Collections Edited from British Library Manuscripts, Additional 32085 and Royal 12.C.xii. *Speculum*. Vol. 61, No. 4: 859–882.

Hill, Christopher. 1958. *Puritanism and Revolution. Studies in Interpretation of the English Revolution of the 17th Century*. Secker and Warburg, London.

Hill, Georgiana. 1865. *The Breakfast Book*. Richard Bentley, London.

Hooper, Mary. 1873. *Handbook for the Breakfast Table*. Griffith and Farran, London.

Hooper, Mary. 1883. *Good Plain Cookery*. Ward Lock, London.

Howell, Sally. 2003. Modernising *Mansaf*: The Consuming Contexts of Jordan's National Dish. *Food and Foodways*. Vol. 11: 215–243.

Hughes, Kathryn. 2005. *The Short Life and Long Times of Mrs Beeton*. Fourth Estate, London.

Humble, Nicola. 2005. *Culinary Pleasures: Cookbooks and the Transformation of British Food*. Faber and Faber, London.

Hunter, Jackie. 2009. The Power Breakfast: No Longer Toast. *Intelligent Life*, Spring.

Ishige, Naomichi. 2001. *The History and Culture of Japanese Food*. Kegan Paul, London, New York and Bahrain.

James, Allison 1997. How British is British Food? In Caplan, Pat (Ed) *Food, Health and Identity*. Routledge, London and New York.

Jekyll, Lady (Agnes). 1922. The Woman's View: A Country Breakfast Table. *The Times,* September 2, 1922. Pg 9, Issue 43126; col D. London.

Jewry, Mary. 1879. *Warne's Domestic Cookery and Housekeeping Book.* Frederick Warne and Co, London and New York.

Johnson, Samuel. 1971. *A Journey to the Western Islands of Scotland edited by Mary Lascelles.* Yale University Press, New Haven.

Kenney Herbert, Colonel Arthur Robert. 1894. *Fifty Breakfasts.* Edward Arnold, London.

Keynes, Simon. 1999. The Cult of King Alfred the Great. In Lapidge, Michael (Ed) *Anglo-Saxon England,* Volume 28. Cambridge University Press, Cambridge.

Khare, R.S. 2005. Food With Saints. In Korsmeyer, Carolyn (Ed) *The Taste Culture Reader: Experiencing Food and Drink.* Berg, Oxford and New York.

Kirby, Chester. 1937. *The English Country Gentleman: A Study of Nineteenth Century Types.* James Clarke and Co, London.

Kopytoff, Igor. 1986. The Cultural Biography of Things: Commoditization as Process. In Appadurai, Arjun (Ed) *The Social life of Things: Commodities in Cultural Process.* Cambridge University Press, Cambridge and New York.

Kumar, Krishnan. 2003. *The Making of English National Identity.* Cambridge University Press, Cambridge.

'L..., Major' (Major James L. Landon). 1887. *Breakfasts, Luncheons and Ball Suppers.* Chapman and Hall, London.

Lane, Maggie. 1995. *Jane Austen and Food.* The Hambledon Press, London and Rio Grande.

Lee, Paul. 1976. Preface. In Cadwallader, Sharon and Judi Ohr. *Whole Earth Cook Book.* New York and London, Bantam Books.

Logan, Thad. 2001. *The Victorian Parlour.* Cambridge University Press, Cambridge.

Lytton, Edward Bulwer (Lord Lytton). 1875. *Harold: The Last of the Saxon Kings.* Routledge, London.

Macauley, Rose. 1942. *Life Among the English.* William Collins, London.

MacClancy, Jeremy. 1992. *Consuming Culture.* Chandler Publishers, London.

Magee, Paul. 2005. Introduction: Foreign Cookbooks. *Postcolonial Studies.* Vol. 8, No. 1: 3–18.

Maitland, Agnes C. 1926. *What Shall We Have for Breakfast?* John Hogg, London.

McNeil, F. Marian. 1932. *The Book of Breakfasts.* Alexander MacLehose & Co, London.

McNeil, F. Marian. 1971. *Recipes from Scotland.* Albyn Press, Edinburgh.

Melman, Billie. 1991. Claiming the Nation's Past: The Invention of an Anglo-Saxon Tradition. *Journal of Contemporary History.* Vol 26: 575–595.

Mennell, Stephen. 1985. *All Manners of Food: Eating and Taste in England and France form the Middle Ages to the Present.* Basil Blackwell, Oxford.

Miller, Daniel. 1987. *Material Culture and Mass Consumption.* Basil Blackwell, Oxford.

Millers' Mutual Association. 1940s. *120 Ways of Using Bread for Tasty and Delightful Dishes.* Northern Publishing Company, Liverpool and London.

Mintz, Sidney. 1985. *Sweetness and Power: The Place of Sugar in Modern History.* Viking, New York.

Mintz, Sidney W. 1996. *Tasting Food, Tasting Freedom.* Beacon Press, Boston.

Mintz, Sidney W. and Christine M. Du Bois. 2002. The Anthropology of Food and Eating. *Annual Review of Anthropology.* Vol. 31: 99–119.

Moore, D.C. 1981. The Gentry. In Mingay, G. E. (Ed) *The Victorian Countryside,* Volume Two. Routledge and Kegan Paul, London, Boston and Henley.

Moore, D.C. 1981. The Landed Aristocracy. In G. E. Mingay (Ed) *The Victorian Countryside,* Volume Two. Routledge and Kegan Paul, London, Boston and Henley.

Morphy, Countess. 1936. *British Recipes: The Traditional Dishes of England, Scotland, Ireland and Wales.* Herbert Joseph Limited, London.

National Council for Hotel and Catering Education. 1947. *The Waiter.* Practical Press Ltd., London.

Norwak, Mary and British Bacon. 1979. *The Best of British Bacon Recipes.* British Bacon Marketing Board, The Sales Machine, London.

Opie, Robert. 1985. *Rule Britannia: Trading on the British Image.* Viking, London and New York.

Orwell, George. 1941. *The Lion and the Unicorn: Socialism and the English Genius.* Secker and Warburg, London.

Orwell, George. 1945. In Defence of English Cooking. *Evening Standard,* December 15, London.

Orwell, George. 1946. A Nice Cup of Tea. *Evening Standard,* January 12, London.

Orwell, George. 1949. *Down and Out in Paris and London.* Secker and Warburg, London.

Palmer, Arnold. 1984. *Moveable Feasts: Changes in English Eating Habits.* Oxford University Press, Oxford and New York.

Palmer, Catherine. 1998. From Theory to Practice: Experiencing the Nation in Everyday Life. *Journal of Material Culture.* Vol. 3, No. 2: 175–199.

Pocock, David. 1985. Introduction. In Palmer, Arnold. *Moveable Feasts.* Oxford University Press, Oxford.

Priestley, J. B. 1970. *The Edwardians.* Heinemann, London.

Purcell, Nicholas. 2003. The Way We Used to Eat: Diet, Community and History at Rome. *American Journal of Philology.* Vol. 124: 329–358.

Robertson, Laurel with Carol Flinders and Bronwen Godfrey. 1976. *Laurel's Kitchen.* Routledge and Kegan Paul, London.

Sackville-West, Vita. 1944. *English Country Houses.* William Collins, London.

Sahlins, Marshall. 1976. *Culture and Practical Reason.* University of Chicago Press, Chicago.

Scott, Walter. 1848. *Ivanhoe.* Robert Cadell, London.

Scully, Terence. 1995. *The Art of Cookery in the Middle Ages.* The Boydell Press, Woodbridge, Suffolk.

Selfridges Department Store. 1950s. *Household List.* Selfridges, London.

Senn, C. Herman. 1923. *Breakfast Dishes and Savouries.* Ward Lock, London.

Shand, P. Morton. 1930. *A Book of Food.* Jonathan Cape, London.

Short (Pseud). 1880. *Breakfasts and Luncheons at Home.* London.

Smollett, Tobias George. 1884. *The Expedition of Humphrey Clinker.* George Routledge, London.

Strabo (Translated by Hamilton, H. C.). 1912. *The Geography,* Volume I. Bell and Sons, London.

Streatfield, Noel. 1956. *The Day Before Yesterday.* William Collins, London.

Surtees, R.S. 1940. *Jorrocks' Jaunts and Jollities.* The Folio Society, London. (First published 1838).

Surtees, R.S. 1926. *Hawbuck Grange*. George Bayntun, Bath. (First published 1847).

Surtees, R.S. 1926. *Mr Sponge's Sporting Tour*. George Bayntun, Bath. (First published 1852).

Sutton, David E. 2005. Synesthesia, Memory and the Taste of Home. In Korsmeyer, Carolyn (Ed) *The Taste Culture Reader: Experiencing Food and Drink*. Berg, Oxford and New York.

Tacitus, Cornelius (Translated by Anthony R. Birley). 1999. *Agricola*. Oxford University Press, Oxford.

Tacitus, Cornelius (Translated by Maurice Hutton). 1914. *Germania*. W. Heinemann, London.

Tannahill, Reay. 1988. *Food in History*. Penguin Books, Harmondsworth.

Tchumi, Gabriel. 1954. *Royal Chef*. William Kimber, London.

Terry, Josephine. 1947. *Food Merry-go-Round*. J. P. McNulty & Co Ltd, London.

Thomas, David St John. 1980. *The Breakfast Book*. David & Charles, Newton Abbot.

Tibbott, S. Minwel. 1976. *Welsh Fare: A Selection of Traditional Recipes*. Wales, National Museum of Wales.

Tibbott, S. Minwel. 2002. *Domestic Life in Wales*. National Museum of Wales, Cardiff.

Vanden Bossche, Chris R. 1987. Culture and Economy in Ivanhoe. *Nineteenth Century Literature*. Vol. 42, No. 1: 46–72.

Walford, L. B. 1883. *Margaret Sim's Cookery Book*. William Blackwood and Sons, Edinburgh and London.

Waterstone, Merlin. 1985. *The Country House Remembered*. Routledge and Kegan Paul, London, Melbourne and Henley.

White, Florence. 1932. *Good Things in England*. Jonathan Cape, London.

White, Florence. 1934. *Flowers As Food*. Jonathan Cape, London.

White, Florence. 1952. *Good English Food*. Jonathan Cape, London.

Wilk, Richard R. 1999. 'Real Belizean Food': Building Local Identity in the Transnational Caribbean. *American Anthropologist*. Vol. 101, No. 2: 244–255.

Wilson, C. Anne. 2010. *The Book of Marmalade, Second Revised Edition*. Prospect Books, Totnes.

Young Ladies' Journal, Extra Supplement (No. 4). *Breakfast and the Breakfast-Table*.